# SHAKESPEARE'S
# LIFE AND ART

By
PETER ALEXANDER

*Regius Professor of English Language and Literature
in the University of Glasgow*

New York University Press 1961

First published in Great Britain
by James Nisbet and Co. Ltd.
All rights reserved.

SHAKESPEARE'S LIFE AND ART

## By Professor Peter Alexander

SHAKESPEARE'S HENRY VI AND RICHARD III

*(Shakespeare Problems, Vol. III)*

# CONTENTS

v

# PROLOGUE

THE idea that Shakespeare is a dramatist of sovereign genius, a poet with a gift of expression ' eminent and unrivalled,' and yet, for all his powers, entitled to no more than secondary rank among the literary artists of the world, is the root of almost every error about the man and his work.

To explain this imagined discrepancy some have dwelt on the accidents of his birth and education. David Hume thought of Shakespeare as born in a rude age and educated in the lowest manner, without any instruction from the world and from books. Shakespeare's plays were, it was argued, for the amusement of the least refined of his ignorant contemporaries, and the playwright could not have afforded to cherish artistic ideals, especially with a mind as set as Shakespeare's seemed to his critics to be on financial success. Such was the slander which Pope, the most business-like of men of letters, put in circulation, when he told how Shakespeare

> For gain not glory winged his roving flight,
> And grew immortal in his own despite.

For what he envied Shakespeare as a man he could, as a critic, put to the dramatist's discredit. ' That all these contingencies,' he wrote in his Preface to his edition of the Plays, ' should unite to his disadvantage seems to me almost as singularly unlucky, as that so many various (nay, contrary) Talents should meet in one man, was happy and extra-ordinary.' In the later judgment of Warton, an age so unversed in criticism as the Elizabethan did not permit of the sustained propriety of thought desiderated by Hume, and Shakespeare's excellencies and faults were in consequence so equal and opposite that he stood in this 'like Virgil's majestic oak—

Quantum vertice ad auras
Aetherias, tantum radice in Tartara tendit.'

These are but types of the explanations that have multiplied themselves from generation to generation of Shakespearean critics. But the careful and protracted inquiries of historians and antiquaries have at last discovered this picture of a benighted Stratford in an illiterate England to be merely fanciful, reflecting no reality but the self-satisfaction that every generation is prone to in its contemplation of the past. The historical and bibliographical researches that have swept away these reasons for Shakespeare's failure as an artist are summarized in Chapters I and II, which clear the ground for the handling of the central notion round which so many misconceptions have accumulated. The verdict that Shakespeare is not among the supreme artists of the world cannot be upset, it is true, by historical considerations, but only by an analysis of his work, and Chapters III–VI are an essay towards such an analysis. A brief consideration here, however, of the circumstances in which the unfavourable judgment was first pronounced will show that it comes in so questionable a shape as to invite inquiry ; and this, though it may since have been approved by critics who had not merely a real knowledge of the great literatures of the world but were themselves the possessors of a goodly portion of ' the vision and the faculty divine.'

When Shakespeare was writing his greatest dramas modern European criticism was only struggling into life. The Renaissance had liberated the artist from conventions in which he could no longer work with freedom ; and the genius of Europe, ' spiritualized by the reverie of the middle age,' found in the art of antiquity an aid to the expression of that divine ideal of which Michelangelo speaks,[1] and of which he and Shakespeare are among the great masters. But Renaissance criticism was too feeble to rise to the height of such heroic argument ; it tended to stress what was accidental in the masterpieces of Greece and Rome, formulated ' rules ' based on an imperfect observation of these masterpieces, and condemned more modern work merely because this was in externals very different from the chosen models. The error was not confined to literary criticism, and can be most easily exposed in the field of architecture.

To Vasari, the pupil of Michelangelo and the cultivated historian of Italian art, the cathedrals of the Middle Ages were German fabrications, and therefore outstanding embodiments of ignorance and barbarism. Gothic was a term of contempt for a style attributed to the savage destroyers of Roman civilization. This was the view maintained for two hundred years and more. Vasari died in 1572, but only towards the end of the 18th Century, when Lessing and others in Germany had advanced criticism by a profounder interpretation of Classical art, was the way prepared for Goethe's famous defence [2] of the art he still spoke of as German.

Since that day the architect and archæologist, in their enthusiasm for this once despised art, have traced its motifs and dispositions beyond the Roman world, through such hidden channels as the catacombs of Rome itself, into the Hellenistic world that cradled Christianity, and even across the sands of Syria into furthest Persia. And these tireless inquirers can no longer regard this marvellous creation of

[1] See Hollanda's *Four Dialogues on Painting*. There is a translation by A. F. G. Bell.

[2] *Von Deutscher Baukunst* (1773). A translation, *On German Architecture* is included in *Goethe's Literary Essays* edited by J. E. Spingarn.

the 12th and 13th centuries as coming almost ready-made
from the wild woodland homes of the Teutonic invaders.
Its foundations are laid deep in the ancient civilizations of
the world, and whether one considers the colour of its
glass, of which the flame was kindled in the Persia of the
Sassanids, or the Euclidean precision of its framework,
that speaks of the mathematical genius of Greece, the
elements that make up its perfection are in their variety
only less wonderful than the unity in which all coalesce.
And this in its highest form, as at Chartres, or Amiens, or
what once was Rheims, is the supreme creation of the
artistic genius of France.

If an artist of so gifted a race as Vasari, taught by the
most illustrious masters, in an age remarkable for its force
and genius, could yet feel in Gothic so little of all that
subsequent research has made plain to the intellect; if
his attention was so given to the precepts of Vitruvius and
the study of the styles of Greece and Rome that he could
talk without understanding of

This glorious work of fine intelligence,

no one need wonder that the studious Jonson, even as he
placed Shakespeare in all sincerity above the greatest names
of Greece and Rome, felt that his friend's art was not equal
to his genius.  For Shakespeare's work is like Gothic so
different in form from that of the masters Jonson admired,
that the theories of the critic could not but contradict his
feelings.

In a later generation, when Shakespearean criticism made
its systematic beginnings, French theory dominated the
dramatic practice of Europe; and France had now con-
stituted herself the jealous guardian of the rules the Renaissance had discovered as essential to artistic perfection.
French taste now turned with shame from the noblest

monuments of France's genius, and even Molière could write of

> Le fade goût des monuments gothiques,
> Ces monstres odieux des siècles ignorants.

It is not surprising, therefore, to find Voltaire, in spite of his admiration for certain qualities in Shakespeare's work, calling the tragedies monstrous farces and their author a barbarian. Shakespeare knew nothing, he thought, of the three Unities that must govern the construction of the plot, and of that essential decorum which forbade the inter-mixture of tragic and comic, and which made princes on the stage speak with the dignity which they always show in reality, or ought to show. The age of 'enlightenment' had as little perception of the structural integrity of Shakespeare's work as it had of the engineering science of the Gothic builders.

English criticism moved on parallel lines. 'What Reformation,' says our learned Rymer at the beginning of his *Short View of Tragedy* (1693), 'may not we expect now, that in France they see the necessity of a Chorus to their Tragedies? The Chorus was the root and original, and is certainly always the most necessary part of Tragedy.' And he had concluded his previous study of this subject by observing, 'I have thought our Poetry of the last Age as rude as our Architecture.' His views seemed even in his own age extreme; but they were often only the logical expression of premises accepted by almost everyone; for though many fine and true things were said of Shakespeare in England during the 18th century, there still persisted, except in Morgann's famous essay,[1] the old contradiction between men's feelings about Shakespeare's genius and their theories about his art.

[1] *An Essay on the Dramatic Character of Sir John Falstaff*, by Maurice Morgann, 1

This contradiction was not resolved till the Romantic Revival and the rediscovery of Gothic. Men now saw that they could understand the structure of Gothic not by comparisons between its external features and those of Greek buildings but only by a consideration of how far these features expressed the idea that gave life and meaning to the work as a whole. And Gothic was seen to be at its best a wonderful example of how an almost infinite variety may be the expression of one fundamental idea. This method of inquiry vindicated Shakespeare's art. Coleridge could now maintain that Shakespeare's judgment was equal to his genius, and that his tragedies attain that final degree of artistic organisation in which ' each part is at once end and means.' ' How long,' adds Wordsworth, ' may it be before it becomes universally acknowledged that the judgment of Shakespeare in the selection of his materials, and in the manner in which he has made them, heterogeneous as they often are, constitute a unity of their own, and contribute all to one great end, is not less admirable than his imagination, his invention, and his intuitive knowledge of human Nature ? ' Nor did this judgment involve any surrender of classic loyalties. It was rather the consequence of a deeper devotion to classic conceptions. For this architectonic power, unless such interpreters of antiquity as Lessing, Goethe and Arnold, were mistaken, is what the Greeks took to be the distinguishing mark of the great artist.

But this is the very power which amazed Shakespeare's first critics when they subscribed to the view that

Nature herself was proud of his designs,

for the challenge to the artist in Nature's designs lies not only in their variety but in their vital unity. And that Shakespeare attained to this cunning only at the price of

constant endeavour, the analysis of his technical methods
has at length made plain. Mouldings and tracery hardly
reveal the development of Gothic more clearly than do
the details of Shakespeare's verse and diction his ceaseless
search for adequate expression.

It is because of this inward vital power that there is
between the Greeks and Shakespeare, as there is between
Greek and Gothic, for all their outward and obvious
differences, a profound artistic kinship, deeper than that to
be attained by any direct imitation, however zealous and
scholarly. This is the point of the question put by Keble,
who so truly felt the spell of both Greek and Gothic art that
he could say : ' Who would wish the architect of Canterbury cathedral to have been deeply versed in the proportions
of the four regular orders of Greece ? ' To which one
may answer in this context : only those who, like Rymer,
would have had Shakespeare recast *Hamlet* in the form
required by the Unities of Time and Place, or rewrite *Lear*
with Choruses, imitated from the Greek.

But old fallacies take new forms, and Arnold, who
insisted so strongly that a work of art can be judged only
as a whole was himself misled by a theory about the ' great
style,' a theory that is a survival from 18th Century criticism.
which gave a special place in its estimation to the epic,
To suppose that Shakespeare lacks ' sureness of perfect
style ' because his diction and phrasing would be out of
place in *Paradise Lost* is like criticising the south spire at
Chartres because it will not fit St. Paul's or St. Peter's.
Yet the old conviction that Shakespeare takes second rank
as an artist dies so hard that the critic who has done
most in our time to vindicate Shakespeare's judgment as a
dramatic craftsman can yet say as he examines *Hamlet* :
' Let us cheerfully admit that he " wanted art " ; he was the
genius of the workshop.' Had Mr. Granville-Barker

described the man who planned Chartres or Amiens as a stone-mason of genius, he would be understood to put with ironic emphasis the point he has so convincingly argued in his *Prefaces* : that Shakespeare thought in terms of the medium in which he worked ; and that he can be regarded, to use the words a French archæologist has applied to the architect of Amiens, as 'un de ces maîtres enracinés dans le métier.' But were Mr. Granville-Barker to go on to deny to this genius, as he does to Shakespeare, a scheme of consistent principles, the reply would be that this is just what posterity has discovered in his work. It is the wonderful consistency with which he has worked out a body of principles in Amiens that has made his cathedral worthy to be called the Parthenon of Gothic. It is, indeed, this noble effort towards consistency that has given the Gothic style at its best 'a profound and a commanding beauty' which probably, as Newman has said, 'the Church will not see surpassed till it attain to the Celestial City.' Mr. Granville-Barker's comparison between Shakespeare and this type of genius forces one to ask if it is not a comparable rigour in the treatment, and a comparable energy in carrying a fundamental idea into the remotest detail of the many branching superstructure, that give such power to Shakespeare's masterpieces. But though Mr. Granville-Barker's criticism points to these conclusions, many of the views most fashionable to-day would rule them out.

Shakespeare's first works constitute, if the analogy is not abused, a kind of Romanesque period, when he is adapting to the needs of a new age the remains of classical antiquity nearest to his hand. He begins with certain set situations, sometimes from Plautus or Seneca, and he improvises for them, with an ever growing skill, his characters, till at length these figures tend in their vigorous life to

rise above the stations for which their creator designed
them. But to make this the whole story of Shakespeare's
artistic development is to miss its most characteristic feature.
Yet Mr. Bernard Shaw is only summarising in his own
trenchant manner much learned opinion when he says of
Shakespeare :

> He never found the inspiration to write an original
> play. He furbished up old plays, and adapted popular
> stories, and chapters of history from Holinshed's Chron-
> icle and Plutarch's biographies, to the stage. All this he
> did with a recklessness which showed that his trade lay
> far from his conscience. It is true that he never takes
> his characters from the borrowed story, because it was
> less trouble and more fun to create them afresh ; but
> none the less he heaps the murders and villainies of the
> borrowed story on his own essentially gentle creations
> without scruple, no matter how incongruous they may
> be.
>
> *Back to Methuselah*, p. lxxxii

And Mr. Bernard Shaw continues :

> He forced himself in among the greatest of play-
> wrights without having once entered the region in which
> Michael Angelo, Beethoven, Goethe and the antique
> Athenian stage poets are great.

But when one asks how Shakespeare holds his audience
that has grown more numerous with the passing of time
and, presumably, more critical, since it has included such
minds as Beethoven and Goethe, the answer is by ' his
extraordinary natural gift in the very entertaining art of
mimicry.' For even Mr. Bernard Shaw cannot come to
any but some such absurd conclusion when the hypothesis
from which he starts contains a fundamental contradiction.
His astonishment at Shakespeare's success takes us back
three hundred years to Beaumont's wonder

> How far sometimes a mortal man may go
> By the dim light of Nature,

and to the old opposition between Shakespeare's genius and art ; though Mr. Bernard Shaw has made them change ends by giving Shakespeare's genius the secondary position and attributing his immortality to the art or artifice, as some modern critics delight to call it, with which he has imposed his second-rate mind on posterity.

To escape this and similar entanglements a more careful study of Shakespeare's development is necessary. But just as it is almost impossible to say at times where the Romanesque period ends and Gothic begins, though Gothic is the expression of an ideal that was to transform completely the whole structure, so in Shakespeare's work there is no sharp division between those plays where his characters are still, as it were, improvised on a given situation, and those in which the situations themselves are chosen to give the character at once its sharpest individuality and its most universal significance. By the time of the great tragedies, however, the situations selected exhibit the fullest potentialities of the hero, and because of the moral forces for which they provide a field, give rise to great actions. It is true that Shakespeare adapted these situations, sometimes from Roman history, sometimes from a half legendary British past ; but the Greek dramatists also worked on themes already familiar, ' permanent problems ' as Arnold described them, ' perpetually offered to the genius of every fresh poet.' The originality of the Greek dramatists lay not in devising new and ingenious combinations of circumstance, but in their treatment of the problem, and in the one moral impression they obtained from a great action treated as a whole. Shakespeare's way of working may differ as widely from the Greek method as does the structure of Amiens from that of the Parthenon, but the unity and

profoundness of moral impression which give their immortality to the *Oresteia* or the *Antigone* are equally characteristic of *Hamlet* or *King Lear*. And Shakespearean
criticism, however elementary, must attempt to realize
in intellectual terms what the enthusiasm and study of
every generation of Shakespeare's readers and spectators
have implied, that Shakespeare lives as the Greek dramatists
live, because, like theirs, his works are indeed

Fictions in form but in their substance truths.

\*     \*     \*     \*     \*     \*

The most complete collection of documents bearing on
Shakespeare's affairs has been brought together by Sir
Edmund Chambers in his *William Shakespeare* ; and to his
transcriptions and valuable comments on their matter I
have made constant reference. In clearing away the conjectural history of the 18th century that represented the
poet as illiterate and his text as a patchwork from many
hands, I have done little more than summarize in Chapter I
the arguments of the late Dr. Smart, and at times of Professor
Quincy Adams, and in Chapter II those of Professor A. W.
Pollard, and the bibliographical school that will always be
associated with him, of which the leading scholars are
Dr. Greg, Dr. McKerrow, and Professor Dover Wilson.
In later chapters I am often indebted to Mr. Granville-
Barker. I must also acknowledge my debt to the three
distinguished scholars who have in turn occupied the
English Chair at the University of Glasgow : A. C.
Bradley, Walter Raleigh, and W. Macneile Dixon ; and
to their names I would add that of Mr. Ritchie Girvan.

If I do not now mention the critics and scholars of
previous generations it is because my indebtedness is beyond

acknowledgment, since a work of this sort must everywhere contain

> Old things repeated with diminished grace.

To Professor Pollard, who has added to what I owe him by reading the early proofs and contributing corrections, and to Professor Rennie of the Greek Chair at Glasgow, who has spared no pains in the castigation to which he has submitted the work, I offer my sincerest thanks.

PETER ALEXANDER

# STRATFORD

THE first published life of Shakespeare was written in the reign of Queen Anne by the dramatist, Nicholas Rowe.[1] Although nearly a hundred years had elapsed since the poet's death, historians and scholars had as yet made no systematic search for documents concerning his affairs, and Rowe was content with the hearsay stories of his circle and the information that a friend, the actor Betterton, obtained at Stratford from a hasty examination of the Parish Register and from local gossip. Nor had Rowe any real historical knowledge of the Elizabethan age that would have enabled him to interpret the few facts about Shakespeare which he did know ; he could only guess at their significance from the practice of his own time. Such conjectural history is almost inevitably wrong ; and the prejudices of Rowe's age strangely distort his picture of Shakespeare. He saw from his reading of the plays that Shakespeare generally ignored the Unities of Place and Time, often representing on the stage what must have occupied years in reality, and bringing together scenes that in fact lay leagues apart. The importance, however, the Unities had assumed in the critical convention of Rowe's day led him to conclude that Shakespeare's neglect of them must have been due to sheer ignorance and lack of education. 'We are,' Rowe tells us in his *Life*, 'to consider him as a man that liv'd in a state of almost universal licence and ignorance,' and he goes on to represent Shakespeare as a man of no education who wrote his plays by what he calls the 'mere light of nature.' He failed to note that Shakespeare's contemporaries, Marlowe and

[1] For his edition of *Shakespeare*, 1709.

Greene, also ignored these rules when constructing their dramas, though they would have passed with him for educated men, being graduates of Cambridge University.

Rowe's view that Shakespeare's schooling was so incomplete ' that he had no knowledge of the writings of the antient poets ' persisted during the 18th century ; but when the minuter examination of later commentators revealed a greater familiarity with the classics than Rowe seemed to have observed, his views were not set aside as mere conjecture contrary to the plain facts, but were maintained by the addition of further conjecture.

In 1767 Richard Farmer, Master of Emmanuel, published his *Essay on the Learning of Shakespeare* to maintain substantially the same view as Rowe, that Shakespeare, though he remembered enough of his ' *schoolboy* learning ' to quote a tag or two from his Latin grammar, never had any real first-hand acquaintance with the classical writers ; and Farmer further maintained that Shakespeare had no working knowledge of any of the modern European tongues. Farmer's reading in Elizabethan literature enabled him to point to a number of passages where Shakespeare borrowed directly from a translation ; but he assumed that the use of a translation argues total ignorance of the original ; and when he came to a number of passages that could not be accounted for by pointing to an available translation, he either ignored them or assumed that the particular passage, or in some instances the play itself, was from a hand other than Shakespeare's.

This simple way of maintaining Rowe's argument, by ruling out all that contradicts it, has, however, in recent years been carried so far as to expose the fundamental absurdity of the position. As minuter examination has extended the catalogue of Shakespeare's reading, and as more stress has been laid on the felicity and copiousness of his reminiscence, more and more would, on Farmer's argument, have to be taken from Shakespeare ; till at last a school of writers has arisen who do not hesitate to deny the whole of Shakespeare's work to an illiterate actor from Stratford. The theories of the Baconians and others of that way of thinking are the logical outcome of the view that Shakespeare's only equipment for dramatic composition was the ' mere light of nature.'

Fortunately there is no need to choose between Bacon or Lord Oxford and a miraculous but ignorant genius called Shakespeare ; for Shakespeare's work, though it reveals a rare cultivation of mind and an exquisite literary sense, does not afford evidence of a painful and laborious scholarship, or of a reading beyond the powers of one educated in 16th century Stratford ; since the minute research of modern scholars has shown that Rowe's picture of Shakespeare's early environment is the very opposite of the truth.

Stratford was made a corporate borough by Royal Charter in 1553, and the local government entrusted to a Council, consisting of a Bailiff, Aldermen and Burgesses ; provision was also made for a Grammar School to be maintained from the endowments handed over to the Corporation. This Charter must not be interpreted, however, as the effort of an enlightened central authority to civilize a benighted provincial hamlet ; it was merely a partial restitution of funds that had been confiscated some years earlier, and the recognition of an order the inhabitants had achieved for themselves. Centuries before the reign of Edward VI there was an active corporate life at Stratford, and a school.

The communal spirit of the place had found expression in the Guild of the Holy Cross. This fraternity cared for the souls of the living and of the dead brothers and sisters, ministered to the poor, and undertook educational and public work. Though granted a new Charter by Henry IV, the Guild, according to a report by two responsible members in 1389, was founded 'in times whereunto the memory of man reacheth not,' and it is known to have been in existence in 1269.[1] The Guild was a wealthy body with its own Chapel and almshouses in the newer part of Stratford, at some distance from the Parish Church ; near the Guild Chapel it built in 1427 a school. This was not, of course, the first school in Stratford, as there is evidence of a school-master there in 1295. One at least of the schools of Warwickshire dates from before the Norman Conquest,[2] and that at Stratford, like many of the others, was certainly of ancient foundation. In 1482 John Jolyf left a sufficient endowment to enable the Guild to educate the children of the town free of charge. The public spirit of another Stratford man, Hugh Clopton, who had become Lord Mayor of London, is commemorated in the fine bridge that still spans the Avon at Stratford. The beautiful chapel, the almshouses, the school, the bridge, are sub-stantial monuments to the energy and enlightened policy of the Guild and its members.

The income of the Guild by the reign of Edward VI was about £50, and this was confiscated under the Chantries Act. A chantry was an endowment to provide masses for the souls of the departed ; and pious benefactors generally directed that masses were to be said for their souls by those who administered their charity. The schoolmaster at Stratford, therefore, who was a cleric, though his business was to teach the children and only incidentally to say masses for the souls of Jolyf and his wife, was technically a chantry priest. His endowment with other Guild pro-

---

[1] *Victoria History of Warwickshire*, p. 113.
[2] *The Schools of Mediaeval England* by A. F. Leach, p. 241.

perty was therefore forfeit. Besides despoiling the Guild, the Government confiscated the property of the College of Priests attached to the Parish Church. This was first endowed by another distinguished man of the place, John de Stratford, Archbishop of Canterbury from 1333–49. At the time of its dissolution the College had the considerable income of £125 per annum.

It was their own confiscated property, therefore, that the inhabitants of Stratford were fortunate enough to recover, though only in part, in 1553. And the Common Council of the new free borough carried on the Guild tradition —almost all its members having held high office in the old fraternity. They now maintained, according to Charter, the vicar and his assistant at the Parish Church, the Guild almshouses, the bridge, and the Guild school, renamed the King's New School of Stratford-upon-Avon. The importance of the school is indicated by the salary of the master, which was fixed at £20 per annum and a house ; the masters at Eton did not get more, and Stratford was able to attract graduates of standing from Oxford and Cambridge.

Under the new order the borough continued to show the old vitality ; in the days of the Guild it had given London a Lord Mayor, and England an Archbishop of Canterbury ; no greater miracle than the birth of genius was needed to give Stratford a still more illustrious son. The past generations had not left the way unprepared for him, since nothing could be further from the universal licence and ignorance imagined by Rowe than the Stratford into which Shakespeare was born.

The first mention found in Stratford records of John Shakespeare, the poet's father, is dated 1552, when he was fined along with two important townsmen, Adrian Quiney and Humfrey Reynolds, for making a new and unauthorized

refuse-heap in Henley Street.[1]  By this date John Shakespeare was renting the western house (which he purchased
in 1575 for £40) of the two now preserved by the Shakespeare trustees in Henley Street, and was carrying on there
the business of a glover or whitetawer, dealing not only in
gloves, girdles, purses, but parchment and articles made
from the softer leathers.  He must have left his home in
Snitterfield, 4 miles north of Stratford, where his father was
a yeoman farmer, some time before 1552, for he could  not
have been a member of the Craft of Glovers, Whitetawers
and Collarmakers, without serving an apprenticeship to the
mystery.  By 1556 he was able to buy the eastern house
of the pair, possibly for business purposes.  In 1557 he
married Mary Arden, the youngest daughter of Robert
Arden of Wilmecote, his father's landlord.

Robert Arden's father was Thomas Arden, the second
son of Walter Arden [2] of Park Hall.  The Ardens had been
the most important family in Warwickshire for many
generations, having settled there before the Conquest, and
their ancestor, Turchill, appears in Domesday Book as the
owner of large estates.  The family name of Arden was
taken from the district in Warwickshire where his possessions lay.  Robert Arden being the son of a younger son
had not inherited any large estate, but he was much better
off than most younger sons, possessing, besides his property
at Wilmecote, land in Snitterfield, part of which was rented
by John Shakespeare's father, Richard.  His most important
possession, an estate called Asbies, consisting of a house and

---

[1] This does not prove the indifference of the magistrates to sanitation,
as some have argued, but the reverse.  The Corporation sold the public
refuse-heaps from time to time, so that their financial interests were
also threatened.

[2] Walter Arden married Eleanor Hampden, daughter of John Hampden,
an ancestor of the great Hampden of the Civil War ; so that through
Eleanor Hampden, Shakespeare was connected with the patriot and statesman.

sixty acres in Wilmecote, he left at his death in 1556 to Mary, his other daughters and his second wife being provided for by previous settlements.

The first two children of the marriage were daughters, Joan (September 1558) and Margaret (December 1562) ; both died in infancy ; the third was a son, who was christened William on 26th April, 1564. His birthday is usually fixed from this as 23rd April, St. George's Day. There were three more sons, Gilbert (October 1566), Richard (March 1574), and Edmund (May 1580), who all died before the poet, and two more daughters, Joan (April 1569), mentioned in her brother's will, and Ann (September 1571), who died when eight years old.

By 1564 John Shakespeare was taking an important part in the affairs of the borough, having been elected to the Common Council in 1557, the year of his marriage ; after holding several of the minor offices, such as constable and affeeror, he was in October 1561 appointed one of the two Chamberlains who looked after the town's finances. During 1562 and 1563 he served with John Taylor, but although their term of office came to an end in 1563, they continued to do the work for William Tyler and William Smith, who were the titular Chamberlains for 1564 and 1565. The account presented in February 1566 is headed *The account of William Tyler and William Smith Chamberlains made by John Shakespeare.*[1]

It has been assumed by some scholars that John Shakespeare could neither read nor write because he regularly puts a mark against his name in the Council proceedings.[1] The town clerk wrote out the list of the Council and each man present signed or put a mark against his name. But the conclusion is another piece of conjectural history.

[1] See *In Shakespeare's Warwickshire*, by Oliver Baker. At p. 203 he shows that ' made ' in this context means ' written by.' At p. 188 he gives instances of burgesses who could write making their marks in Corporation Minutes.

Though the use of a mark to-day is good evidence of illiteracy, this does not hold for Elizabethan times. Even in the Stratford Council minutes there is found a mark by Adrian Quiney, some of whose letters in his own hand still exist. John Shakespeare could not possibly have kept the fairly lengthy borough accounts (that for 1565 has nearly 80 entries) without being able to give and accept receipts and make the necessary entries. His extra service as Chamberlain points to his being not only zealous in public business but particularly qualified for its discharge. In 1568 he was appointed to the highest office in the borough, that of Bailiff.

The poet then was born not only into an enlightened community but of parents whose connections and position suggest that from his earliest days he would lack neither breeding nor education. It has been supposed, however, that the difficulties his father had soon to encounter, and what has been represented as his own thoughtless and even culpable conduct, must have interfered with his education.

John Shakespeare was absent from the Council meeting of 23rd January, 1577, and although he had been a most energetic member for 20 years, he never attended again, except possibly on one occasion.[1] The first explanation offered of this change in John Shakespeare's conduct was that he had become so involved in financial difficulties that he could no longer afford the expenses of an alderman. On 29th January, 1578, when the other aldermen were entered for 6/8 to pay for three pikemen, two billmen and an archer, he is put down for 3/4 ; a year later it is noted that the sum was unpaid. He was also excused his contribution of 4d. a week for the poor. At this time, November 1578, he mortgaged his wife's property at Asbies to her brother-

---

[1] *Minutes and Accounts of the Corporation of Stratford-on-Avon,* R. Savage and E. Fripp, p. xxxiv. The details of John Shakespeare's progress in the Council are there well set out.

in-law, Edmund Lambert, for £40 ; and sold out a share
in the Snitterfield estate that had come to his wife since her
father's death, probably at the death of a sister. By
September 1580, however, he was ready to redeem Asbies,
and there is further proof that in 1580 he was, at least by
general report, a man of some substance.

In 1577 John Whitgift was made Bishop of Worcester,
and at once set about prosecuting all those in his diocese
who did not submit to the church as then established. He
punished both Puritans and Catholics, transmitting to the
Privy Council a list of those who were ' noted to bee
greate myslikers of the religion now professed and do absent
themselves from the churche with the valewes of their
landes and goodes, as they are thought to be worthe by the
common voyce and opynyon of men, and not otherwise ' ;
and the Bishop asked that some discipline be provided for
these offenders. When, therefore, John Shakespeare was
cited before the Queen's Bench in Westminster in June
1580, and fined £20 for failing to appear and provide
security that he would keep the Queen's peace, and when
he was at the same time fined another £20 for failing to
present a certain John Audley of Nottingham before the
court, it seems probable he was a victim of Whitgift's zeal
for conformity. In 1592 his name appears on a return of
recusants as one who had been ' heretofore presented,'
and the note is added that he is said to absent himself from
church for fear of arrest for debt. But as this is said of
others on the same list who are known to have been well-
to-do, and as there is no record of any process for debt
against him at the time, it may have been the kind of excuse
Whitgift had complained of, when he noted the difficulty
of procuring sufficient evidence against the Puritans. The
severe fine of 1580 indicates that the Government did not
regard John Shakespeare as a poor man.

The entries, therefore, in the Corporation minutes may indicate the Council's sympathy with a colleague whose well-known public zeal had brought him into collision with the authorities. This would explain his complete withdrawal from public affairs, and even the temporary transference of his wife's estate, for recusants were known to 'convey all their lands and goods to friends of theirs before their convictions.'[1] In September 1580, however, when John Shakespeare came to redeem the property Lambert refused to surrender it, claiming other monies as well. At Lambert's death John Shakespeare lodged a complaint against his son's inheriting the property, but only in 1597 did he venture to take the matter to the Court of Chancery, when his recusancy would no longer be held against him. He never, however, recovered the property.

At no time, in spite of his difficulties, can John Shakespeare have been in serious poverty, for he continued in possession of his valuable Henley Street houses and his business.

In view of the father's position and credit, the picture that has been drawn of his eldest son in destitution in London, driven there by 'the terror of a criminal prosecution,' waiting at the playhouse door to hold horses, hiring boys to help him, and then finding mean employment in the theatre, could be accepted only on good testimony. But the horse-holding story was not put into print till 1765, a hundred and fifty years after Shakespeare's death, when Dr. Johnson added it as a kind of postscript to Rowe's *Life*, with the note that it was said to have been related by Pope as coming from Rowe. Rowe, if he had ever heard of this remarkable adventure, did not include it among his anecdotes, though he had given currency to the deer-stealing story, to which it forms a natural sequel. This

[1] Thomas Carter, *Shakespeare, Puritan and Recusant.*

adventure is often represented as the turning point in Shake-speare's life, the accident that set him on his path to fame. Having robbed a deer-park belonging to Sir Thomas Lucy, he was prosecuted, so we are told, severely, and when he replied with a bitter ballad, the prosecution was so increased that he had to shelter from it in London, and take any mean employment that came his way. But there was no deer-park at Charlecote till 1618, when Sir Thomas Lucy's grandson obtained the licence, without which there could be no park. Had his grandfather possessed such a licence, it would have passed to him, as such licences did, with the estate.[1]

Nor does Shakespeare's marriage, as some suppose, support the view that he spent a wild and irregular youth of which the deer-stealing story retains some echoes, however distorted. In November 1582 he obtained a special licence from the Bishop of Worcester to marry Ann Hathaway in the church at Temple Grafton, near Stratford. For such a licence the Bishop required security to the extent of £40 that there was no impediment to the marriage. Shakespeare's father's name is not on the bond, as he did not wish to draw the attention of the ecclesiastical authorities to his standing ; but the licence could not have been ob-tained without his written consent, as his son was not yet nineteen. The first child of the marriage, Susanna, was born in May 1583, six months after the church ceremony, and on this fact much conjecture has been built. But this rests on ignorance of the customs of the time. Marriage in England at that time, as in Scotland to-day, required neither church, nor priest, nor document of any kind, only the declaration of the contracting parties in the presence of witnesses. Such a marriage was recognized by Church and State, and reflected in no way on the respectability of

[1] The story is examined by Smart, *Shakespeare Truth and Tradition*, p. 96.

the man and woman. It was customary, though not necessary, to follow the marriage proper at a convenient season by a ceremony in church.[1] To suppose that we have any evidence here of irregularity in Shakespeare's behaviour is merely to argue from procedure to-day to that of Elizabeth's time, and to provide another instance of the dangers of conjectural history.

In 1585 Hamnet and Judith Shakespeare were born, and christened on 2nd February in the parish church at Stratford, as was Susanna before them. If the story of the flight to London, first circulated nearly a hundred years after Shakespeare's death, is accepted, it must be supposed that he had to abandon his wife and family ; and the question of their support suggests itself. One must also inquire how he supported them before his departure for London. Fortunately we are not without information concerning his occupation between leaving school and turning dramatist.

This information comes from John Aubrey, who lived from 1625 to 1700, and is remembered for his valuable series of notes, left in manuscript at his death, about poets and men of letters. He visited Stratford and recorded what he heard there in this note :

> His father was a Butcher, and I have been told heretofore by some of the neighbours, that when he was a boy he exercised his father's Trade, but when he kill'd a Calfe, he would do it in a high style, and make a Speech. . . . This Wm being inclined naturally to Poetry and acting, came to London I guesse about 18 and was an Actor at one of the Play-houses and did act exceedingly well. . . . He began early to make essayes at Dramatique Poetry, which at that time was very lowe ; and his Playes took well : He was a handsome well shap't man : very good company, and of a very readie and pleasant smooth Witt.

[1] For an amusing instance of this procedure in most respectable society, see Hotson's *I, William Shakespeare*, p. 138 and 203 *seq.*

But the Stratford neighbour who told Aubrey that
John Shakespeare was a butcher was wrong : he was a
glover. There is no reason to suppose that the neighbour
was any better informed about the poet's own early business,
and his story is contradicted by what Aubrey learnt elsewhere.

Aubrey was advised to visit William Beeston, then an
old man, but called by Dryden—because of his long stage
experience and what he had heard from his father, who was
an actor and manager before him—' the chronicle of the
stage.' During the visit the talk turned to Jonson's
panegyric on Shakespeare and the statement that he had
' small Latine, and less Greeke ' ; for Aubrey made this
entry :

> Though as Ben Johnson sayes of him, that he had but
> little Latine and lesse Greeke, He understood Latine
> pretty well : for he had been in his younger yeares a
> Schoolmaster in the Country.

In the margin marking off this note from the rest of his
information, Aubrey put ' from Mr. Beeston.'

In estimating the value of this and other traditions about
Shakespeare it is well to have in mind the rule laid down by
the great Shakespeare scholar Malone :

> Where a tradition has been handed down, by a very
> industrious and careful inquirer, who has derived it from
> persons most likely to be accurately informed concerning
> the fact related, and subjoins his authority, such a species
> of tradition must always carry great weight along with it.

Since Aubrey was a very careful and industrious in-
quirer, and Beeston was in a position to know what he was
talking about, as his father, Christopher Beeston, had acted
with Shakespeare for at least six years, and since Aubrey
has subjoined his authority, the schoolmaster story satisfies
Malone's three requirements ; and this is the only tradition

about Shakespeare that does. Beside it the gossip of some Stratford neighbour, who was obviously not very sure of his facts, can carry no weight. Aubrey did not sift and arrange his notes for publication ; he set down what he heard ; we have to judge for ourselves the various degrees of credibility that attach to them. The schoolmaster tradition is not merely strong in itself ; it is supported by the type of play with which Shakespeare started as dramatist.

Aubrey, it is clear, heard nothing about the flight from Sir Thomas Lucy to London and Shakespeare's entering the theatre as by accident, and his explanation of Shakespeare's beginnings as an actor and dramatist, though less sensational, is certainly more natural than the later story. As Dr. Smart has pointed out, the early comedies have many happy references to the impulses that carry young men beyond the bounds where they were born.

> Such wind as scatters young men through the world
> To seek their fortunes further than at home,
> Where small experience grows,

blew strongly in that adventurous age ; and what we know of Stratford and its inhabitants, of his family, and of his own occupation there, suggests that Shakespeare left his native place not ill-equipped to make the most of his adventure. His earliest works plainly declare his literary ambitions ; and where could a young man with such ambitions, and with a wife and family to support, go but to London ?

## HIS OWN WRITINGS

SHAKESPEARE did not live to publish a collected edition of his works, but in 1623, seven years after his death, two of his old friends and fellow actors produced the First Folio edition of his Plays. The editors were John Heminge and Henry Condell, the last of a group of sharers which Shakespeare had joined some thirty years earlier and which had formed the inner circle of the Lord Chamberlain's Company. Shakespeare remembered in his will the survivors of this association : Burbage, Heminge, and Condell ; and when Burbage died in 1619, the two who remained inherited the pious task which they finally discharged in 1623, 'without ambition either of selfe-profit, or fame,' as they declare in their dedication to Shakespeare's noble admirers, the Earls of Pembroke and Montgomery, 'only to keepe the memory of so worthy a Friend, and Fellow alive, as was our SHAKESPEARE.'

The fellowship which laid this duty upon them had also given them peculiar knowledge and authority for its discharge. They had acted in the plays for some thirty years, and many they must have seen from the first rehearsal. And they could be in no doubt which were ' his owne writings,' for they were not only actors but the managers of the company. When, therefore, they declare in their address *To the great Variety of Readers*,

> His mind and hand went together : And what he thought, he uttered with that easinesse, that wee have scarce received from him a blot in his papers.

they are not merely mentioning a gift they admired in their

friend, but indicating that the ground of their assurance that they have given the public an authoritative text is the good condition of the papers they had from Shakespeare himself.

Such a combination of advantages for the task as Heminge and Condell possessed could have been found in no one except the author ; and with Shakespeare gone their very limitations were something of a blessing. They might have handed over the papers to some man of letters, for the modern editor with his facsimiles and brackets was still unborn ; but in the circumstances it was all to the good that the players, with no literary views to express save an admiration for the genius of their friend, should give the plays to the public as they found them. And a certain consequent ' roughness ' in their text, which was to be counted against them by generations of critics, is now welcomed by the modern editor as giving him a far better grip on Shakespeare's original manuscripts than would the smoother finish of some literary polisher.[1]

In the 18th century, however, this roughness, now regarded as a proof of their fidelity, was made the main ground for doubting the sincerity of their text. Pope and his contemporaries encountered in the early editions many obsolete words, technical terms and unfamiliar idioms, as well as a style of versification of which the refinements and variety were beyond their comprehension. The spelling and punctuation were also unfamiliar and puzzling. Lacking the historical knowledge necessary for dealing with these difficulties, the eighteenth century editors too readily explained away as the illiteracy of Heminge and Condell what did not conform to their own usage. For those who thought of Shakespeare as ' without the advantage of education ' naturally dismissed the first editors as ' mere

---

[1] ' The very roughness of the text before us is a guarantee of its authenticity. Professor Dover Wilson, *Introduction to Antony and Cleopatra*.

players,' and talked of Shakespeare's works being left to
' the Care of Door-keepers and Prompters,' and as ' long
neglected amongst the common Lumber of the Stage.'

But while Pope and his contemporaries ignored the
most explicit statements by Heminge and Condell about
the fidelity of their text, they accepted without criticism
one passage in the address to the general reader which
seemed to discredit all versions previous to the First Folio.
During Shakespeare's lifetime, and some thirty years before
the publication of the First Folio, his plays began to appear
singly in Quarto editions, and by 1623 some twenty had
been so printed, though of these only fourteen were in
versions at all similar to those in the First Folio. But it
seemed that Heminge and Condell characterised all alike
as pirated and mutilated versions when they wrote :

> It had bene a thing, we confesse, worthie to have bene
> wished, that the Author himselfe had liv'd to have set
> forth, and overseen his owne writings ; But since it hath
> bin ordain'd otherwise, and he by death departed from
> that right, we pray you do not envie his Friends, the
> office of their care, and paine, to have collected & publish'd
> them ; and so to have publish'd them, as where (before)
> you were abus'd with diverse stolne, and surreptitious
> copies, maimed, and deformed by the frauds and stealthes
> of iniurious impostors, that expos'd them : even those,
> are now offer'd to your view cur'd, and perfect of their
> limbes ; and all the rest, absolute in their numbers, as
> he conceived them.

Heminge and Condell, it was thought, condemned all
the Quartos as the mutilated productions of thieving
publishers. But this condemnation returned on their own
heads. For it was discovered that the Quartos and Folio,
though in many instances offering a very different text, in
others gave so similar a version as to make it certain that the
Folio was here little more than a reprint of the Quartos.

The more, therefore, the minute examination of the text during the 18th century restored as authoritative the readings of Heminge and Condell, the more it emphasized the partial dependence of the Folio on the Quartos. Thus any decisive answer to Pope's ill-founded criticism was difficult, while Heminge and Condell were thought so lost to ordinary standards of decency as to have passed off on the public in the body of their work what in their preface they denounced as imperfect and fraudulent.

Pope saw the most important textual fact about the first editions of Shakespeare's plays : the printers had worked from papers intended for use in the theatre ; for actors' names are sometimes substituted for the characters they played, and the stage directions are for the stage, not for the study. But Pope went on to argue that texts printed ' from no better copies than the Prompter's Book ' must necessarily give a version of Shakespeare's original that had been ' cut or added to arbitrarily ' by ignorant players.

In support of this view Pope cites the famous passage where Hamlet inveighs against clowns who speak more than is set down for them, and who hinder with their untimely jests the necessary business of the stage. But it is clear that Shakespeare disliked such gagging on the stage, and that the company as a whole were with him, though Kempe had left them just before Shakespeare wrote the scene, perhaps for this very reason. What Hamlet would have said, if the clown's ambition had stretched to inserting his jests in the prompt book, cannot have been sufficiently considered by Pope.

Pope's hasty conclusion, however, was accepted as a self-evident truth : Theobald talks of the first editors printing from parts ' which had gone through as many Changes as Performers ' ; and Dr. Johnson only enlarged

on current opinion when he wrote of Shakespeare's work
as having been

> Multiplied by transcript after transcript, vitiated by
> the blunders of the penman, or changed by the affectation
> of the player ; perhaps enlarged to introduce a jest, or
> mutilated to shorten the representation ; and printed at
> last without the concurrence of the author, without the
> consent of the proprietor, from compilations made by
> chance or by stealth out of the separate parts written for
> the theatre.

Johnson has exploited with all the rigour of his logic
the confusion that follows from Pope's view that Shakespeare's text was handed down by thieving publishers and
dishonest editors. Fortunately his premises were mistaken.
Careful examination of the theatrical documents that
survive from Elizabethan and Jacobean times, and the study
of the conditions then governing book production, especially the printing of play books, not only give no support
to Pope's views of general illiteracy, dishonesty and theft,
but prove the truth in most instances to be the exact opposite
of what he maintained.

The few Elizabethan and Jacobean plays that survive in
manuscript do not bear out the statement that their parts
' went through as many changes as performers.' Indeed,
an author's manuscript might be sent in the author's auto-
graph direct to the Master of the Revels for the allowance
without which there could be no legal performance ; and
the ' allowed book ' might then pass to the prompter for
annotation. Massinger's *Believe as You List* passed thus from
author to prompter with no mutilation of the author's text.
Had all Shakespeare's plays been printed from prompt
books, this would give no ground for Pope's criticism of
their text. But many of the irregularities that so offended
the earlier editors are of a kind that mark the printer's copy
not as a prompt book but as a draft in the author's own

hand before it had been put in working order by the prompter.[1]

This internal evidence, taken with that from the relevant available manuscripts, often points to the printed text having been set up directly from Shakespeare's own papers. And as this conclusion applies as often to the Quartos as to the Folio texts, it would by itself overturn the idea that all the Quartos give stolen and mutilated versions. But it is supported by the evidence now available about the printing and publishing of the period.

There was no copyright in the modern sense in the reign of Elizabeth, or for many years after. A printer or publisher, however, could by an entry in the Day Book of the Stationers' Company, of which he was bound to be a member, secure the sole right of issuing a work in his possession, provided the Master or one of the Wardens was satisfied that the manuscript had been licensed for printing by some recognized authority. The entry in the Stationers' Register for the First Folio is as follows :

8th November 1623.

Master Blounte    *Entred for their Copie under the hands*
Isaak Jaggard.    *of Master Doctor Worrall and Master*
                 *Cole warden Master William Shakspeers*
                 *Comedyes Histories, and Tragedyes soe manie*
                 *of the said Copies as are not formerly*
                 *entred to other men.      viz$^{t}$.*
                    *The Tempest*
                    *The two gentlemen of Verona*
Comedyes.         *Measure for Measure*
                    *The Comedy of Errors*
                    *As you like it*
                    *All's well that ends well*

[1] *The Elizabethan Printer and Dramatic Manuscripts,* by R. B. McKerrow. *The Library,* December, 1931.

*Twelfe night*
*The winters tale*

---

Histories        *The thirde parte of Henry the sixt*
*Henry the eight*

---

                *Coriolanus*
Tragedies.       *Timon of Athens*
                *Julius Caesar*
                *Mackbeth*
                *Anthonie and Cleopatra*
                *Cymbeline*

Mr. Cole is the Warden of the Company who makes the ' entrance ' in the Register ; Doctor Worrall, one of the licensers appointed by the Archbishop of Canterbury, gives the ' authority ' for printing.

The entries for the early Quartos mention or name the Warden or Wardens, but usually omit that of the licenser ; later the signature of the Master of the Revels in a play-book was sufficient authority for printing.[1]

Though it was possible for a printer who had indirectly come by a manuscript to enter it in the Register as his copy, without the author's permission, and even to oppose with success the author's efforts to have it printed for himself;[2] yet Shakespeare's Company had a powerful protector in the Lord Chamberlain, since this official was a member of the Privy Council under whose authority the Stationers' Company acted. In the end the Players made use of this authority. In 1637 the Lord Chamberlain, who was the Earl of Pembroke and Montgomery, and the second of the noble brethren to whom Heminge and Condell

[1] R. Crompton Rhodes, *Shakespeare's First Folio*, p. 28.

[2] " *The Spanish Tragedy* "—*A Leading Case ?* by W. W. Greg. *The Library*, June 1925.

dedicated the First Folio, wrote to the Master and Wardens :

*I am informed that some copies of playes belonging to the King and Queen's servants, the players, . . . having been lately stolen or gotten from them by indirect means, are now attempted to be printed . . . that if any playes be already entered, or shall hereafter be brought unto the hall to be entered for printing, that notice thereof be given to . . . the players, and an enquiry made of them to whom they do belong; and that none be suffered to be printed until the assent of their Majesties' said servants be made appear to the Master and Wardens.*

He refers to the complaints formerly addressed to ' my dear brother and predecessor ' by the players about the unauthorized publication of their plays ' by means whereof not only they themselves had much prejudice, but the books much corruption to the injury and disgrace of the authors,' and he repeats his brother's instructions of May 1619 [1] that the plays belonging to Their Majesties' Servants are not to be printed without their consent.

The powers of such officials as the Lord Chamberlain had no doubt become better defined since Elizabeth's day, but already in Shakespeare's lifetime his Company were able to enter playbooks in the Stationers' Register as their own property with the note that they were ' to be staied.' The Players, however, would hardly appeal to the Lord Chamberlain, or to the special power that seems to lie behind

---

[1] These documents were recorded by Malone. Crompton Rhodes used them in his *Shakespeare's First Folio*, p. 44. See Chambers' *William Shakespeare*, p. 136. The letter of May 1619 is not preserved but is mentioned in the following entry from Court Book C. This is still unpublished, and I have to thank Dr. Greg for the information.

3rd May, 1619.

*Hen. Hemmings.   Upon a letter from the right Noble the Lo. Chamberlain.*
*It is thought fit and so ordered that no plays that*
*his Majesty's players do play shall be printed without*
*consent of some of them.*

The letter of 1637 is printed in the Malone Society's Collections, ii(3), 384-5.

such an entry, if simpler methods were available ; and they sometimes protected themselves by having a friendly printer enter as his any book of which they feared to lose control. At the cost of sixpence, the fee for entry, they blocked against the pirate the regular path to publication. Both ' staying ' and ' blocking ' entries are found for Shakespeare's plays.

Professor Pollard [1] has thus replaced the old opinion that the Stationers and their Company were merely a gang of pirates whenever they touched Shakespeare's plays by the more probable view that piracy is a possibility but not necessarily the rule. And he has established the division of the Quartos into Good Quartos and Bad Quartos ; for though the distinction was recognized in practice, almost from the first, by Shakespeare's editors, its critical implications were ignored in discussions of the text. Professor Pollard's first definition, however, of a Bad Quarto as one giving a mutilated text and having, at most, an irregular entry in the Stationers' Register requires modification. For such early Bad Quartos as *The Contention* and *A Shrew* were regularly entered ; but this was at a time when the Companies, badly hit by the long continuance of the Plague in London and the closing of the town theatres, were reorganizing and changing patrons, and when the confusion must have made it unprofitable to argue about the ownership of disputed plays. Those texts, however, which internal evidence marks as good are all regularly entered in the Register, except when they replace pirated versions. The testimony of the Stationers' Register supports the finding of the successive editors that fourteen of the Quartos give authoritative texts.

---

[1] Some earlier editors, notably Knight in his *Cabinet Shakespeare*, Vol. XII, pp. 230-5, maintained much the same opinion as Professor Pollard ; but it was Pollard's *Shakespeare's Fight with the Pirates* that made further argument, except on details, unnecessary.

The simple distinction between the Bad and the Good Quartos not only gives a new standing to fourteen of these early texts ; it completely restores the good name and authority of Heminge and Condell ; for it can now be shown that their statements square with the facts.  The ' diverse stolne and surreptitious copies ' which they declare ' maimed and deformed ' are the seven or eight Bad Quartos which had been put together piecemeal from actors' parts or imperfect reports.  Some of them Shakespeare did not trouble to replace with good versions ; but ' even those,' Heminge and Condell tell us, ' are now offer'd to your view cur'd and perfect of their limbes.' As for ' all the rest,' Heminge and Condell had the necessary papers in their possession.  But they did not always have the printing done directly from these papers.  Among the Quartos were some issued with the express purpose of replacing versions of important plays so mutilated that they could not but bring the dramatist into discredit with the judicious reader.  Such good versions would naturally carry with them special authority.  What is surprising is not that Heminge and Condell were content to have such versions of *Romeo and Juliet* and *Love's Labour's Lost* reprinted in the Folio more or less as they stood in the Quartos, but that they had *Hamlet* printed from manuscript, though the Good Quarto of that play replaced a Bad one, and gives a text of peculiar authority.  It is clear, however, that they reprinted Quarto texts not of necessity but from choice, and even when they did use a Quarto, they compared it with papers in their own possession.

Though all the notable differences and resemblances between the First Folio texts and the Quartos, Good or Bad, have not so far been explained with certainty and precision, enough has been done to make it clear that a quite intelligible order is emerging from the confusion, an order that at once illustrates and is explained by what is known from other sources of the theatrical and publishing conditions of the day. Like the irregularities of their text, the reprinting of the Quartos by Heminge and Condell, when carefully considered in this new light, so far from weakening actually strengthens their authority.

If the textual evidence drawn from a comparison of the Quartos with the First Folio is all in favour of the good faith of Heminge and Condell, the very history of the printing of their volume reveals their determination to make it as complete a record as possible of Shakespeare's theatrical pieces.

Heminge and Condell gave the printing of the volume to William Jaggard [1] and his son Isaac. What is known, however, of the earlier dealings of this house with Shakespeare's work raises the question how they came to be chosen for the task. In 1599 William Jaggard had put Shakespeare's name to a collection of poems called *The Passionate Pilgrim*, though five only of its twenty pieces were by Shakespeare. In 1612 he added to the third edition ' two love epistles, the first from Paris to Hellen and Hellen's answer back to Paris,' from a work, the *Troia Britannica*, which he had printed in 1609 for Heywood. On the title page he put ' newly corrected and augmented, by W. Shakespeare.' Heywood, in a dedicatory epistle to his *Apology for Actors*, informed the public, in self-defence as he explained, of the dishonesty of this device, and added that Shakespeare was ' much offended with Mr. Jaggard that altogether unknown to him presumed to make so bold with his name.' The title page was cancelled, no doubt because of these protests.

But after Shakespeare's death Jaggard took an even greater liberty with his name, putting it on eight of the

---

[1] Who died shortly before the entry of the First Folio on 8th Nov. 1623.

nine title pages to a collection of ten plays which he issued in 1619. The titles and imprints are as follows :

| | |
|---|---|
| *The Whole Contention* [1] | Printed at London, for T.P. |
| *Pericles* | Printed for T.P. 1619. |
| *A Yorkshire Tragedy* | Printed for T.P. 1619. |
| *Merry Wives of Windsor* | Printed for Arthur Johnson, 1619. |
| *Merchant of Venice* | Printed by J. Roberts, 1600. |
| *Midsummer Night's Dream* | Printed by James Roberts, 1600. |
| *King 'Lear* | Printed for Nathaniel Butter. 1608. |
| *Henry V* | Printed for T.P. 1608. |
| *Sir John Oldcastle* | London printed for T.P. 1600. |

All, with the exception of *Henry V*, he ascribed to Shakespeare. But only three, *Merchant of Venice*, *Midsummer Night's Dream*, and *Lear* were good Shakespearean texts ; the others were pirated versions, or plays by other hands than Shakespeare's. As almost all these composite volumes had in the course of time been broken up into single plays, scholars were puzzled by the existence of what they took to be two editions of *Merchant of Venice*, dated 1600 but with very different imprints, two of *Midsummer Night's Dream* in 1600, and two of *Lear* in 1608, with the same puzzling differences. Professor Pollard, however, saw two surviving copies of Jaggard's volume, and Dr. Greg, following up the clue this gave, proved that all the plays in this volume, whatever the date of the imprint, had been printed in 1619. The statement, *Printed by James Roberts, 1600,* on *Merchant of Venice* and *Midsummer Night's Dream* was in one sense true, for Roberts had printed the first for Hayes in that year ; but it was incorrect in form and misleading on an edition printed by Jaggard in 1619, not in 1600 by Roberts. Jaggard no doubt put it in this form to strengthen his claim to reprint derelicts, works not reprinted

---

[1] This includes *The Contention* and *The True Tragedy*.

for twenty years, since he had taken over the business of their first printer, Roberts. The son of Hayes, however, had an entry inserted in the Register indicating that he inherited his father's rights in *The Merchant of Venice*. And it was doubtless Jaggard's publication that roused the players to seek redress from the Lord Chamberlain, and occasioned his letter (*see* page 34 *n.*) to the Stationers' Company, directing them to forbid the publication of plays belonging to the King's men ' without consent of some of them.'

But Jaggard's irregularities proved that he had every confidence in the commercial value of Shakespeare's name, and Heminge and Condell may well have been glad to come to terms with so willing a collaborator.[1]   Jaggard was also in a position, through his friends Pavier and Butter, to smooth away any difficulties about the printing rights of a number of the plays.   In this venture he was joined by three publishers : Blount, to whom Heminge and Condell gave the publishing rights of the sixteen plays entered on 8th November, 1623, Aspley and Smethwick, who between them had rights in six more. If the rights covered by what has been called the Pavier Shakespeare of 1619 are added to those of these three publishers, the only outstanding claims are three by Law and a fourth by Bonian and Walley ; for doubtless Walkley was given *Othello* in 1621 only on conditions that reserved the right of publication in the collected edition, then arranged for.[2]   The detailed record of the printing of the First Folio that Mr. Edwin E. Willoughby [3] has put together from an examination of the ornaments and typographical features of the volume

---

[1] Even Shakespeare himself, no doubt to save argument, allowed Ling, who had published the Bad Quarto of *Hamlet*, to issue the authentic text.

[2] See Appendix, Table E.

[3] *The Printing of the First Folio of Shakespeare*, 1932.

indicates the trouble and delay that could come from such claims.

Jaggard advertised the First Folio in the Catalogue of the Frankfort Book Fair as ready by October 1622. But a dispute with Ralph Brooke, York Herald, about the responsibility for the errors in a work Jaggard had just printed for him, held up the First Folio, and gave Mr. Willoughby a clue to its problems. Brooke had so offended his colleagues that they were glad their enemy had written a book ; and Augustine Vincent, Rouge Croix pursuivant, annotated the volume with the help of his colleagues to bring out Brooke's responsibility for the mistakes. This *Discovery* Jaggard hastened to print. The volume shared an elaborate tailpiece with the First Folio, and this ornament developed a flaw in the course of printing. It is found in the Folio, as in the *Discovery*, in two states : so that those parts of the Folio with the ornament in the first state date from before the completion of the *Discovery*. As Jaggard pushed on the *Discovery* (S.R. 29th October, 1621) with all the resources at his disposal, since Brooke was printing a vindication elsewhere, the parts of the Folio with the ornament in the second state come after the issue of the *Discovery*.

Beginning late in 1621 Jaggard printed the Comedies, with the exception of *The Winter's Tale*, which has the damaged ornament, and had printed *King John* and two pages of *Richard II*, to the end of quire *b*, when he stopped work on the Folio for Vincent's *Discovery*. Early in May 1623 he began again where he left off, but after finishing quire *c* in *Richard II* he went back and printed *The Winter's Tale* and then proceeded with *Henry V* and 1 2 and 3 *Henry VI* as far as quire *o*. This second break in the printing of *Richard II* and the omission for the time of 1 and 2 *Henry IV* suggest that Law, who had rights in *Richard II* and 1 *Henry IV*, was raising difficulties, especially as he had

*Richard III* and 1 *Henry IV* reprinted in 1622 on his own behalf. In March 1623 the Lord Chamberlain intervened with a letter,[1] and Law must have agreed to terms, for Jaggard then filled in the gap. The only other delay was with *Troilus and Cressida* which was to follow *Romeo and Juliet*. After printing three pages of *Troilus* Jaggard left room for the remainder, but on completing the Tragedies he removed these pages of *Troilus* and substituted *Timon of Athens*. Only after he had completed the Catalogue of the contents, which does not include *Troilus*, did he find the impediment to its printing removed; he then placed it between the Histories and the Tragedies. No doubt Bonian and Walley, who had admitted in their preface to *Troilus* that the actors were against their printing the play, were glad to raise in their turn similar objections.

When the difficulties of choosing the copy for the text are added to the troubles arising from the printing rights of the Stationers, no one can doubt that Heminge and Condell were entitled in offering the plays to the public to mention ' their care and pain to have collected and published them.' And the most searching inquiry having shown their fidelity in these matters, the doubt cast on their repeated statements that the plays they publish are Shakespeare's is merely gratuitous, for contemporary references to these plays, whenever available, support the attributions of Heminge and Condell. Few who have studied the attempts of those who set up to know better than Heminge and Condell what are or are not Shakespeare's plays will hasten to rush in where even great poets and critics can

---

[1] From the unpublished Court Book C. I owe this information also to Dr. Greg.

3rd March, 1623

*Playes. This day a letter from my lord Chamberlain was openly read to all the Master Printers concerning the licensing of Plays etc. by Sir John Ashley, the copy whereof is in the Book of Letters.*

look foolish and untaught.[1]  And the student of to-day
has no longer any excuse for comparing indiscriminately
early with later work and declaring them incompatible.
The early plays are very different from the later masterpieces ; but one can point to such differences in the work
of poets, musicians, and artists, of every age.  Indeed it is
in the greatest creators that such differences are most marked,
for in them the capacity for work and self-development is
infinitely greater than in ordinary men.  And quite apart
from the peculiar difficulties that beset such dramatists as
Shakespeare and Molière, on whom the daily fortunes of a
company largely rested, Shakespeare is one of the great
innovators who are constantly calling upon their brain to
conceive and their hand to execute things to which all
previous achievement in the arts has shown no certain road.
When these human limitations have been allowed for, the
work contained in the First Folio can be seen as a whole in
all its massive proportions, a range of plays in which the
pinnacles and steeps of godlike hardship are securely
buttressed by the more accessible slopes below.

## ORDER OF COMPOSITION OF THE PLAYS

Heminge and Condell did not, unfortunately, think it
necessary to indicate the date of composition or production of
any of the plays.  Generations of scholars have therefore had
to search for the evidence that would establish, approximately
at least, their chronology.  And here, as in other lines of Shakespearean investigation, careful inquiry has shown that the early
conclusions about the irregularity of the poet's genius are but
hasty assumptions which run counter to the facts.  At the
beginning of the 18th century Rowe could say : ' Perhaps we
are not to look for his beginnings, like those of other authors,
among their least perfect writings ; art had so little, and nature

---

[1] Examples of this are discussed in *Essays and Studies for the English
Association*, Vol. XVI, p. 96, *seq.*

so large a share in what he did, that, for ought I know, the performances of his youth, as they were the most vigorous, and had the most fire and strength of imagination in 'em, were the best.' By the end of the century the labours of its editors, particularly Malone, had shown that Shakespeare's art attained its perfection, as Knight observes, only ' by repeated experiment and assiduous labour.'

The evidence for date may be classified as follows :

### 1. *Date of Publication, or Entry in the Stationers' Register*

These dates fix the lower limit of composition, but as the players were unwilling to print new and successful pieces, there is usually a considerable lag to be allowed for. But *Troilus* (1603), *As You Like It* (1600), and *Antony and Cleopatra* (1608), were entered some time before publication, probably in special circumstances and not long after their production. The entry for *Lear* (1607) mentions a court performance of the previous year, December 1606.

The publication of a Bad Quarto, such as *A Shrew*, proves the existence of the original at that date.

### 2. *Record of Performance*

(a) *Revels Accounts*, which record among other court performances : *Othello* (1604), *Measure for Measure* (1604), *The Winter's Tale* (1611), *The Tempest* (1611).

(b) *Henslowe's Diary* is important for the early period, and for the combination of negative evidence about Shakespeare's plays during the season when Lord Strange's men occupied the Rose, and of positive evidence for the short season (June 1594) at Newington Butts, when the same company, now the Lord Chamberlain's men, played in *Titus Andronicus*, *The Shrew* and an early *Hamlet*.

(c) *Other diaries, letters, records.* *Comedy of Errors* was performed at a Christmas entertainment at Gray's Inn (December 1594). Platter saw *Julius Caesar* (September 1599) ; Manningham, *Twelfth Night* (February 1602) ; Forman, *Macbeth, Cymbeline* and *Winter's Tale*, all in 1611 ; Sir Henry Wotton, the first

4

performance of *Henry VIII* (June 1613), at which the Globe was burnt down. *Richard II* was played (December 1595) at the house of Sir Edward Hoby.

### 3. *References or Quotations in Contemporary Publications*

The most important is by Francis Meres in his *Palladis Tamia: Wits Treasury* (1598) :

'As *Plautus* and *Seneca* are accounted the best for Comedy and Tragedy among the Latines : so *Shakespeare* among the English is the most excellent in both kinds for the stage ; for Comedy, witness his *Gentlemen of Verona*, his *Errors*, his *Love labors lost*, his *Love labours wonne*, his *Midsummers night dreame*, & his *Merchant of Venice* : for Tragedy his *Richard the 2, Richard the 3, Henry the 4, King John, Titus Andronicus* and his *Romeo and Juliet.*'

Before this he mentions ' his *Venus and Adonis*, his *Lucrece*, his sugred Sonnets among his private friends.'

Nash refers to 1 *Henry VI* in *Pierce Penilesse* (August 1592) : Greene quotes from 3 *Henry VI* in his *Groatsworth of Wit* (September 1592). Daniel made certain alterations in his *Cleopatra*, reprinted in 1607, which it has been argued were suggested by Shakespeare's *Antony and Cleopatra*.

Gabriel Harvey mentions *Hamlet* in a manuscript note in his copy of Chaucer (probably before February 1601).

The Bad Quarto of *Hamlet* (1603) incorporates matter from *Othello* and *Twelfth Night*, and the Bad Quarto of *Merry Wives of Windsor* (1602) includes a line from *Hamlet* (v, i, 283).

### 4. *References in the Plays to contemporary History ; or Quotations from contemporary publications*

The Chorus of *Henry V* tells of Essex in Ireland, *Macbeth* alludes to the trial of Father Garnet (1606), *The Tempest* to the wreck on the Bermudas reported in London in the autumn of 1610, 2 *Henry IV* to Amurath's slaughter of his brothers (February 1596), *Merry Wives of Windsor* indicates a Garter feast as its first occasion, and other references suggest the year ; the Prologue to *Troilus* refers to that of the *Poetaster* (1601). *As You Like It* contains a quotation from *Hero and Leander* (1598), *Lear* includes names from Harsnet's *Declaration of Popish Impostures* (1603). *Richard II* borrows from Daniel's *Civil Wars* (1595).

### 5. *Style and Versification*

Evidence from the foregoing sources establishes an order among the plays that reveals the gradual development of Shakespeare's art. The conduct of the action becomes less mechanical, the characterization more searching, the thought and feeling more profound. The diction and versification show a corresponding development in richness and variety. Attempts have been made to isolate certain elements of the versification that can be shown statistically, in the hope that these figures may confirm or refine on the conclusions from other sources.

In the earlier blank verse the unit is the line ; later the sense is drawn out variously from line to line. What are called ' run-on lines ' and ' light and weak ' endings are devices to obtain this continuity, and they tend to increase in numbers from period to period, till the paragraph replaces the line as the unit of versification, speeches tending to break the line, which itself becomes freer and less mechanically decasyllabic.

### (a) *Rhyme and Prose*

The later plays have little rhyme except in songs, masques and special pieces ; these features set aside, *The Winter's Tale* has none. On the other hand, *Love's Labour's Lost* has about a thousand rhyming lines. But it would be wrong to place it or *A Midsummer Night's Dream*, which is also rich in rhyme, for this reason alone among the very earliest pieces. A rhyming period seems to come about the time of *Venus and Adonis* and *Lucrece* and to include *Romeo and Juliet* and *Richard II*.

The early histories have little prose : *Richard II* and *John* have none : *2 Henry VI* is an exception in the half-comic Cade scenes. Prose increases rapidly in comedy, and one can see why it is so prominent in the discursive *Hamlet*, while used so sparingly in the earlier *Julius Caesar* or the later *Macbeth*.

These features provide no mechanical means for dating the plays.

### (b) *End-stopt and Run-on Lines*

The many degrees between the definitely end-stopt and the obviously run-on line make differences in reckoning these features inevitable. The distinction, however, can be clearly seen by comparing the following passages. The second is from about 1603-4, the first from before 1592.

> The birds chant melody on every bush,
> The snake lies rolled in the cheerful sun,
> The green leaves quiver with the cooling wind
> And make a chequer'd shadow on the ground.
> Under their sweet shade, Aaron, let us sit,
> And, whilst the babbling echo mocks the hounds,
> Replying shrilly to the well-tun'd horns,
> As if a double hunt were heard at once ;
> Let us sit down and mark their yelping noise.
>
> *Titus Andronicus*, II, iii, 12-20.

> Ay, but to die, and go we know not where ;
> To lie in cold obstruction and to rot ;
> This sensible warm motion to become
> A kneaded clod ; and the delighted spirit
> To bathe in fiery floods, or to reside
> In thrilling region of thick-ribbed ice ;
> To be imprison'd in the viewless winds
> And blown with restless violence round about
> The pendent world ; or to be worse than worst
> Of those that lawless and incertain thought
> Imagine howling.
>
> *Measure for Measure*, III, i, 119-129.

### (c) *Light and Weak Endings*

These mark an extension of the principle governing the run-on line. *Light endings* may be formed by such words as : *I, thou, he, she, them, am, is, are,* and auxiliaries like, *do, have, may, shall.* Even lighter are the *Weak endings : and, or, at, by, or, from,* etc. They appear in numbers somewhat suddenly with *Antony and Cleopatra,* and form a very characteristic feature of the final style as found in that tragedy, *Coriolanus* and the Romances.  The following passage, dating from about 1610, illustrates this further development : its opening line has a *light* and its second a *weak* ending.

> Not for Bohemia, nor the pomp that may
> Be thereat glean'd, for all the sun sees or
> The close earth wombs or the profound sea hides
> In unknown fathoms, will I break my oath
> To this my fair belov'd.  Therefore, I pray you,
> As you have ever been my father's honour'd friend,
> When he shall miss me—as, in faith, I mean not
> To see him any more—cast your good counsels
> Upon his passion : let myself and fortune
> Tug for the time to come.
>
> The Winter's Tale, IV, iv, 480-489.

### (d) *Double Endings*

These are frequent in some early plays.  In the later plays they again become a notable feature as the fifth, seventh, eighth and ninth lines of the foregoing passage show : but they are now often used to produce a new and peculiar form of rhythm, which finds its extremest expression in *Henry VIII* (*e.g.*, Wolsey's farewell, III, ii, 351-373).  Fletcher greatly affects this rhythm, and parts of *Henry VIII* have for this reason been ascribed to him.  But all the peculiarities in this form of verse are in rapid growth in *The Tempest* and *The Winter's Tale* :—

> if 'twere a kibe,
> 'Twould put me to my slipper : but I feel not
> This deity in my bosom : twenty consciences,
> That stand 'twixt me and Milan, candied be they
> And melt ere they molest ! Here lies your brother,
> No better than the earth he lies upon,
> If he were that which now he's like, that's dead ;
> Whom I, with this obedient steel, three inches of it,
> Can lay to bed for ever.
>
> The Tempest, II, i, 267-275.

These lines, like many more in the play, show so plainly the caesura after the seventh syllable, the over-riding rhythm, the double endings and other features of the verse of *Henry VIII*, that the common authorship cannot be questioned merely on metrical grounds. This form, more mechanical than the fourth period style at its best, suits the declamatory nature of much of *Henry VIII*.

Numerous other features of the verse, such as the internal pauses in the line classified carefully according to their precise position and nature, have been proposed for counting and in part enumerated. Such investigations at least emphasise, from the outside, the complexity of the verse, which is an index of the poet's inward development ; but they have not yet helped to date any play more certainly than the available external evidence, when combined with the broadest considerations of style and manner.

Mr. Hart has pointed out that since the average prose line in many editions contains fewer words than the average verse line, we should select, when counting, an edition in which they are approximately equal ; otherwise comparisons of length between the plays will be misleading. He also demonstrates how the figures in column 1, Table F, are by themselves evidence of the fact that Shakespeare was ' first and above all, a poet and creative artist.' Since the ' two hours traffic of the stage ' would not permit of the declamation of more than 2,500 lines at the very outside,[1] the 3,799 lines of *Hamlet* could never have been intended for performance. Shakespeare must have known that it could be presented only in an abridged version, though, like Ben Jonson, he chose to put on paper his conception in its full and perfect form.

The tables in the Appendix summarise the evidence afforded by verse tests and the Stationers' Register.

TABLE A *includes details of the Quarto publication of plays included in the First Folio.*

---

[1] A. Hart, *Shakespeare and the Homilies*, p. 110. The play began at 2 o'clock (p. 98) and the performance, including the jig, was probably over well before 4.30 p.m. (p. 113).

TABLE B, *of plays previously entered but not published, and of Pericles.*

TABLE C, *of two plays on plots used by Shakespeare.*

TABLE D, *of the Poems.*

TABLE E *indicates the ownership of Quarto printing rights in 1623.*

TABLE F *contains a summary of the metrical characteristics of the plays.*

NOTE—The extracts from the Stationers' Register are taken from Arber's *Transcript of the Register of the Company of Stationers*, except where another source is named.

The numbering of acts, scenes, and lines, is that of *The Cambridge Shakespeare* (1891).

# III

## THE FIRST PERIOD

FROM SHAKESPEARE'S ARRIVAL IN LONDON TO HIS JOINING
THE CHAMBERLAIN'S MEN (1594)

SHAKESPEARE joined the Chamberlain's men not later than 1594, and with this Company he was to continue for the rest of his life. From that year his career as a dramatist is known at least in outline ; but it is natural that the evidence of his earlier activities, when he was still a newcomer with his way to make, should be very imperfect, and that only when he is emerging as an author and dramatist of reputation should we hear of him at all. Not till the end of this first period are there any certain references to his work on the stage, but these throw back some light on his previous history.

The first printed reference to Shakespeare deals with his work as a dramatist. On 3rd September, 1592, Robert Greene, the poet, pamphleteer and dramatist, died in poverty and distress. He had lived an irregular and, financially at least, an unprofitable life ; and on his death-bed he wrote a work whose title summarises its contents :

*Greenes, Groats-worth of witte bought with a million of Repentance. Describing the follie of youth, the falshood of makshifte flatterers, the miserie of the negligent, and mischiefes of deceiving Courtezans*

At the conclusion he placed a letter,

*To those Gentlemen his Quondam acquaintance,
that spend their wits in making plaies, R. G.
wisheth a better exercise, and wisdome
to prevent his extremities.*

As this superscription tells us, the letter is a warning against the folly of working for actors, whom Greene represents as an ungrateful tribe that have abandoned him in his need ;

from such creatures his friends need expect no better treatment in the distress to which, he warns them, they are
heading. It was an old complaint with Greene that the
actors took the profits and left the dramatist to starve,
though they were merely the puppets who spoke from his
mouth ; in their prosperity they had become a race of
upstarts, 'proud with Aesop's crow,' as Greene in his
*Franciscoes Fortunes* reminded one successful performer,
'being dressed in the glory of others feathers.' But to
this Greene has now to add a new complaint : one of
these puppets had actually taken to writing, and was
challenging the best of Greene's friends on their own
ground ; and since the actors would naturally favour a
playwright from their own ranks, the prospects of the
scholar dramatist were worse than ever.

> Yes trust them not : for there is an upstart Crow,
> beautified with our feathers, that with his *Tygers hart*
> *wrapt in a Players hyde*, supposes he is as well able to
> bombast out a blanke verse as the best of you : and beeing
> an absolute *Iohannes fac totum*, is in his owne conceit the
> onely Shake-scene in a countrey.

The actor dramatist, as the quotation and the play on
the name indicate, is Shakespeare ; and Greene regards
him as a successful rival, though he affects to despise his
merits as a poet, contemptuously misquoting one of his
lines to ridicule his style and blacken his character. The
line that Greene parodies,

> Oh Tygres Heart, wrapt in a Womans Hide

is from 3 *Henry VI*, I, iv, 137, but it is also found in a
publication called *The True Tragedie of Richard, Duke of
Yorke*. Though Thomas Tyrwhitt, who first recovered the
allusion for modern students, had explained it correctly,
Malone, misled by the appearance of the line in what
seemed to him two different plays, understood Greene to

mean by ' beautified with our feathers ' that Shakespeare had stolen his verses from Greene. Malone therefore attributed *The True Tragedie* to Greene and regarded 3 *Henry VI* as a mere revision of it by Shakespeare ; hence the reason of Greene's attack. But Malone could not explain how Greene should claim a line as his own by misquoting it in this way. Nor is *The True Tragedie*, as Malone supposed, an original work by Greene, but merely a pirated and mutilated version of 3 *Henry VI.* Further ' beautified with our feathers,' like the phrase Greene uses earlier in his letter, ' Anticks garnisht in our colours,' merely points at Shakespeare's profession as actor. Nash, in his *Epistle* to *Menaphon*, used a similar expression in talking of gentlemen poets who have ' tricked up a company of taffata fooles with their feathers.' Shakespeare was an actor, and Green's quotation is meant to indicate to us the kind of stuff we must expect from an actor.

Greene makes no charge of plagiarism ; his complaint was that Shakespeare's success was taking away from him and his acquaintances the little the actors had so far thrown their way. The letter is a pathetic document ; and it is impossible not to sympathise with the author, who at that time had none of the copyright protection that now enables him to bargain for a share of any profits that his plays may bring. But Greene's remarks on Marlowe, as well as those he directed against Shakespeare, reveal him as a disappointed man, galled by his own follies and failures, and so bitter in spirit as to be venomous in detraction.

The *Groats-worth of witte* was not published till after Greene's death, but it was not well received, even by those whom Greene claimed as his acquaintances.

Of these acquaintances Greene picked out three for particular admonishment. The first, whom he addresses as ' thou famous gracer of Tragedians,' and whom he reproves for atheism, was Marlowe ; young *Iuvenall* was probably Nash ; and the third, George Peele. Nash called the publication ' a scald, trivial, lying pamphlet.' And Chettle, who had seen to the publication of the work, felt obliged to print by way of a Preface to his *Kind Harts dreame* (entered S.R. 8 December, 1592) a disclaimer which indicates that Marlowe, as well as Shakespeare, resented Greene's insinuations. Atheism was then a serious charge, and Marlowe's examination by the Privy Council, ostensibly for a heretical pamphlet seized among the papers of Kyd, author of *The Spanish Tragedy*, was only prevented by his sudden death (*see* page 56). In earlier days Greene had regarded Marlowe as his most dangerous rival, had sneered at Marlowe's blank verse, and encouraged Nash to ridicule a group of rival dramatists, among them Marlowe. And now, under cover of attacking Shakespeare, whom he represents as their common enemy, he openly exposes, with as it were the best intentions, the most dangerous side of Marlowe's reputation. But though Chettle refused to admit he had wronged Marlowe, claiming that he had even cut out some further charge against him by Greene, ' what then in conscience I thought he in some displeasure writ, or, had it beene true, yet to publish it was intollerable ' ; he freely offered a full apology to Shakespeare :

> With neither of them that take offence was I acquainted, and with one of them I care not if I never be : The other, whome at that time I did not so much spare, as since I wish I had, for that as I have moderated the heate of living writers, and might have usde my owne discretion (especially in such a case) the Author beeing dead, that I did not, I am as sorry as if the originall fault had beene my fault, because my selfe have seene his demeanor no lesse civill than he exelent in the quality he professes : Besides, divers of worship have reported his uprightnes of dealing, which argues his honesty, and his facetious grace in writting, that aprooves his Art.

By September 1592 Shakespeare had written 2 and 3 *Henry VI*, since Greene could quote from the latter. But some have held that Greene's epithet ' upstart,' and Chettle's statement that he was not acquainted with Shakespeare, prove that Shakespeare can only just have started as a dramatist. Yet Greene would have called an actor an upstart however long he had been writing plays, and Chettle was not acquainted with Marlowe, who had been known as a dramatist for five years and more. Shakespeare was well known as a man and a writer to ' divers of worship.' In addition, the records of the theatre at that time, however imperfect, as well as references in the plays themselves, support the view that he was already an established dramatist.

Though Chettle speaks of Shakespeare's excellence as an actor, the first explicit information about his theatrical connections is found in a record of a payment of £20 made for Court performances on 26th and 28th December, 1594.

> To William Kempe, William Shakespeare, and Richard Burbage, servants to the Lord Chamberlain, upon the Council's warrant, dated at Whitehall 15 March 1594.

Shakespeare, however good as an actor, was never the rival of Burbage and Kempe in that art, and we are entitled, if other evidence points the same way, to suppose he took his place beside the others because of his standing as a dramatist. This is certainly two years after Greene called him an upstart, but had he not made his position by 1592, he could hardly have made it in the interval, the Companies being on tour because of the plague in London.

That Shakespeare came to the Chamberlain's men as a dramatist is further established by a very significant change in their repertory after their return from the provinces. The plague and various disturbances had closed the London theatres to them from 23rd June, 1592, to 29th December. They had a short season in town from 29th December, 1592, to 1st February, 1593, and the next record of their playing in London is at Newington Butts in June 1594.[1]  Before their tour in the provinces they had been Lord Strange's men, and had played for some time at the Rose, Henslowe's theatre.  With them was associated Alleyn, the famous tragic actor, who was married to Henslowe's step-daughter. His company, the Admiral's, was on tour abroad.  Of the plays performed by Strange's men at the Rose, Henslowe kept a careful record, and, although they produced some twenty-six pieces, only one, *Henry VI*, has a name that coincides with a title in the First Folio ; and, as there were several plays by various hands on Richard II and Richard III, other dramatists than Shakespeare may also have handled Henry's reign.  After the plague, however, on their appearance at Newington Butts, three out of the four pieces they put on have Shakespearean titles : *Titus Andronicus, Taming of a Shrew, Hamlet.*

How they had come by these plays is made clear by a letter dated 28th September, 1593, which Henslowe sent Alleyn, when on tour with Strange's men, in answer to his inquiry about the fortunes of the rival company of Lord Pembroke :

> as for my Lord Pembrokes which you desire to know where they be they are all at home and have been this five or six weeks for they cannot save their charges with travel as I hear and were fain to pawn their apparel for their charge (*see* Greg's *Henslowe* III, 40).

That they were forced to part with their plays, as well as their apparel, is proved by the new entries in the repertory of Strange's, now the Lord Chamberlain's men.

[1] See W. W. Greg's edition of *Henslowe's Diary*. Henslowe was a financier and theatre owner whose detailed records of his transactions have in large part survived.

For though *Titus Andronicus*, and *The Taming of the Shrew*, printed in the following year, one in a good, the other in a bad quarto, are, as well as the bad quarto of 3 *Henry VI* printed in 1595, described on the title page as Pembroke plays, the circumstances of their publication (*see* page 78) explain why they were ascribed to their former owners.

The sudden appearance of Shakespeare as a leading man in the Chamberlain's company, and the equally sudden appearance of his plays in their repertory, can hardly be a coincidence. The evidence points to his having been before these plague years one of Pembroke's company.

It is unlikely that Shakespeare toured with Pembroke's men, for he was during the plague years writing his *Venus and Adonis* and *Lucrece*, and his dedications to Southampton suggest that he had formed a new set of connections. Why he left Pembroke's men we shall probably never know. The suggestion that he left them because they were in difficulties is a conjecture of the kind some enjoy making about great men ; but it is more likely that they fell into difficulties because he left them, and his withdrawal may have been caused by the attitude of the Company's patron.

This view is at least not contrary to the facts. In 1592 the Privy Council, fearing an attack on foreign craftsmen in London, had search made for evidence of a conspiracy. The lodgings of the dramatist Kyd were entered, and though no proof was found of his complicity in any such plot, a heretical pamphlet among his papers was made the pretext for committing him to prison. In a letter to the Lord Keeper (transcribed in Tucker Brooke's *Life of Marlowe*), Kyd explains how two years earlier he had been working in the same room as Marlowe, and that the document had passed by mistake from Marlowe's papers to his. This association came about because the noble lord, Kyd's patron, whom he had served six years, engaged Marlowe to write for his Company. On discovering Marlowe's reputation for atheism, so Kyd declares, his lordship dispensed with his services. The name of this noble lord is probably that which stands on the one play by Marlowe not written for the Admiral's men, especially as it can be, and usually is, dated 1591, the year of Kyd's association with Marlowe. The title page describes *Edward II* as a Pembroke play. If this identification is correct, the patron of Shakespeare's early company not only dismissed Marlowe but abandoned Kyd in his need. With this in mind we can hardly insist that Shakespeare's break with his service was necessarily to the poet's discredit.

On Shakespeare's connection with Southampton, which probably began about this time, something will be found in the section dealing with the poems and sonnets.

For Shakespeare's new theatrical connections one must turn again to theatrical documents. The leading actors of the Chamberlain's men are named in the warrant from the Privy Council, dated 6th May, 1593, under which they travelled :

> Edward Allen, servant to the right honourable the Lord High Admiral : William Kemp, Thomas Pope, John Hemminges, Augustine Phillipes and George Brian, being all one company, servants to our very good Lord the Lord Strainge.

When Alleyn rejoined his own company, his place was taken by Richard Burbage, and the company as it was after reconstruction (with the exception of Shakespeare, Kempe and Heminge) is detailed in a Plot in which the actors' names are given against their parts in the *Seven Deadly Sins* (Greg's *Henslowe*, II, 374 and R.E.S., I, 257-274).

Now began their association with the Burbages which first took them to *The Theatre*.

The plays that can be assigned with confidence to the

period preceding this partnership are : *Titus Andronicus,
The Comedy of Errors, The Taming of the Shrew,* 1, 2 and
3 *Henry VI.* To these may be added *The Two Gentlemen
of Verona,* and possibly *Love's Labour's Lost, Richard III* and
*King John.*

All these plays critics have, at one time or another,
assigned in part or in whole to other hands than Shakespeare's. Some find them too deficient in poetic and
dramatic interest to be by the author of *Hamlet* or *Lear ;*
others regard them as too learned for the ignorant young
man from Stratford. But these early pieces, and Beeston's
story that Shakespeare had been in his younger years a
schoolmaster in the country, provide the strongest mutual
support. In Elizabeth's time, the superficial omniscience,
as Lamb has called it, that later became fashionable was not
yet required, so that only some Latin need be assumed as his
equipment. The early plays reveal no scholarship beyond
the reach of such learning : their author had read in Plautus,
Seneca and Ovid, as a junior schoolmaster might have done.
In setting up as an author, the schoolmaster would naturally
turn his Latin to account, since for anyone with literary
ambitions, and Shakespeare declared his ambitions though
in the modesty of a Latin motto, the Latin authors were
the most convenient models. It is true that country
schoolmasters are not necessarily men of genius ; but the
young Johnson kept a school in the country, though he
may have called it an academy, and Milton taught boys,
though we have his nephew's word for it that he was no
ordinary schoolmaster. Shakespeare was doubtless a
humbler pedagogue than either Milton or Johnson, but
this early employment would not be incompatible with the
literary interests displayed or the learning demanded by his
first compositions.

Shakespeare in his first tragedy, *Titus Andronicus,*

imitated Seneca ; in his first comedy, *The Comedy of Errors*,
Plautus ; and in his first poem, *Venus and Adonis*, Ovid.
Since then taste has changed : the immense superiority of
the Greek dramatists to Seneca is now common report, if
not common knowledge. But it is to Seneca that Elizabethan drama is so heavily indebted. However distorted
the tragic sense of the Greeks may now appear in the horrors
of Seneca, the Roman poet transmitted something of value
from the untainted sources of tragedy ; and like others of
the silver age, he has a style that is obvious even to the un-
scholarly, and, as Quintilian observed, attractive to the young.
The Elizabethans read him with the enthusiasm of youth,
and *Titus Andronicus* is a spirited imitation, as clearly inspired by literary ambition as *Venus and Adonis* or *Tamburlaine*.

These early plays reveal two great natural gifts that
Shakespeare was to develop, and then unite in the perfection
of his tragic masterpieces.

He is first a poet, and, like other youthful poets, a lover
of beauty in language, art, and nature. Keats, speaking of
his own delight in language, said, ' I look upon a fine phrase
like a lover,' and Shakespeare's early works betray the
same passion. And Shakespeare found, as Keats was to do,
and as Chaucer had done, ready material for phrase and
epithet in classical legend and story. And like the others,
he draws no less directly on nature itself for imagery and
illustration. The picture of how

> wild geese that the creeping fowler eye,
> Or russet-pated choughs, many in sort,
> Rising and cawing at the gun's report,
> Sever themselves and madly sweep the sky,

forms itself in Puck's description of the panic among
Bottom's friends as spontaneously as does the Image of

> Dido with a willow in her hand
> Upon the wild sea-banks

5

in the moonlight at Belmont.  These various strains are heard from the beginning.

To question the authorship of the early poetry, because there is not here the ' moral interpretation' of Shakespeare's maturity, is to ignore all that the great Romantic poets and critics have taught of the development of the imagination.  Here is the ' natural magic,' the delighted communion of the senses with the world, which forms, as Wordsworth taught and Keats believed, a necessary stage in the progress to what Keats called the nobler life of poetry. Here in the more than normal sensibility and delicacy of organization revealed by the early poetry is the essential soil for that comprehensiveness of mind demanded of a great poet.  The famous lines on the ' cockled snail,'

> Or, as the snail, whose tender horns being hit,
> Shrinks backwards in his shelly cave with pain,
> And there, all smother'd up, in shade doth sit,
> Long after fearing to creep forth again.

*Venus and Adonis,* 1033-36.

speak openly to every reader, through the chance of their subject matter, of a sensibility that is in the very texture of the poetry as a whole.

But if the author of these early plays is a poet, he is also a dramatic craftsman of skill, and he seconds the passion of his utterance with an admirably cool and directing mind. *The Comedy of Errors* and *Titus Andronicus* show him the master of the plot of intrigue.  Kyd's *Spanish Tragedy* is the only piece from these early times put together with a comparable skill.  But Shakespeare exercises it continuously : it is in *The Taming of the Shrew* as well as in *The Comedy of Errors;* and even in the historical plays, as in 2 and 3 *Henry VI,* where the material is obviously refractory, he contrives a vital circulation of interest wanting in such similar ventures as *Edward II.*

In this early period the poet and the craftsman often work independently. The poetry is often a decoration that fails to follow or emphasize the structural lines of the work. But as they develop they grow together, till in his maturity Shakespeare is the poet of his plots. The great tragedies are no longer merely skilfully contrived stories for the stage, some sequence of strange events and no more. The poet now interprets for us through the living symbolism of his characters and their actions the dreams or intimations of our destiny that so disturb this earthly life. Shakespeare has put eternity into the hour or two allowed by the traffic of the stage. To this end he sacrifices everything unessential, such as the external consistency and verisimilitude so missed by some critics : from this standpoint alone can his plays be understood. And if the action becomes the heart of the poetry, the poetry is the vehicle to carry its pulsations through the entire body of the play. Such a line as

> The setting sun and music at the close

is perhaps more beautiful out of its context than in it, but in Macbeth's,

> To-morrow, and to-morrow and to-morrow,

and Lear's

> Never, never, never, never, never,

the poetry has ceased to exist for us, if we cannot hear in it the throb of the action.

The plot and the poetry unite through the third element in drama—characterization. And while this is still rudimentary in the early plays, compared with those of his maturity, it yet shows glimpses of the treatment that Shakespeare was to find most satisfying in his study of character, and his growing interest in what was to prove his real inspiration.

Taking *Lear* as Shakespeare's greatest achievement, Mr. Granville-Barker would justify the choice by quoting Anatole France's

> La pitié, voyez-vous, M. le Professeur, c'est le fond même du génie.

But the tragic poet's pity goes out not to the weakness but to the strength of man. The paradox is perhaps put most clearly to us by Wordsworth at the end of his *Simon Lee,*

> I've heard of hearts unkind, kind deeds
> With coldness still returning.
> ( Alas ! the gratitude of men
> ⟨ Has oftener left me mourning.

That the old man's afflictions could not deprive him of his capacity for gratitude, or deaden his response even to a passing show of goodwill, came as a revelation to Wordsworth of the native strength of the heart. It was the discovery of this invincible virtue in his fellows that made Wordsworth a poet and a great interpreter of the business of poetry. It is true, he tells us, that poetry has no celestial ichor in its veins, sheds no tears ' such as angels weep ' ; but the tears that all Satan's scorn and pride could not keep back were for a constancy of heart in his followers,

> Yet faithful how they stood,

not more heroic than that over which Wordsworth mourned in the old huntsman.

For if Wordsworth was right in supposing that one being is elevated above another in proportion as he possesses the capacity to respond to what he himself calls the great and simple affections of our nature, then Simon Lee's tears that could rise from such profound depths of affliction in answer to simple courtesy reveal a force of heart and a heroism that dignify the man more than all his earlier feats of courage and endurance. That Shakespeare and Milton

would have agreed with Wordsworth is proved by their
making such a response by Satan and Lear in the midst of
their distresses the crowning stroke in the picture of their
greatness. For Lear, though unsubdued by the malice of
his daughters and the elements,

> this heart
> Shall break into a hundred thousand flaws
> Or ere I'll weep,

does weep at the touch of the returned Cordelia. But
such tears have no self-pity in them,

> If you have poison for me I will drink it,

coming as an irresistible tribute to a goodness that he feels
to be worthy of a better world.

And this passionate admiration for the disinterested
and unselfish in others that moves the poets beyond tears
is the secret of their own hold on men. For the poet
' the true sorrow of humanity consists in this,' as Wordsworth wrote some ten years after his *Simon Lee*, ' not that
the mind of man fails, but that the course and demands of
action and of life so rarely correspond with the dignity
and intensity of human desires.' But this very lack of
correspondence between the infinite within and the limited
world without, while it calls forth the poet's sympathies
to redress the balance, also reveals most plainly to him the
real nature of the heart. And Mr. Granville-Barker, like
so many other critics, chooses *Lear* because he finds there
Shakespeare's clearest revelation of the strength of that
soul of sensibility in the heart of man that so transcends
the material objects that engage it.

And so strongly does this revelation grow upon the poet,
and the reader to whom his virtue goes out, that in tragedy,
at least, the sense of pity for virtue in an unrewarding world
gives place to the assurance that such virtue is above the
rewards the world can give : the mind, as Aristotle held.

is thus purged of pity, and longs to play a part in what it now holds as a victory, however dearly bought.

But though pity understood in this sense is the inspiration of Shakespeare's tragedies, his early masterpieces are with one exception comedies. And so naturally did this mode of writing come to him that Johnson ventured to say :

> In comedy he seems to repose or luxuriate as in a mode of thinking congenial to him. His tragedy seems to be skill, his comedy to be instinct.

But where can one find words more natural than the simple phrases that so often mark the culminating points of the tragedies ?

you must bear with me.
Pray you now, forget and forgive ; I am old and foolish.
Her voice was ever soft,
Gentle and low : an excellent thing in woman.

These are the spontaneous overflow of powerful feeling, but of one who, to add Wordsworth's own qualification, had thought long and deeply on human life. And this is so, because the tragedies are no more than the supreme expression of a mode of thought and feeling that can be seen maturing in the comedies themselves.

It has often been observed that there gradually grows up in the comedies a tragic interest that sometimes runs counter to the general drift of the plot. The victories of Henry V are vain shows after the defeat of Falstaff. A year or two earlier Shylock disrupted *The Merchant of Venice*. And even *Twelfth Night*, perhaps the most brilliant of the comedies, is infected with the same malady. Charles I, that connoisseur whose grave melancholy drew him to Shakespeare as it did to Rembrandt, crossed out the title *Twelfth Night* in his copy of the plays, and wrote in its stead, *Malvolio*, anticipating the criticism of Lamb, who could never see Bensley play this character without feeling in it a tragic dignity.

Shakespeare's comedy is not unique in possessing this tragic intermixture, for it is characteristic of Cervantes and Molière. The comic artist may begin by seeming to ask us to laugh at the follies of others, but the heartiness of our response becomes less a product of the diaphragm and spleen as we realize we may be seeing ourselves as others see us. But the great comic artists are even more ruthless with men's virtues than their vices. To see the most cherished convictions of the heart as the best jest of all, and as a never failing source of mirth to the wise of this world even more than to the foolish, is the last stage in that self-criticism which is the true glory of laughter. Moralists like Rousseau have denounced Molière as the enemy of virtue—the parallel in the criticism of Tragedy is Johnson's complaint about the morality of *Lear*—but the laughter to which Molière has exposed his honest man is the expression of a self-watchfulness beyond the imagination of Rousseau.

Cervantes and Molière make us aware of a virtue that can endure even laughter. And virtue is indeed often hardly to be discerned till laughter unlooses the knot in which humanity's strength and weakness are so distractingly bound together. The jests of Lamb, as well as Wordsworth's thoughts too deep for tears, may open our eyes to courage, constancy, faith, gratitude, love, in a world where their opposites would have been so much more profitable and even natural. The paradox that comedy and tragedy are only diverse aspects of a fundamental knowledge of life is as old as Plato or his master ; and it is most unfortunate that Aristodemus was in no condition the morning after the famous banquet to report the line of argument by which Socrates forced Aristophanes and Agathon, who were hardly in a state to profit by it, to admit that the man who could, by a fully conscious art, master one would be necessarily the master of the other.[1]

Shakespeare is from the first and to the end as confirmed a punster as Lamb ; but his laughter ventures where Lamb dare not go, and only Chaucer and Burns in these islands can accompany him. It has often been suggested that Shakespeare's fun was a deliberate concession to the groundlings, but the aristocratic circle at the Court of Edward III or Richard II no doubt enjoyed their Chaucer as freely as the natives of Tarbolton or Mauchline their Burns ; and Shakespeare's worst offences were not for the most ignorant of his hearers. But an excess of this kind does not justify Bridges' contention that Hamlet's praise of the play where ' there were no sallets in the lines to make the matter savoury ' is really an admission by the poet that he spiced his own work, because a vulgar taste demanded such seasoning. For those with no stomach for such humour Hamlet is himself among the greatest offenders. Charles Bathurst, who showed real quality as a critic in his *Shakespeare's Versification*, complains of his author's extravagant coarseness. He clears him, however, of taking delight in it except in *Othello*, ' nor altogether in *Hamlet* where it is much more improper.' But Hamlet's grim obscenity is an essential trait in the portrait. There is a comparable brutality in some of Shakespeare's own sonnets. But so far is this from being the evidence of an insensitive mind, that it is the cry of one touched to the quick by the strange accidents of our existence. In the tragedies this element finds its appropriate form, whether as a continuous commentary as in the scurrility of Iago, or in a brief and sudden

---

[1] Plato embodied his idea of Comedy in the Rabelaisian fable he gave to Aristophanes, where the extravagance of love, though set forth with a verve worthy of the great comedian, is yet seen as an effort to regain man's original harmony and strength. It is a comic illustration of the great doctrine of recollection.

outburst as in the Porter scene in *Macbeth*.  The jesting of
the comedies, when transposed into the tragic key, can be
seen as a necessary criticism of life, permitting the dramatist
to obtain those contrasts, the ' bold projections and recesses
deep,' without which both the strength and sublimity of his
structure would be impaired.  The early jesting, once its
direction is found, cannot be dismissed as mere wantonness.

And from the first Shakespeare begins to create a soul
within the ribs of the convention he adopted.  In the *Errors*,
one of the most comic scenes shows the wife of the married
twin claiming his brother as her husband.  But in the full
flow of the farce Shakespeare gives us not merely a jealous
woman, clamouring for rights whose very assertion reduces
human beings to mere possessions and ludicrous chattels,
but a wife not unconscious of a love whose dignity should
go hand in hand with the vows of marriage.  And Katherine
in *The Shrew*, though her role is rigidly prescribed by the
plot, shows a strength and independence that make us wish
that Shakespeare could have contrived in the end to show
more clearly that she stoops to conquer.  Again in *Love's
Labour's Lost* there is the queer dignity, noted both by
Mr. Masefield and Mr. Granville-Barker, in Armado, as he
reproves the courtiers who mock his Hector.  In such
moments the characters live, for they are exposed to the
full rigour of the situation by what is human and best in
their nature.  Here are the seeds of the Promethean fire
that was to give life to his later patterns of excelling nature.

## THE COMEDY OF ERRORS

**S.R. 8th November 1623 ;** first printed in the **First Folio.**
The comedy is mentioned by Meres, and was certainly composed before 28th December, 1594, when the Chamberlain's
men played it at Gray's Inn as part of the prolonged Christmas
celebrations there.  On this particular evening the members of

Gray's Inn had invited the Inner Templars to witness the performance, but there was serious overcrowding, and the Templars withdrew in displeasure. The *Gesta Grayorum*, a mock heroic chronicle of the season's doings, calls this ' The Night of Errors.' The piece was not composed specially for this occasion, as it contains a topical reference from an earlier period.   In the fooling about the kitchen girl's looks (III, ii), Antipholus of Syracuse after asking, ' in what part of her body stands Ireland ? ' continues, ' Where France ? ' and is answered by Dromio :

> In her forehead : armed and reverted making war
> against her heir.

In June 1584, the death of the Duke of Anjou, brother of the childless king, left Henry of Navarre heir to the French throne.   Although the king, Henry III, was still alive, the Catholic League took up arms against the heir, but was defeated at Coutras, a victory that spread Henry of Navarre's fame throughout Europe.   When the king died on 12th August, 1589, Henry of Navarre was now by right king, and was recognized in England, though only after 19th July, 1593, when he became a nominal Roman Catholic, did he obtain possession of Paris. He was heir, therefore, between 1584 and 1589.   It is in these years that Jonson's admittedly rough estimate places *Titus Andronicus*.   Till there is something better to go on, the ' heir ' allusion, taken with the other evidence of Shakespeare's dramatic work before 1592, may be regarded as dating the *Errors* before August 1589.

The play as a whole supports the view that it was composed when its author was still a beginner, fresh from his reading of Plautus, and designing his play with his eye not so much on the Elizabethan stage as on the ' scene individable ' of classic convention.   The characters encounter one another in a marketplace on which open the three doors of the Priory, the house of Antipholus and the house of the courtesan—the two latter indicated by their signs, the Phœnix and the Porpentine, respectively. One side entrance leads to the Bay, the other to the Town. This was the proper classic setting for the stage, since the Comedy, which was Shakespeare's model, was born at Athens between the Bay and the Town. And the courtesy of convention allowed Comedy to enjoy the advantages she was born to, even in cities where they were unsanctioned by the laws of nature. Plautus in his *Amphitruo* gives a harbour to Thebes, and Shakespeare has in the same way added to the attractions of several of the towns of North Italy.

The plot also, a contamination of two pieces by Plautus, the *Menaechmi* and the *Amphitruo*, has good classical precedent in the Roman adaptations from Greek comedy. The twin masters come from the *Menaechmi*, but the twin servants were required by the incorporation among the errors of the famous scene from the *Amphitruo*, where master and man are shut out while Jupiter and Mercury impersonate them inside, and are entertained by the unsuspecting mistress.

Instead of a father, as in Plautus, Shakespeare gives the wife of Antipholus a sister, and so adds further to the confusion ; for the wandering twin falls in love with her, to the great distress of both the ladies. But this addition makes for the neater solution of the puzzle, since the unmarried brother can now be paired off with the sister. To bind all this together Shakespeare has contrived a romantic setting in the story of Aegeon, which to begin with serves instead of the Roman Prologue, putting the spectators in a position to follow the ensuing complications, and at the end operates very effectively in securing the final discoveries.

## THE TAMING OF THE SHREW

**S.R. 2nd May, 1594.** *Peter Shorte. Entred unto him for his copie under master warden Cawoodes hande a booke intituled A plesant Conceyted historie called ' the Tayminge of a Shrowe.'*

Cuthbert Burby published **Q1 1594** (printed by Peter Short) and professed on the title page to give it *As it was sundry times acted by the Right honorable the Earle of Pembrook his seruants.* But this is a pirated and mutilated version of Shakespeare's play, peculiar however among the Bad Shakespeare Quartos in the manner of its construction. The pirate anticipated the procedure adopted by Tate Wilkinson, manager of the Theatre

Royal at York, when he put together a version of Sheridan's *Duenna*.

> I locked myself in my room ; set down first all the jokes I remembered, . . . and by the help of a numerous collection of obsolete Spanish plays, I produced an excellent comic opera.

Like ' this illiterate paraphrase,' *The Taming of a Shrew* attempts to reproduce the jests of the original as well as the plot, and is filled out with much ludicrously inappropriate material from Marlowe's *Tamburlaine* and *Faustus*, not to speak of other sources. Shakespeare's own version, *The Taming of the Shrew*, passed from Pembroke's men to the Chamberlain's men, who played it in June 1594 at Newington Butts on their return from the provinces. It was first printed in the First Folio. Meres does not mention it, unless this is his *Loves Labours Won*.

*The Taming of the Shrew* dates, therefore, from before the plague years, and at least from Shakespeare's Pembroke period, which ended in 1592. Like *The Comedy of Errors* it owes much to Latin models, but indirectly, now, through Italian comedy. Shakespeare, however, took the names Tranio and Grumio from the town and country slaves in the *Mostellaria* of Plautus. But the main debt is to Ariosto, who gave a fresh start to European comedy by the pieces he wrote for performance at the Court of Ferrara. These were in part adaptations from Plautus and Terence ; among them is *I Suppositi*, translated by Gascoigne as *The Supposes*. Shakespeare read the translation, if not the original, since he adopted the name of one of Gascoigne's minor characters, Petrucio, and reduced its plot to the intrigue that centres in Bianca, with the disguised lover, the masquerading servant and the supposed father, as in Ariosto. This he combined with the Petruchio-Katherine business, and Johnson's verdict on the result is a fair one :

> . . . the two plots are so well united, that they can hardly be called two without injury to the art with which they are interwoven. The attention is entertained with all the variety of a double plot, yet is not distracted by unconnected incidents.

Those with no relish for the high spirits of this extravaganza should not dismiss it as of little interest except as evidence of the brutality of Elizabethan taste. Part of its attraction was no doubt the sense of escape from reality it afforded even Elizabethans ; but any hopes we may suppose such an audience may have entertained of transferring the discipline of the stage to daily life must have been checked by the reminder in the Epilogue of what may be in store at home for the drunken Sly, into whose fuddled mind the piece seems to have put some dangerous notions. The Epilogue, unfortunately, can only be reconstructed very imperfectly from the Bad Quarto, as some error in the printing house, or in the preparation of the copy, has led to its omission from the Folio. The Quarto gives a feeble version of the Induction, which was alive with allusions to Warwickshire characters like ' Marian Hacket, the fat alewife of Wincot,' that still give weight and substance to this piece of realism that is so happily contrasted with the main fantasy. Though the Quarto obviously gives an equally poor report of the Epilogue, enough survives to show us that it is not Shakespeare's fault if we take his comedy too literally.

Those on the other hand who see in the continued hold the piece has on the stage not only proof of its dexterous stage craft, but evidence that some essential substance must go with the effervescence, can regard it as a version of one of the great themes of literature, a comic treatment of the perilous maiden theme, where the lady is death to any suitor who woos her except the hero, in whose hands her apparent vices turn to virtues.

## THE TWO GENTLEMEN OF VERONA

**S.R. 8th November, 1623 ;** first printed in the **First Folio.**

The earliest reference to the piece is by Meres in his *Palladis Tamia* (1598) ; but the construction, style and temper of the work support an early date. It is probably the first of the Romantic comedies, and is a very nest of the devices Shakespeare was to conjure with so freely in later times. He used a story from Montemayor's pastoral romance *Diana*. Yonge's translation from the Spanish was not published till 1598, but there was an earlier French translation, and the record in the Revels Accounts for 1584–85 of a performance by the Queen's company before Her Majesty of *Felix and Philiomena* suggests that the story was dramatized by that date.  In *Diana* Felix sends a letter to Felismena by her maid, is followed by her to court, and over-heard serenading another lady ; employs Felismena as his page, and recognizes her after a fight in a forest.  Here is the girl disguised as a boy Shakespeare was to employ so regularly in after years ; and her dispatch to plead her lover's suit with her rival, her earlier discussion of her suitors with her maid, the banishment of the true lover, the friar and the rope ladder, the flight to the forest and the outlaws, remind us in turn of *Twelfth Night*, *Merchant of Venice*, *Romeo and Juliet* and *As You Like It*.

Shakespeare crosses the theme of love with that of friendship by introducing Valentine, and handles the complications in the thorough-going manner we might expect from the author of *The Shrew*.  The tide of love is sudden and full, but may ebb as quickly, and on these turns the interest is carried violently to and fro ; and Shakespeare can hardly reconcile the perjured Proteus and his friend without some such hazardous device as he adopts when he makes Valentine say to the man he has taken laying violent hands on his sweetheart—after five lines of repentance however—

once again do I receive thee honest.

. . . . . . . .

All that was mine in Silvia I give thee.

This is the most out and out use of the David and Jonathan convention of male friendship, and of the doctrine of repentance ; but to look for some one other than Shakespeare on whom to fix the blame for this drastic cutting of the  knot is as unnecessary as it would be to relieve Shakespeare of the final scene in *The Shrew*, where the doctrine of wifely obedience, however accept-able in moderation to the majority of men, is enforced in all its rigour.  Shakespeare also treats Sir Eglamour most shabbily, introducing him as a chivalrous knight and dismissing him as a poltroon. But it is only in the days of his easy mastery of events that he allows such humble helpers to stand up for themselves and to refuse, as does Bernardine in *Measure for Measure*, to be made a convenient property. Even there the disposal of Isabella warns us not to look for too much compunction at the close of a comedy by Shakespeare.

The play, however, is full of admirable passages ; at every turn there is struggling to extricate itself a poetry that surprises us with a fine excess. It was here that Thomas Hardy found the motto for the most tragic of his heroines,

> Poor wounded name, my bosom as a bed
> Shall lodge thee,

though Julia, as she says this, is only picking up the scraps of a letter she has torn in her caprice and looking for her lover's name among the pieces. And the serenading of Silvia is a remarkable piece of counterpoint. The artful complaining of the music, the pleading of Proteus, the disdain of Silvia, are admirably contrasted, and go well with the undersong between Julia and the Host, whose parts in their turn run in such musical contrariety. It is the perfect setting for Julia's feverish wakefulness, with the comfortable Host so sleepy in the night air that he can only enjoy as in a luxurious twilight the strings and the fine changes in the music. But the scene is not merely a poetic triumph ; it contributes most effectively to the economy of the drama by its way of bringing Julia into the main current of the intrigue.

And here is the gnomic Shakespeare whose precepts have delighted the generations with their moral prudence, whether it comes from the youthful and sententious Valentine, with his

> Home-keeping youth have ever homely wits,

or in the more familiar and proverbial wisdom of Launce's

> Blessing of your heart you brew good ale.

And here in Shakespeare's prose, so downrightly effective in *The Shrew*, there comes at times a more humorous inflection. As in most of the Comedies, there is fooling of the kind that is repeated in every generation, but only completely acceptable when in the ruling fashion; critics, however, are agreed in praising the humours of Launce. Speed is usually underrated. Yet when he reminds Proteus that it is dinner time,

> Ay but hearken, sir : though the chameleon Love can feed on the air, I am one that am nourished by my victuals and would fain have meat,

and more so when he comments on the clearness of his master's malady, he has a turn of phrase that would not have disgraced the youthful Falstaff.

## TITUS ANDRONICUS

**S.R. 6th February, 1594.** *John Danter. Entred for his Copye under thandes of bothe the wardens a booke intituled a Noble Roman Historye of Tytus Andronicus.*

Q1 1594 states on the title page that it was played by *the Right Honourable the Earle of Darbie,*[1] *Earle of Pembrooke, and Earle of Sussex their Servants.*

The Servants of Sussex played it on 23rd January, 1594, at the Rose, and Henslowe marked it in his diary as 'ne,' a mark he put to a piece 'the first time it was plaied.' But here this can indicate no more than the first performance at his theatre, and he no doubt obtained a copy in 1593 when Pembroke's men were bankrupt. As a Pembroke piece it must date before the touring years, 1592–93, and it is referred to in *A Knack to know a Knave,* 'ne' at the Rose on 10th June, 1592.

> As Titus was unto the Roman Senators
> When he had made a conquest of the Goths.

The Chamberlain's men played it on 7th and 14th June, 1594, at the Newington Butts. It was not in their repertory during the long Rose season of 1591–92, the *Tittus and Vespacia* of 15th January, 1591, being a different play, though the name

---

[1] Lord Strange became Earl of Derby on 25th September, 1593 and died 16th April, 1594. During that period his company were called 'Derby's' men. After his death the Lord Chamberlain became their patron. On his death, 23rd July, 1596, his heir, George Carey, Lord Hunsdon, took over the company, which again became the Chamberlain's men on 17th March 1597, when he succeeded to his father's office.

Vespasian was incorporated, either because of some memory of this piece, or because of its historical association with Titus, in the pirated version of *Titus Andronicus* circulated in Germany (*see* Cohn's *Shakespeare in Germany*). Now that Shakespeare had joined the Chamberlain's men, they took over *Titus Andronicus* with his other plays.

Those who do not accept its inclusion in the Folio, or its ascription to Shakespeare by Meres, as proof of Shakespeare's authorship point to a statement by a Restoration dramatist named Ravenscroft :

> I have been told by some anciently conversant with the stage, that it was not originally his, but brought by a private Author to be Acted, and he only gave some Master-touches to one or two of the Principal Parts or Characters.

Ravenscroft had re-written *Titus Andronicus* in the manner of his age ; and on being censured for his presumption, defended himself by declaring the original ' rather a heap of Rubbish then a Structure,' and denying it to Shakespeare ; though he had, as Langbaine reminded him, ascribed the play to Shakespeare in the original Prologue (now declared lost) to his revision, and had been impudent enough to excuse his rewriting Shakespeare by saying :

> So far he was from robbing him of's Treasure
> That he did add his own, to make full measure.

Ravenscroft's statement is an excuse devised to cover up this impertinence ; without corroboration it is worthless. Internal evidence gives it no support.

*Titus Andronicus* is like *Venus and Adonis* the offspring of youthful ambition. In the motto of his poem Shakespeare announced the tradition he worked in. *Titus Andronicus* reveals the same aim and method. As in the poem, Shakespeare decorates a groundwork of classic myth or story with the most prodigal enrichment of imagery and reflection. Neither Seneca nor Ovid is the severest of classic models, and those familiar with the austerer masterpieces of Aeschylus and Sophocles may

6

wish that Shakespeare had had different masters. Professor Housman has imagined Virgil welcoming Shakespeare to the Elysian fields with the words tradition attributes to Paul, when he visited the tomb of Virgil : ' O Chief of poets, what would not I have made of thee, had I but found thee living ! '

> ' Quem te ' inquit ' reddidissem,
> Si te vivum invenissem
> Poetarum maxime ! '

' Virgil and the Greeks would,' Professor Housman thinks, ' have made Shakespeare not merely a great genius, which he was already, but, like Milton, a great artist, which,' Professor Housman ventures to assert, ' he is not.' But the labours of many scholars and humanists had to go to enrich the general stock before even a man of genius, who was not also a finished scholar, could realize what the Greeks had made of tragedy. The understanding Milton gained through the long and isolated discipline of his studies was probably impossible in Shakespeare's age, and certainly impossible in Shakespeare's circumstances ; and that kind of retirement was no doubt incompatible with his genius. Even Milton had to pay for his isolation. ' The " Paradise Lost," ' wrote Keats, ' though so fine in itself is a corruption of our language . . . a northern dialect accommodating itself to Greek and Latin inversions and intonations.' Shakespeare is master of a purer English. His worst manner is, perhaps, his most Latinised style. And what is unpleasing in *Titus* is not untutored barbarism but the artificial and imitative. The crowning horror of Tamora's feasting on her own children Shakespeare took from the *Thyestes*.[1] There he could find not only the fatal banquet, but such preliminaries as the account of their murder and the spluttering of the livers on the spits. He was only too ready, perhaps, to make his own selection of horrors, and present what he could on the stage ; he may have added the faults of his own age to the faults of his

---

[1] The story of Philomela was a favourite with Shakespeare, as with so many other poets, and is mentioned in passing in other of his plays ; but here it is wrought into the texture of the plot in the rape and mutilation of Lavinia, perhaps because it, too, tells of a parent feasting on his child.

model, but not because he was illiterate. He was a beginner at
the beginning of English Tragedy, and he had to make what he
could of it. Many years later, in the *Induction* to his *Bartholomew
Fair*, Jonson was to refer to *Titus* as a popular success, like
Kyd's *Spanish Tragedy*, in a style long out of date :

> He that will sweare, Ieronimo, or Andronicus are the
> best plays yet, shall pass unexcepted at, heere, as a man
> whose Iudgement shewes it is constant, and hath stood
> still, these five and twentie, or thirtie yeeres.

Jonson produced *Bartholomew Fair* in 1614, so he gives
1584–89 as a rough date for *Titus*. But though this tragedy is
an early work, and Shakespeare's genius was to raise itself by
its own virtue far above the Elizabethan-Senecan manner to a
sphere where only the greatest masters dwell, yet *Titus* shows
the purpose as well as the vigour of his youth. Skilfully put
together, its phrasing at every turn reminds the reader of memorable lines from later works, as Aaron, Tamora and others show
glimpses of characters to come.

## I, 2 AND 3 HENRY VI

**S.R. 8th November, 1623.** I *Henry VI*, first printed in the
**First Folio,** is entered as *The thirde parte of Henry the sixt*.
This was to distinguish it from the other parts already published
in pirated versions. The stolen text of 2 *Henry VI* has a regular
entry.

**S.R. 12th March, 1594.** *Thomas myllington. Entred for his
copie under the handes of bothe the wardens a booke intituled, the
firste parte of the Contention of the twoo famous houses of York and
Lancaster withthe deathe of the good Duke Humfrey and the banishe-
ment and Deathe of the Duke of Suffolk and the tragicall ende of the
prowd Cardinall of Winchester with the notable rebellion of Jack
Cade and the Duke of Yorkes ffirste clayme vnto the Crowne.*
This is **QI 1594** of 2 *Henry VI*.

Next year Millington, without further entry, printed the
sequel, **QI 1595** of 3 *Henry VI*, putting on the title page,

*The true Tragedie of Richard Duke of Yorke . . . as it was
sundrie times acted by the Right Honourable the Earle of Pembrooke
his seruants.*

When he transferred the Bad Quartos of 2 and 3 *Henry VI*
to Pavier in 1602, the Register describes them as *The firste and
Second parte of Henry the vi^t*.

In the Register, therefore, though not, of course, in the
Folio, 1 *Henry VI* is called the ' thirde parte.'

The first authentic texts of 2 and 3 *Henry VI* were printed
along with 1 *Henry VI* in the 1623 Folio ; for *The Contention*
and *The True Tragedie*, as Millington's Quartos are generally
called, give a very mutilated version of their originals. These,
as the title page of *The True Tragedie* indicates, belonged at one
time to Pembroke's men, but probably passed from their hands
when the company broke in 1593. The actors, however, would
still remember something of their parts, and might, in some
instances, even possess written copies of these parts. It is
largely from the memory of two actors who had played Warwick and Suffolk (doubling Clifford) in 2 *Henry VI* that *The
Contention* is compiled. For one small passage they had a
theatrical scroll such as would be used on the stage, and besides
this there remained with them some fragments in manuscript.
The same pair of actors were also largely responsible for *The True
Tragedy*.[1] This combination of memory and transcript was
an obvious resource for a pirate actor, and was used with considerable success by John Bernard, the actor, when he put together
for performance in the provinces a version of Sheridan's *School
for Scandal*.[2] These unauthorised provincial versions of a later
date sometimes found their way into print, and the two Shakespeare piracies may have first been made for playing in the

---

[1] In *Shakespeare's Henry VI and Richard III*, Cambridge Press, 1929, the
evidence is set out in detail. The first to prove that *The Contention* and *True
Tragedy* are no more than Bad Quartos of 2 and 3 *Henry VI* was Thomas
Kenny in his *The Life and Genius of Shakespeare*, 1864. His book, however,
was neglected, and was not included in the bibliographies of Chambers
or Ebisch and Schücking (1931). Much of his argument is repeated in
my discussion, because I did not in 1929 know of his work.

[2] See the edition of Sheridan's *Plays* by R. C. Rhodes.

provinces by a remnant of the ruined Pembroke's men ; the chance of raising something extra on them from a publisher would not be refused.

The Contention and The True Tragedy, being merely Bad Quartos, give no support to the view maintained by Malone, though he made them the foundation of his argument, that Shakespeare began as a reviser of the work of others, and that 2 and 3 Henry VI are examples of his work in this kind. Further, since Greene is quoting from 3 Henry VI (see page 51), not from The True Tragedy, both 2 and 3 Henry VI date from before the plague years. Greene died in September 1592, but the theatres were closed on 11 June, 1592, for three and a half months because of a riot, and the plague then kept them shut till the last week in December ; so that 2 and 3 Henry VI must date before June 1592, and so must 1 Henry VI. Nash, in his Pierce Penilesse (1592), replying to an attack on stage plays, instances, as a popular and profitable piece, one showing the death of ' brave Talbot, the terror of the French.' This may well be a reference to Shakespeare's 1 Henry VI. We cannot, however, identify 1 Henry VI with the Henry VI played on 3 March, 1592, at the Rose by Strange's men and marked as ' ne ' in Henslowe's diary. To take 1 Henry VI as a ' new ' play in March 1592 would make it an afterthought in the form of a prologue to the York and Lancaster plays, unless we suppose 2 and 3 Henry VI composed between then and June ; but the links in 1 Henry VI inserted to join it with 2 and 3 Henry VI (the scene between Margaret and Suffolk and the final scene arranging her marriage) are clearly later additions put in to join it to pieces to which it was not originally designed as an introduction. Again, The Contention contains in its opening scene a clear reminiscence of the final and additional scene in 1 Henry VI. Actors reproducing a piece from memory naturally introduced lines and phrases from other plays they had known : the Bad Quartos of 2 and 3 Henry VI are full of phrases from Edward II, because that was also a Pembroke piece. But it would be strange to find them introducing the phrase they did from a new play by another company. Nor can we suppose that ' ne ' may mean that the play had been transferred to Strange's men, for there is no trace of any connection between Strange's men and Shakespeare and his plays till after the breaking of Pembroke's men. That there would be more plays than Shakespeare's on the reign of *Henry VI* may be taken as certain.

Nor need there be doubt about the authenticity of 2 and 3 *Henry VI*. Greene's quotation supports their attribution by Heminge and Condell to Shakespeare. Internal evidence confirms it. The Cade scenes are, no one doubts, by the hand that added the 147 lines on the encounter between the May-day rioters and More to the play of *Sir Thomas More*.[1] Shakespeare, not in the capacity of some obscure botcher, but as an acknowledged master whose casual contribution was welcome, assisted some others to alter this play in an attempt to make it acceptable to the censor, and the manuscript still preserves for us three pages in the poet's own hand. Here, as in the Cade scenes, Shakespeare shows himself ' sympathizingly cognizant with the talk of the illogical classes ' ; there is the same absurdity and good humour in the mob, the same capacity for deeds of savagery, the same instability. Even Cade in 2 *Henry VI* has fair play from the dramatist, for if he is something of a monster in his success, in his distress he is certainly a man.

But in ' the 147 lines ' Shakespeare not only sketches the English mob in a style identical with that in 2 *Henry VI*, he outlines in More's speech to the rioters the thoughts that, as his maturest as well as his earliest works show, habitually occurred to him at the mention of lawlessness and civil disorder. That the ordinary citizen has no profit in rebellion is one of the themes of More's speech. ' Had there such fellows lived when you were babes,' he tells them, ' not one of you should live an aged man.' There is the same turn of thought in *Troilus and Cressida*. Take but degree, that is due subordination, away, says Ulysses, ' And the rude son should strike his father dead.' In 3 *Henry VI* Shakespeare presents these very thoughts almost in dumb show

[1] *Shakespeare's Hand in The Play of Sir Thomas More*, by A. W. Pollard and others ; and Professor R. W. Chambers' expansion of his contribution to this volume in *M. L. R.*, July 1931.

to the very eyes of the spectator.   In II, v, is this stage direction :

> *Enter a Sonne that hath kill'd his Father, at one doore :*
> *and a Father that hath kill'd his Sonne at another doore.*

Both victors at first think there is profit in the business. ' Ill blows the wind that profits nobody ' says the son, and the father, ' Give me thy gold ' ; but in the end they join in the lament with the wretched king over times when civil order is broken.

The thoughts suggested to Shakespeare by the struggle of the Roses are those of More's speech : without rule and government, he says,

> men like ravenous fishes
> Would feed on one another ;

or of Albany's warning in *Lear*, that with such dissensions,

> Humanity must perforce prey on itself,
> Like monsters of the deep ;

or of Ulysses showing that appetite, given free play,

> Must make perforce a universal prey
> And last eat up himself.

Like ravenous fishes the opposing factions feed on one another, York kills old Clifford, and young Clifford, York.   Warwick and his party slay young Clifford, and Warwick in turn is killed in battle.   Meantime the pious Henry can only comment on the misery of the times.   This dark background certainly shows up more clearly the ambitious emulation of the contending nobles.   Shakespeare could sympathize like Keats when ' a man in his quarrel shows a grace.'   Already ' he could discern in the differences, the quarrels, the animosities of man, a beauty and truth of moral feeling, no less than in the everlastingly inculcated duties of forgiveness and atonement ' ; and his nobles form a living and vigorous group.   There is little in *Edward II* to compare in dramatic vitality with Margaret, Suffolk, Warwick, or Cade and his bustling henchmen, and beside their quickly shifting intrigues the doings of Marlowe's characters are slow and incoherent.   Yet while it is not Shakespeare's business to preach any formal doctrine, his thought gives the whole dreadful pageant a social significance and depth of meaning unsounded by Marlowe.

There is, perhaps, no sufficient evidence for determining the question of the relation between 2 and 3 *Henry VI* and *Edward II*. It is often assumed that Marlowe was first in the field, and that this form of history is another of his examples to the age. But it is a marked departure from his previous work, showing an attempt to construct a more complicated plot and organize the action of a group of characters, instead of allowing everything to depend on one figure. But Shakespeare was master of the intrigue plot from the first, while some more simple and archaic form would probably have suited Marlowe's genius better : it seems more likely, therefore, that Marlowe is here the imitator rather than the master. The 1592 Quarto of *Edward II* gives us the play according to the title page : *as it was sundrie times publiquely acted in the honourable citie of London by the right honourable the Earle of Pembrooke his seruants.* When writing this piece for Pembroke's Company Marlowe would be closely associated not only with Kyd but with Shakespeare (*see* page 57).

Once 2 and 3 *Henry VI* are recognized as the work of the early Shakespeare, the probability that he wrote 1 *Henry VI* is greatly strengthened. Some critics desire so strongly a modern portrait of Joan that, though she stands out a stout champion of her country, ready to sacrifice even salvation for it, they cannot reconcile the somewhat coarse treatment (in spite of finer touches here and there) on the lines of the Chronicles with Shakespeare's authorship. But no work of this period in which Talbot was the hero could be expected to do justice to the French heroine. Elizabethan patriotism had tougher strands in it than mere self glorification. But in presenting the English exploits in France a dramatist had to argue, as did Joan, with the unpatriotic Burgundy—

> One drop of blood drawn from thy country's bosom
> Should grieve thee more than streams of foreign gore.

Shakespeare did not hesitate to exploit the drum and trumpet music in *Henry V;* we can hardly insist that he was a more delicate artist in his youth.

# RICHARD III

**S.R. 20th October, 1597.** *Andrewe wise. Entred for his copie under thandes of master Barlowe, and master warden man. The tragedie of kinge Richard the Third with the death of the Duke of Clarence.*

Wise issued **QI 1597**, and five other editions appeared before the First Folio text was printed. The Quarto gives a shortened version, adapted, as the stage directions show, for performance by a limited cast. The Folio gives a fuller version, but the printer used a late Quarto in conjunction with a manuscript, or a Quarto with numerous corrections and additions entered in it.

Meres includes the play in his list.

In 3 *Henry VI* the figure of Richard Crookback is already beginning to emerge from the murder and civil confusion as ' the bug that feared us all,' the inevitable sequel to such anarchy. And so History tends to pass into Tragedy, becoming less of a fateful pageant and more the adventure of an individual soul. In the great tragedies history hardly exists except as part of the hero's story ; but in them Shakespeare draws on the legendary parts of *Holinshed*, where, if history survive, it does so as the doings of individuals, or he uses the *Lives* into which Plutarch had cast Roman history. Crookback, however, had, thanks to the account of him by More (who served Morton, who knew Richard, and appears as Bishop of Ely in the play), already become something of a legend, and Shakespeare took full advantage of this aspect of his story.

*Richard III* gives us a brilliant portrait by a youthful artist, in the full flood of his advancing power, of a type of man whom it is a pity not to have met, and folly not to understand. As well as the villain here is, as Lamb points out, ' the lofty genius, the man of vast capacity—the profound, the witty, the accomplished Richard.' Here is visible in its supreme state the energy and power that may put a man who knows no conscience but the promptings of his own will and interest at the head of a College or a Trade Union, in a Bishopric or St. Peter's chair itself; the man whose progress is accompanied by curses not loud but deep, whose character is an open secret that few care or dare to mention except in whispers. Here is the exploitation of the susceptibilities of ordinary men, the use of their catchwords to yoke them to his purposes. Nothing could be better than the appearance of Richard between two Bishops before the Mayor and his subdued Aldermen, or this arch-hypocrite's rebuke to Buckingham's profane enthusiasm,

O do not swear my Lord of Buckingham.

Shakespeare's Richard has often been cited as evidence of the influence of Marlowe and his supermen. Marlowe is, indeed, the poet of the aspiring mind that moves like the restless spheres whether after knowledge or power. There is a touch of the Promethean in such figures as Tamburlaine and Faustus; their impossible designs suggest something of the immortal longings that must always trouble the spirit of man. But Marlowe was as yet unable to give adequate expression to his theme, for Faustus has nothing to do in the middle of the play but some childish conjuring tricks, and Tamburlaine can only pass from one 'lune' to another. Marlowe has shown us the intensity rather than the dignity of human desires. *Richard III* falls below the highest tragic level in the same respect; but Shakespeare, instinctively recognizing this, allows for it in his treatment, and we have the unstrained mirth with which this wolf assumes the clothing of the lamb. 'Nowhere in any of Shakespeare's plays,' says Lamb, 'is to be found so much of sprightly colloquial dialogue, and soliloquies of genuine humour, as in *Richard III*.'

Villainy is not a tragic theme even when raised to the level of genius. It can only contribute to tragedy when it so ruins a soul as to reveal the moral foundations which, but for the catastrophe, might have remained unseen. Beside the thick-coming fancies of Macbeth the ghosts of Richard's victims are a melodramatic addition. Compared with the melancholy grandeur of Macbeth's features, worthy of the fallen archangel himself, Richard's are those of a light-hearted fiend. But this is after all a portrait from the artist's youth. If it lacks depth when compared with the masterpieces of his maturity, its energy is superb and worthy of the subject.

## KING JOHN

There is no entry in the Register for *King John*, first printed in the **First Folio**, and the publication of *The Troublesome Reign of King John* in 1591 must for some reason have been taken as covering it.

*The Troublesome Reign* is generally taken to be an original work by an anonymous writer, which Shakespeare used as the basis of his *King John*. But it is difficult to understand how this work, so well digested in the scenes as to permit Shakespeare to follow it nearly scene by scene, should yet show so little corresponding modesty or cunning in its writing as to appear like a tissue of borrowed and only half-assimilated phrases from *Henry VI, Richard III*, as well as *King John* itself. This reasoning would date all these pieces before 1591 ; the present consensus of critical opinion, however, places *King John* considerably later.[1] Meres in 1598 included it in his list.

Shakespeare follows the tradition established in the Chronicles which represents John as an early English champion of national and religious liberty. But the Arthur intrigues round which the plot is cleverly constructed, as well as the other main events, give John so unheroical a part that Shakespeare accepts or invents the figure of the Bastard to keep the spirit of Cœur de Lion alive in the hour of England's humiliation.

As a picture of the sensible, humorous and determined man of action, Shakespeare has not improved on the Bastard : he has nothing more plain, downright and humane. His disquisitions on ' Commodity, the bias of the world ' and on ' worshipful society ' might seem too mature for the youthful Shakespeare, were it not certain that *The Shrew* is not later than 1592. Petruchio has a similar verve and gusto. The famous lines,

> This England never did, nor never shall,
> Lie at the proud foot of a conqueror,

[1] See *King John*, edited J. Dover Wilson, xvii *seq.*

But when it first did help to wound itself.
Now these her princes are come home again,
Come the three corners of the world in arms,
And we shall shock them.   Naught shall make us rue,
If England to itself do rest but true,

are no intrusive top note to bring down the house, but a natural
utterance of the character that throughout seems to breathe much
of Shakespeare's early idealism.

There could be no better contrast to this forceful man of the
world than Prince Arthur, whom Shakespeare has invested
with the appeal that a warlike cavalcade always gives to the
face of extreme youth riding in its ranks ; and Shakespeare
has placed him amidst the boisterous events of the story as
tenderly as Uccello has framed the face of the boy in the spears
of his *Rout of San Romano.*

## LOVE'S LABOUR'S LOST

S.R. 19th November, 1607, when it was transferred from
Burby to Ling.   But Burby had printed **Q1 1598** ' *As it was
presented before her Highnes this last Christmas.   Newly corrected
and augmented.*'   The absence of an initial entry in the Register,
the words ' *Newly corrected and augmented,*' as well as its publisher,
link this Quarto with that of *Romeo and Juliet,* of which Burby
published a Good Quarto to replace a Bad one.   It is almost
certain, therefore, that his *L.L.L.* Quarto was issued in similar
circumstances, though no copy of this Bad Quarto is known
to survive.

The text given to replace the pirated and mutilated version
might be expected to prove of peculiar authority, and it is
probable that it was printed directly from a manuscript in
Shakespeare's hand, many of the peculiarities in spelling being
forms favoured by the poet, which the printer has failed to
normalize.[1]   Unfortunately, the printer, instead of working
solely from his manuscript, used in places (as did the printer of
*Romeo and Juliet,* Q2) the Bad Quarto, and this may explain a

[1] *Love's Labour's Lost,* Cambridge, 1923, p. 103.

number of confusions in the text, particularly the double version in Berowne's defence of love (IV, iii, 292–313 and 314–50). The Folio reprints the Quarto : this is natural, since Heminge and Condell must have known the authority of Burby's edition. They had it checked, however, as certain changes in stage-directions and speech-headings show, with a stage version in their possession.

At a time when verse tests were interpreted more mechanically than now seems admissible, the large amount of rhyme and the end-stopt nature of much of the verse gave this play first place among the comedies ; but the subject and its treatment suggest a social experience not possible to a newcomer to town ; and the piece should stand either at the end of the first or the beginning of the second period. 'The first and second cause' (I, ii, 167) is from Segar's *Book of Honor and Arms* (1590), and John Banks began showing his 'dancing horse' (I, ii, 53) in 1591. Harvey's *Pierces Supererogation*, which Shakespeare echoes, was published in 1593. The features of the dark lady of the sonnets seem to appear at III, i, 185–187.

The adventures of Henry of Navarre, which had greatly interested England, suggested some of the features of the story. Biron, Longaville, Dumain, were prominent, though not all of the same party, in the struggle between Henry and the Catholic League. In 1578 a Princess of France, Marguerite de Valois, paid him a visit, taking with her a group of ladies on whose fascinations she could rely. She was Henry's wife, though separated from him, and wished to bargain about her dowry that involved possessions in Aquitaine (II, i, 8). Further the lines (V. ii, 14–18),

> He made her melancholy, sad, and heavy ;
> And so she died : had she been light like you,
> Of such a merry, nimble, stirring spirit,
> She might ha' been a grandam ere she died ;
> And so may you, for a light heart lives long,

seem to refer to the death of Helène de Tournon, which happened two years before the visit, and which is recorded in the Queen's *Mémoires*. These were not then published, but Marguerite's story was not unknown in England ; and Shakespeare's fantasia on foreign affairs smacks of the observation prescribed by Falconbridge in *John*. His tale of ' worshipful society,' with your traveller and his toothpick at his worship's mess, and of how with ' my picked man of countries '

> talking of the Alps and Apennines,
> The Pyrenean and the river Po,
> It draws towards supper in conclusion so,

all seems to find an echo in the knowledge displayed in *Love's Labour's Lost*.

The personages of the underplot were suggested by the stock figures of the Italian Commedia dell' Arte, the Captain, the Pedant, the Clown. These provide a pedantic chorus to the pedantry of the Principals. For this of all Shakespeare's comedies is the one that depends most openly on an idea. His earlier comedies are of situation, as his later are of character. The progress seems a natural one, and is parallel to Molière's. The early farces on stock situations that he played in the provinces give way to the comedy of ideas, *Les Précieuses Ridicules*, with which he took Paris ; and, eventually, comes such a work as *Le Misanthrope*, where character dominates everything. In *Love's Labour's Lost* Shakespeare, like Molière, glances at some of the follies of his time, working into his historical medley a criticism of what are now called educationists.

Some have recognized John Florio, the translator of Montaigne, in Holofernes ; and Shakespeare certainly puts into this character's part a proverb taken from Florio's *First Fruits*. This and his *Second Fruits* were manuals designed to teach Italian on a conversational method, imitated from the Latin dialogues then popular in the Grammar schools. Recently Miss Yates [1] has shown how familiar Shakespeare was with these modern language text books, as he was with those in Latin, and that he quotes not only from Florio's dialogues but from a book of French dialogues, the *Ortho-epia Gallica* of John Eliot. *Eliot's Fruits for the French*, as it is called in the sub-title, is not merely

---

[1] A Study of *Love's Labour's Lost*,' by Frances A. Yates, 50 *seq*.

instructional, but attacks the French refugees who were taking over the teaching of modern languages from Englishmen, and parodies their pedantic style and matter. In one question that Shakespeare treats at length in *Love's Labour's Lost* Eliot is diametrically opposed to Florio. In his *Second Fruits* Florio had taught that English plays were ' neither right comedies, nor right tragedies,' but merely ' representations of histories without any decorum.' Like Holofernes he adopted what was regarded as the classical point of view. Eliot, on the other hand, regarded this learned imitation that passed for Art as mere pedantry ; and Gabriel Harvey, another partisan of learning, in his *Pierces Supererogation*, referred to by Shakespeare at IV, ii, 79–85, cites Eliot as one who preferred ' Sanguine witt' in a man of letters to ' Melancholy Arte,' and who rated experience and native invention taught in such a school above mere learning. Shakespeare, as *Love's Labour's Lost* proves, was familiar with the works of these disputants, and in the play handles in his own way the question of art and learned imitation that was so unhappily debated by his own early critics and that so long delayed the understanding of his art. Holofernes and Armado should not be taken as portraits of Florio and Harvey ; the characters express sentiments, and perhaps reveal mannerisms, that would remind the better informed in the audience of these scholars ; but they are types of the pedant found in all ages, and among the warnings Shakespeare has given his commentators.

To the theme of Art, Shakespeare has joined that traditionally associated with it, Love. And once more he found in a contemporary debate the occasion for a contribution to this eternal question. Florio in his *First Fruits* had declared ' that it were labour lost to speak of Love,' a phrase that may have given Shakespeare his title ; but in the *Second Fruits* Florio treats this matter at length, and, in setting forth the arguments for and against love, recalls the exhortations addressed to Sir Philip Sidney, then writing his sonnets to Stella, by Giordano Bruno, when that celebrated disciple of Copernicus visited England. This debate had been revived by the utterances of some of the members of a circle of scholars and gentlemen interested in the new science and particularly the theories of Copernicus.  Chapman, in the dedication of his poem *The Shadow of Night* (1594) to Roydon, another member of this circle, recommends invocation, fasting and watching, as the means to ' skil ' ; and Miss Yates has printed an essay, written about this time by the ninth Earl of Northumberland, in which he holds the pursuit of love to be inconsistent with that of learning.  Thomas Hariot, the mathematician, was the instructor of the school, and numbered among his pupils, Raleigh, Marlowe, Roydon, as well as the Earls of Northumberland and Derby.  This is the ' School of Night ' of IV, iii, 251, and its opinions gave Shakespeare the topical setting for the argument that culminates in Berowne's famous tirade on art and love, and for the intrigue that ends with the disciples of Copernicus discovering in the ladies' eyes the perfect starriness that makes all men astronomers.

' Deep-searching ' Northumberland married and quarrelled with Dorothy Devereux, the sister of Stella and of Essex. Southampton was the close friend of Essex, and Shakespeare was at this time intimate with Southampton ; so that some of the observations in the play may have been taken as glancing at the Earl's conduct.[1]

But when all the topical allusions are set aside, the comedy remains a plea for nature and sense.  ' Learning is to Shakespeare,' Smart has said, ' something that enriches and vivifies ' ; it must not lead to ignorance of ' Nature and the language of the sense,' the ' Life of Sensations ' in Keats's phrase.  To see and not to feel seemed death to Shakespeare as it did to Coleridge :

> These earthly godfathers of heaven's lights,
> That give a name to every fixed star,
> Have no more profit of their shining nights,
> Than those that walk and wot not what they are.
> Too much to know, is to know nought but fame ;
> And every godfather can give a name.   (I. i, 88–93.)

Not that Shakespeare any more than Wordsworth, Keats or Coleridge is an advocate of ignorance and sloth ; and the

---

[1] But the date of the marriage is doubtful.

knowledge and reading shown in this and other early plays allow Smart to apply to the poet himself the words of Navarre to the chief critic of his pedantry,

How well he's read to reason against reading.[1]

Shakespeare's final development of the main theme, in which the king is sent for a year to a hermitage, and Berowne ' to jest a twelvemonth in an hospital,' presents another aspect of experience on which the great Romantic poets were accustomed to dwell. The conviction that Keats expressed in the second *Hyperion*

    ' None can usurp this height,' return'd that shade,
    ' But those to whom the miseries of the world
    Are misery and will not let them rest,'

is here treated in a key in keeping with comedy. But it is prophetic of the later development of Shakespeare's art.

## THE POEMS

### I. VENUS AND ADONIS

**S.R. 18th April, 1593.** *Richard Feild. Entred for his copie under thandes of the Archbisshop of Canterbury and master warden Stirrop, a book intituled Venus and Adonis.*

Richard Field was a printer not a publisher ; but he made the entry for Shakespeare no doubt because they were friends, their fathers having been well known to each other in Stratford, and they themselves of an age. Yet we can hardly suppose he felt any reluctance in associating himself with a publication **Q1 1593** under such influential patronage. Field had come to London when fifteen to be apprenticed to Vautrollier, a Huguenot and one of the leading printers in London ; and on his master's death had married his widow, and taken over the important business.

On 25th June, 1594, Field assigned the publishing rights of

---

[1] So Keats could write to his brothers : 'I am reading Voltaire and Gibbon, although I wrote to Reynolds the other day to prove reading of no use.'

7

the poem to Harrison, to whom Shakespeare's second poem is entered.

## II. THE RAPE OF LUCRECE

**S.R. 9th May, 1594.** *Master harrison Senior. Entred for his copie under thand of master Cawood Warden, a booke intituled the Ravyshement of Lucrece.*

Field was again the printer, QI 1594.

The Archbishop of Canterbury licensed *Venus and Adonis* with his own hand. He was Whitgift, formerly Bishop of Worcester, the prelate who had disciplined Shakespeare's father ; but we cannot say whether he now did this honour to the son because he was asked to by Southampton, or because he himself was an admirer of Shakespeare's genius, and wished to help a poet from his old diocese.

The dedicatory epistle to the Earl of Southampton is throughout modest yet dignified in its attention to the ceremony required by the customs of the time, the barriers between one order of society and another that the independent mind will not, as Dr. Johnson has observed, overlook. Southampton, however, must have disarmed Shakespeare by the continuous courtesy of his reception and his impetuous generosity. But even if Southampton, in keeping with the ideal of the day, did, as Rowe tells us, reward the poet handsomely for his offering, this alone could not have effected the change of tone revealed in the second letter, which went with *Lucrece*. Without the assurance of the Earl's warm friendship, Shakespeare would not have removed the cloak of his reserve and written : ' The love I dedicate to your lordship is without end.'

One must, of course, clear the mind of cant. ' You may say to a man,' as Johnson told Boswell, ' Sir I am your most humble servant. You are *not* his most humble servant.' But these letters, though they belong to a familiar form of literary address, reflect the generous mind we should expect in the creator of Hamlet, and the man of whom Ben Jonson said : ' He was indeed honest and of an open and free nature.' That Jonson could say no more of his friend is clear from Drummond's remark on Jonson himself : ' of all styles he loved most to be named honest.' Without confounding ranks the letters speak of a noble equality.

That it was the attack on Shakespeare's honesty contained in Greene's epilogue to his *Groatsworth of Wit* that suggested the publication of such a work as *Venus and Adonis* is a probability not to be overlooked ; and Southampton may well have been one of the gentlemen of worship who told Chettle what they thought of Greene's observations on Shakespeare as a man and a poet. For though the internal evidence shows that Shakespeare regarded the drama as seriously as Marlowe or Ben Jonson, most plays then as now had no claims to literary merit ; and the dramatist may have agreed to the suggestion of his friends to give the world unequivocal proof of his title to the name of poet. And this would explain the contrast between the modesty of the dedication and the pride of his motto :

> Vilia miretur vulgus ; mihi flavus Apollo
> Pocula Castalia plena ministret aqua.[1]

For the motto is hardly intelligible if Shakespeare had not already given proof of his genius. Certainly in the dedication he refers to the poem as ' the first heir of my invention.' But this need mean no more than his first published work. Those who suppose that Shakespeare till this time was merely a botcher of plays have to explain how this humble occupation had won for him so distinguished a circle of admirers. But if Shakespeare was already recognized as a man of genius by those whose judgment he valued, the motto and dedication are not surprising. ' I would be subdued before my friends,' Keats wrote to Bailey, ' and thank them for subduing me—but among multitudes of men I have no feeling of stooping, I hate the idea of humility to them.' The motto informs us of the royal line from which Shakespeare claimed descent, and that he could speak ' unbonneted ' to as proud a fortune as this that he had reached.

---

[1] Ovid's *Amores*, Elegy 15. Translated by Jonson.
   Kneele hindes to trash : me let bright Phoebus swell,
   With cups full flowing from the *Muses* well.

### III. THE SONNETS

**S.R. 20th May, 1609.** *Thomas Thorpe. Entred for his copie under thandes of master Wilson and master Lownes Warden a Booke called Shakespeares sonnettes.*

In **Q1 1609** the publisher, Thomas Thorpe, inserted this dedication :

TO. THE. ONLIE. BEGETTER. OF.

THESE. INSVING. SONNETS.

Mr. W. H. ALL. HAPPINESSE.

AND. THAT. ETERNITIE.

PROMISED.

BY.

OVR. EVER-LIVING. POET.

WISHETH.

THE. WELL-WISHING.

ADVENTVRER. IN.

SETTING.

FORTH.

T. T.

The interpretation of the expression ' only begetter ' is doubtful. Did Thorpe mean that Mr. W. H. was the fair youth of the sonnets (though on this reading the dark lady also has a claim as a begetter, to some of the sonnets), or was he merely the gentleman who gave Thorpe the manuscript—Mr. William Harvey perhaps, who in 1598 married the widowed mother of Lord Southampton ?  The manuscript can only have come from one in the innermost circle of those who knew Shakespeare and his noble friend.  If Southampton was the friend, William Harvey may have been the ' only begetter.'

That Southampton was the friend seems probable.  The dedicatory epistles to *Venus and Adonis* and *Lucrece* are in terms that agree with those used in the sonnets.  The dedication to *Venus and Adonis* is merely a prose rendering of sonnet xxvi. Further, Southampton was in 1593 in his twentieth year— young, yet already past ' the ambush of young years ' (sonnet lxx).  Lord Herbert, his only serious rival, was not 20 till 1600 ;

and the mention of the sonnets by Meres in 1598, and the publication of Nos. 138 and 144 by Jaggard in the *Passionate Pilgrim*, afford evidence that they were written before Lord Herbert [1] was beyond this ambush—nor do his relations with Mary Fitton bear out the statement that he had emerged ' a victor.' There is no need to suppose that Shakespeare introduced himself to Southampton with the *Venus and Adonis* : the sonnet corresponding to the dedication is xxvi, and the Archbishop's licence points to the poet's moving in influential circles before publication.

One of the difficulties of the sonnet story is the identification of the rival poet. Chapman has been suggested as one to whom the phrase ' the proud full sail of his great verse ' (lxxxvi) is applicable, but he dedicated nothing to Southampton. And not only does the phrase seem more applicable to Marlowe's verse, but the expression in the same sonnet ' his spirit by spirits taught to write ' may have been suggested by the reputation his *Faustus* had made for him. Greene talks of his being bred of Merlin's race and having prophetical spirits. Marlowe's sudden death in 1593 would explain why there is no dedication from him to Southampton. Marlowe, however, can only be considered in this connection if we are prepared to date the meeting of Shakespeare and Southampton some time before the publication of *Venus and Adonis*.

But already all is obscure. To go further, and seek through Southampton's connection with Essex, and his part in the rising of 1601 (*see* pages 116 and 128), a path to the interpretation of

---

[1] This was William Herbert, from 1601 third Earl of Pembroke, to whom (with his brother) Heminge and Condell dedicated the First Folio. His mother is commemorated in Jonson's line ' Sidney's sister, Pembroke's mother.' Though his initials were W. H., he could hardly have been addressed so informally as Mr. W. H.

If Mr. W. H. is William Harvey, T. T. in wishing him ' that eternitie promised by our ever-living poet ' is perhaps, in allusion to the opening theme of the Sonnets,

> And nothing 'gainst Time's scythe can make defence
> Save breed, to brave him when he takes thee hence,

hoping that his recent marriage may be blessed with a son.

Shakespeare's art, is more than hazardous. And those enquirers who have been lured on by the enigma of the dark lady have nothing verifiable to record. Tyler's story, admirably retold by Mr. Bernard Shaw in his Preface to *The Dark Lady of the Sonnets*, in which the friend is Lord Herbert and the lady Mary Fitton, is the most interesting, but can hardly survive as history the discovery of the lady's portrait in which she appears as blue-eyed and fair-haired.

But however interesting the story might be, could we recover it in its entirety—of Shakespeare's relations with his friend, whether Southampton or some other—it would be of very secondary importance to the plain record the sonnets bear on their face of the heart of their author. The generous instincts, the susceptibility to beauty, the moral discrimination, the enthusiasm, the passion that one can feel behind the plays are here more directly revealed. And we can see that it was to the intensity of his own struggles as a man that Shakespeare owed, when he came to interpret as a dramatist the conflicts of a Coriolanus, an Antony or a Hamlet, his supreme power of moving the heart.

### IV. A LOVER'S COMPLAINT

This poem of just over 300 lines in the rime royal stanza of *Lucrece* was published by Thorpe along with the Sonnets, which it follows in the 1609 volume. It is there ascribed to William Shakespeare; and it is not easy to reject this attribution, so difficult is it to suggest any other author who could have written it.

### V. THE PHŒNIX AND THE TURTLE

In 1601 was published a volume entitled, *Loves Martyr: Or, Rosalins Complaint. Allegorically shadowing the truth of Love, in the constant Fate of the Phœnix and Turtle . . . by Robert Chester. . . .*
*To these are added some new compositions, of severall moderne Writers whose names are subscribed to their severall workes, upon the first subject : viz. the Phœnix and Turtle.*

Chester was in the service of Sir John Salisbury, who, coming to London in 1595 when he was 28, became a member of the Inner Temple, and was knighted by the Queen in 1601, the year of this publication. Chester's principal theme is his patron's married happiness. Among the modern writers who contributed new compositions were Chapman, Marston, Jonson, and Shakespeare, no doubt to please Sir John, who was an earnest patron of poets and dramatists. Shakespeare confined himself to a metaphysical treatment of the theme of love and constancy.

# IV. THE SECOND PERIOD

IN the second period references to Shakespeare increase in number, and give a picture of his life at this time which, though lacking in intimate detail, provides a clear enough outline of his professional connections, and the growth of his prosperity and fame.

As a member of the Chamberlain's Company he would act during this period at the Theatre and the Curtain, playhouses situated in the North-East of London. The Theatre dated from 1576, and was the first building of its kind in England. Hitherto the London Companies had played in inn-yards about town. These provided an enclosed rectangle to which admittance was easily controlled ; the galleries that formed a feature of the inner face of the surrounding buildings accommodated the wealthier spectators, while the others—the groundlings—stood in the open yard, into which the improvised stage projected. Burbage's building was on similar lines, though no doubt the stage plan he adopted was formed on Italian models. The raised stage projected into an open yard round which were three galleries carried by the enclosing wall. Though the building as a whole was open to the sky, the galleries had a projecting cover of thatch, and over part of the stage was a canopy called the heavens, supported on pillars.

The builder and proprietor was a carpenter, James Burbage, father of the famous tragic actor, and himself the associate of actors. The financial prospects of such a venture were good. The Corporation of London had among its members many strongly Puritan in their outlook, who disliked the fun and looseness, and the consequent dangers of infection and riot, that were found on the outskirts of such places of resort ; and they were doing their best to make playing impossible in buildings under their control. Burbage, therefore, built his theatre just beyond their jurisdiction in the Liberty of Holywell, beside Finsbury Fields. A Liberty was a piece of ground formerly attached to a religious house that continued, after the dissolution of the fraternity, exempt from City authority. Blackfriars was such a Liberty within the walls, the Bankside another on the south of the river, just across London Bridge. Holywell in the north was a short way beyond Moorgate and Bishopsgate, but on fields much frequented by Londoners.

As Burbage's son had joined the Chamberlain's men it was natural for them to play at the Theatre, and at the Curtain in the vicinity, which had passed in 1585 into Burbage's management. It was this association that was to take the Chamberlain's men from the Theatre, in the north, to a new theatre called the Globe, in the south, on the Bankside.

The lease of the Theatre, which James Burbage held from one Gyles Alleyn, expired in April 1597. Anticipating this Burbage had purchased the old dining hall of the Blackfriars and furnished it as a theatre ; but the inhabitants of the district, many of whom were influential, prevented his using it as a public theatre. Meanwhile Alleyn pretended to be negotiating with Burbage, for there was a clause in the lease giving him possession of the building if it was not removed at its expiry. During his absence in the country, however, on 28th December, 1598, Cuthbert and Richard Burbage, their father having died in February 1597 just before the agreement terminated, took a party of friends armed with swords and axes to the Theatre, and there, according to Alleyn's complaint, ' in very riotous, outrageous and forcible manner ' pulled down the building, after driving off Alleyn's servants by force. The materials they transported to the Bankside, where the Burbages had built by the spring of 1599 an improved version of the Theatre, called the Globe.

Cuthbert and Richard Burbage were not by themselves able to finance this venture ; so, taking between them half the shares in the new building, they distributed the other half among five of the leading actors in the Chamberlain's Company : Shakespeare, Heminge, Phillips, Pope, and Kempe. Kempe, as he left the Company just at this time, did not take up his share in the new venture, and Condell later joined this body of ' housekeepers.' By making the leading actors, hitherto ' sharers ' in the Company's profits after rent and the wages of the hired men had been paid, into ' housekeepers,' who drew a share from the rent charged for the theatre, the Burbages practically secured the Company as permanent tenants for their new house, and through them an assured return on their investment.

Shakespeare's part in this transaction is evidence of his financial position at the end of the period, but throughout this whole time there is ample proof of his affluence.

The subsidy rolls show that for some time before 1596 Shakespeare had been resident in Bishopsgate, and the sum on which he was assessed indicates that he was living in a comfortable style. In November 1597 the collectors report his February tax as unpaid, and a subsequent assessment was recovered from him in Southwark, where he must have settled some time in 1596. This removal took him from the neighbourhood of the Theatre to that chosen for the Globe. After making this change he purchased in May 1597 for £60 New Place, which Sir Hugh Clopton, Lord Mayor of London in 1496, had built to retire to at

Stratford. As Shakespeare's son, Hamnet, died at Stratford in August 1596, it has been suggested by Professor Quincy Adams, that Shakespeare may have had his family with him in Bishopsgate since his assessment was high, and decided, when his son sickened and died after removal to Stratford, to keep the rest of his family in the country for good.

That Shakespeare was now known as a man in easy circumstances appears from some letters, once preserved among the Stratford records. They were written by Shakespeare's friend Richard Quiney, who died in 1602 during his second period as Bailiff of Stratford—his first being in 1592—and were put away at his death with the public papers in his possession. Among them is a letter written by Quiney on 25th October, 1598, from the Bell in Carter Lane, while on Stratford business in London. The superscription runs : *To my Lovinge good ffrend and contreymann Mr. Wm. Shackespere deliver thees ;* and in the letter Quiney requests the dramatist to raise for him at short notice the £30 he needed for his expenses. The letter remained in Quiney's possession, and this circumstance, taken with the letter he wrote the same day to a Stratford friend indicating that he had talked over money matters with Shakespeare, suggests that a personal encounter made its delivery unnecessary.

In two other important transactions during this period Shakespeare must have been closely associated with his father. In 1597 they started a Chancery suit to recover the property mortgaged to the Lamberts in 1578, but without success. The other business also had its beginnings many years before. In 1596 John Shakespeare obtained from the College of Heralds a grant of arms.[1] As a former

[1] The shield ' in a field of gold, upon a bend sable, a spear of the first, the point upward, headed argent ' ; the crest ' a falcon, with his wings displayed, standing on a wreath of his colours, supporting a spear, armed, headed, and steeled silver ' ; the motto ' *Non sans droict.*' See *A Life of Shakespeare*, by Quincy Adams, p. 250.

Bailiff of Stratford he was entitled to this privilege, and the Heralds note at the end of their draft that John Shakespeare had twenty years or so before this—no doubt about the time of his bailiffship—obtained a ' pattern ' of a coat of arms from one of their College, that he was worth £500, and that he had married ' a daughter and heir of Arden, a gent. of worship.' The draft itself states that his grandfather (his great-grandfather in a later version) was advanced and rewarded by Henry VII for his faithful and valiant service. Some take this to refer to his wife's family ; that is unlikely, though nothing is known of any of John's forbears except his father. In 1599 a draft was made of a grant permitting John Shakespeare to impale the Arden arms of his wife's family, but neither John nor his descendants seem to have shown the Arden arms with their own.

By the end of the second period Shakespeare is not only a ' sharer ' in the leading company but a ' housekeeper ' in the chief theatre of the time. He is, in addition, the possessor of a substantial country house and a gentleman entitled to bear arms. But that Shakespeare's main interest throughout the period was his art is borne out by the remarkable development it shows. Bach said that anyone who had worked as he had would have done as well. No one can doubt that work is an essential ingredient in great art, but work so hard that only a pursuit to which one is irresistibly drawn could make it endurable. ' The labour we delight in physics pain ' ; and Shakespeare must have delighted as well as laboured in his vocation, for, in a few years, he passed from plays that many have declared un-worthy of his genius to those all acknowledge as entitling him to the fame he had won, as the best among the English, as Meres expressed it in 1598, both in Tragedy and Comedy.

The plays of this period show the development of all the powers found in the earlier works. Shakespeare is still the maker of the poetical phrase and beautiful speech ; and if the verse in its untroubled perfection has not the sublime note yet to come, it attains a rare lyrical intensity in *Richard II, Romeo and Juliet, A Midsummer Night's Dream*, and *The Merchant of Venice*, the most poetical, in one sense of that term, of all the Histories, Tragedies, and Comedies.

Nor had Shakespeare lost any of his skill in weaving together the diverse threads of his plots. *A Midsummer Night's Dream* is of as varied yarn as the most changeable taffeta, opalescent with incongruities ; heroic figures from Greek mythology, fairies from English folk-lore, craftsmen from Warwickshire, lovers from nowhere, all taking part in the marvellous and happy doings of this middle summer's spring. And the action of *Romeo and Juliet* is built round its crisis with a power that foretells the great tragic architect of *Hamlet* and *Lear*.

But the development of Shakespeare's powers of characterization is the most remarkable feature of the second period. The tendency of the earliest characters to take on themselves more life than is required by their circumstances now becomes a habit. *The Merchant of Venice* needed a villain, and a Jew was a stock figure for the part, particularly in a story with a strong financial interest. The villain must be worsted, and if his defeat comes at the moment he is surest of success, so much the better. It must be admitted that the prime requirements of the plot are admirably met by Portia's learned interpretation of the bond, and her taking Shylock red-handed. But his defeat makes him friends. Yet it would be as absurd to blame Portia and Antonio for Jew-baiting as it would be to reprove Jack in the Bean Stalk story for being a trial to his mother or a disturber of the giant's peace. We are conscious, however, of a discord in the play that even the moonlight and music of Belmont cannot quite resolve. ' The scene is disturbed ; a real man has got in among the *dramatis personæ,* and puts them out.' Lamb, protesting here against the too realistic portrayal of such characters in artificial comedy as the sea-going son in *Love for Love,* concludes : 'We want the sailor turned out. We feel that his true place is not behind the curtain but in the first or second gallery.' But there is no place in the auditorium that would have been acceptable to Shylock. If he is to be in the theatre he must be on the stage ; and since his disturbing reality is no actor's over-doing of a part, but the very nature of the character as it comes from its creator's imagination, the play must be recast to make room for him. And the change from comedy to tragedy in the third period is the natural development of the genius that so threatens to obliterate the limits of comedy.

At this turn in the flood of Shakespeare's genius his greatest comic character makes his appearance. It is a truism that the supreme comic artists give a tragic depth to the shadows with which they set off their most humorous figures, and Falstaff is a portrait that challenges comparison with any in this great tradition. But with Shakespeare it marks the culmination of but one phase of his genius that leads almost inevitably, it seems, to the next.

# A MIDSUMMER NIGHT'S DREAM

**S.R. 8th October, 1600.** *Thomas Fyssher. Entred for his copie under the handes of master Rodes and the Wardens. A booke called A mydsommer nightes Dreame.*

Fisher published Q1 1600. This Jaggard reprinted in 1619, putting on the title page *Printed by James Roberts, 1600.* From this reprint Jaggard's compositors worked when setting up the Folio text ; but it had been compared with a copy in the theatre, for at V, i, 125 the Folio notes, as the characters in the final

Interlude are introduced, *Tawyer with a trumpet before them*, this Tawyer being Heminge's servant.

The conclusion of the play suggests that it was designed as a marriage entertainment. Oberon says,

> To the best bride bed will we,
> Which by us shall blessed be.

But there may have been three marriages on this occasion,

> So shall all the couples three
> Ever true in loving be.

There are, of course, two subsidiary marriages in the play itself, but they may have been there, in the first instance, because two marriages of lesser social importance were to be solemnised on the same day as the principal ceremony that gave the poet his commission.

The guess that the piece was for the marriage of Elizabeth Carey to Thomas Berkeley on 19th February, 1596, is the most likely put forward, since the Lord Chamberlain, who was the bride's grandfather, was also the patron of Shakespeare's Company. There are, however, no details of the ceremony now available to confirm or refute this conjecture. But *The Merry Wives of Windsor*, which like the present piece introduces a fairy episode and dance, was almost certainly produced on an occasion of importance to the Carey family (*see* page 126), and the singing boys maintained by the family would have been available as a fairy contingent.

To continue the conjecture, the framework in which the action is set, the marriage of Theseus and Hippolyta might well have suggested itself to Shakespeare when he was turning over, with his commission in the back of his mind, the new edition of Plutarch's *Lives* issued in 1595 by his friend Field; for from Plutarch come the names at II, i, 78-80, Perigouna, Aegles, Ariadne, Antiopa. The bad weather mentioned in II, i, 88-117 may have reminded the audience of the unusually bad weather of 1594. Another episode of 1594 is also glanced at in Bottom's anxiety about the Lion (III, i, 38) : in August at the baptism

*backwards reasoning*

of James VI's son, Henry, there was among the pageants a car drawn by a blackamoor who had been substituted for a lion which, it was feared, might prove troublesome. *A True Reportarie* of this was entered in the S.R. 24th October, 1594. The play is mentioned by Meres ; and the date 1596 cannot be far out.

Shakespeare drew on Ovid as well as on Plutarch : he knew Golding's translation well, but Titania, a name for Diana not used by Golding, he took straight from the *Metamorphoses*.

It is probable that the main lines of the play, the marriages, the fairies coming to give their blessing, the townsmen to give their play, were all suggested to Shakespeare by the very nature of his task ; but the skill with which he bound them together in one harmonious whole cannot be too greatly admired. The magic juice which sorts out at last the lover's tangle also brings Bottom into the Fairy circle, and Shakespeare's ingenuity passes into inspiration. There is no deep significance in the magic juice, no profound interpretation of life in the adventures of the lovers. Shakespeare gives them at one moment enough poetry to raise an interest in their difficulties,

> As due to love as thoughts and dreams and sighs,
> Wishes and tears, poor fancy's followers ;

at another realism enough, as in the quarrel scene, to hold it. But though they are nothing in themselves they prepare the mind for the central situation in the play.

No comedy of situation, not farce itself can provide a stranger encounter than that between Bottom and Titania ; but it belongs to the purest comedy of character, and Bottom is as much the life of this scene as he is of the Interlude to follow. ' There is a sort of savage nobility about his firm reliance on his own bad taste,' says Professor Housman, speaking of the great Bentley's revision of *Paradise Lost* ; and there is a similar robust independence in all Bottom's thoughts and actions that is not to be extinguished even by the ass's head. What lucidity and sanity are his, how just and straightforward his fashion of thought, whether in Athens or fairyland !

*Quince.*—Is all our company here ?

*Bottom.*—You were best to call them generally,
man by man, according to the scrip,

and then, as Quince still fumbles with the business,

> First, good Peter Quince, say what the play treats on ;
> then read the names of the actors, and so grow to a
> point.

True, he is sometimes himself discursive, even vagrant, for, as
in many brilliant commentators, the energetic current of his
thought eddies at times into a backwater. If there is no difficulty
he must invent one,

> There are things in this comedy of Pyramus and
> Thisby that will never please.

But only that he may restore the situation by some happy stroke,

> I have a device to make all well.

And what an eye for the right authority he discovers when
Quince poses the problem of bringing in moonshine,

> *Snug.*—Doth the moon shine that night we play our
> play ?
> *Bottom.*—A calendar, a calendar ! Look in the al-
> manack ; find out moonshine, find out moonshine.

Bentley himself could not have settled this particular point more
decisively.

Bottom's commonsense corresponds to his manly cast of
mind. Though deserted by his terrified companions he will
sing,

> I will walk up and down here, and I will sing, that
> they may hear I am not afraid.

And he will argue resolutely even with his fancies,

> The finch, the sparrow, and the lark,
> The plain-song cuckoo gray,
> Whose note full many a man doth mark,
> And dares not answer nay ;

for indeed, who would set his wit to so foolish a bird ?
Who would give a bird the lie, though he cry ' cuckoo '
never so ?

8

But there is nothing overbearing or boorish in the man ; and he treats Pease-blossom, Mustard-seed, and their companions, with the same patient courtesy he extends to the Duke himself :—

> *Theseus.*—The wall, methinks, being sensible, should curse again.
>
> *Bottom.*—No, in truth, sir, he should not. ' Deceiving me,' is Thisby's cue : she is to enter now, and I am to spy her through the wall. You shall see, it will fall pat as I told you. Yonder she comes.

Naturally he is not appreciated except by those who know him. To them he is ' Sweet bully Bottom,' with simply the best wit and best person, too, in Athens, ' a very paramour for a sweet voice.' To Puck, untouched by human toil and infirmity, he is merely

> The shallowest thick-skin of that barren sort.

And even the enchanted Titania seems a shade unappreciative, unless it is pure solicitude that makes her say,

> Tie up my love's tongue, bring him silently.

It is easy to laugh at Bottom, and Johnson was able to put his old friend Garrick, and the actors, in their place, when he noted on Bottom's choice of beard :

> Here Bottom again discovers a true genius for the stage by his solicitude for propriety of dress, and his deliberation which beard to choose among many beards, all unnatural.

But what is Johnson himself, in many of his most solemn observations on the plays, but another incarnation of vigorous and humane commonsense lost in the fairy wood of poetry ? Under his remarks on this play Keats wrote, ' The clamorous owl that hoots at our quaint spirits,' and the youthful poet has riddled the criticism of the learned Warburton and Steevens, to him the hard-handed but less gifted sons of a mechanical toil, with a fusillade of such Puckish quotations.[1]

[1] See C. F. E. Spurgeon, *Keats's Shakespeare.*

The character of Theseus provides an admirable point of repose amidst the vivacities of the composition. He is very much Chaucer's complete man of the world, naturally taking first place by a kind of sovereignty of nature. He understands the contradictions of the world well enough to permit him to subdue it, and rule with humanity,

> Love, therefore, and tongue-tied simplicity
> In least speak most, to my capacity ;

but he is royally indifferent to those more curious and more disinterested inquirers into its contradictions, the poets, and he is not carried away by any passion for the arts. ' The best in this kind are but shadows,' he observes of the drama, ' and the worst are no worse if imagination amend them.' Under his eye, however, the Interlude goes forward with less of the unseemly interruption that we have in *Love's Labour's Lost* at the more fantastical Court of Navarre.

Of the poetry of the play nothing need be said, for it overflows in every scene. ' The thing,' said Keats, ' is a piece of profound verdure ' ; and in his early days as a poet its phrases haunted his memory. Speaking of the edition Keats read about 1817, Dr. Spurgeon observes that the markings and wear of the paper prove that *The Tempest* and *A Midsummer Night's Dream* were by far the most read of the plays. These two were also Milton's early choice, and to Milton might be applied Dr. Spurgeon's observation on Keats, ' it is, above all, the fairy poetry and songs he loves.'

But this is only half the marvel. For by putting his intellectual weaver amidst those that need neither toil nor spin, Shakespeare discovers a wonder beyond that of the lilies of the field in poor humanity rehearsing with toil a part that can bring but little thanks in performance ; and yet beyond all pity, since it lives in a glory of its own. This irradiates the humour of the play, as the moonlight shines through its poetry.

## THE MERCHANT OF VENICE

**S.R. 22nd July, 1598.**  *James Robertes. Entred for his copie under the handes of bothe the wardens, a booke of the Marchaunt of Venyce or otherwise called the Jewe of Venyce Provided that yt bee not prynted by the said James Robertes or anye other whatsoever without lycence first had from the Right honorable the lord Chamberlen.*

This was a ' blocking ' entry. Hayes secured the necessary permission and published **Q1 1600.** The printer was Roberts.

**S.R. 28th October, 1600.**  *Thomas haies. Entred for his copie under the handes of the Wardens and by Consent of master Robertes. A booke called the booke of the merchant of Venyce.*

In 1619 Roberts' successor, Jaggard, issued a reprint of Q1 with *Printed by J. Roberts, 1600*, on the title-page. This was true, but not of the edition on which it stood. Lawrence, the son of Thos. Hayes, took steps to reassert his rights to the book, even at the expense of the extra sixpence which the Shakespeare item in this entry cost him.

**S.R. 8th July, 1619.**  *Laurence Hayes. Entred for his Copiestby Consent of a full Court theis two Copies following which were he Copies of Thomas Haies his fathers vizt. A play Called The Marchant of Venice.*

Before being reprinted in the Folio, Q1 was compared with a copy in use in the theatre, some few theatrical directions being added and ' other Lord ' substituted for ' Scottish Lord,' I, ii, 69, a change that would naturally be made in the prompt book and part after 1603.

Dr. Greg has pointed out that the expression in the 1600 entry *A booke called the booke of* . . . suggests that the clerk, having written *A booke*, then copied what follows from the cover of the theatre copy on which would be written ' The book of the Merchant of Venice.' Certainly Q1 was printed from a fair copy of the piece, not from any hasty draft, the songs and letters all being clearly set forth and in order in the text.

The S.R. and Meres fix a date before 1598 for the play. If the lines at IV, i, 133, with their play on the word wolf = lupus, are a reference to the Queen's Jewish physician Lopez, tried for attempting her life and hanged in June 1594, *The Merchant of Venice* may be dated 1595. The next year and part of 1597 are occupied with *Midsummer Night's Dream*, 1 and 2 *Henry IV*, and *Merry Wives of Windsor*. Perhaps this trial, which Essex, the president, and his party made as sensational as possible for their own ends, interested Shakespeare in a story with a Jew in it. For Shakespeare was no doubt ' a man of business,' as Spedding puts it, who thought the story of a wicked Jew good material for such a time ; but, if so, he also did much thinking about the Jew and his relations with Christians that men of business usually spare themselves. The story is found in *Il Pecorone*, a collection of stories by Ser Giovanni of Florence, who was a contemporary of Boccaccio. The test by which the adventurous youth there wins the rich heiress was unsuitable for stage purposes, and Shakespeare replaced it by the casket story ; but in the Italian he would find the bond and the ring episode, the lady's defence of her husband's friend, and the name Belmont. Those who believe that Shakespeare cannot have known a little Italian argue that the casket story was already combined with the main plot in a play called *The Jew*, performed, according to Gosson in his *Schoole of Abuse* (1579), at the Bull, and commended by this severe censor of the stage as ' representing the greedinesse of worldly chusers and bloody mindes of usurers.' Here are, they tell us, the bond and the casket story in English. But, even if this conjecture were certain, Shakespeare may well have gone behind his immediate source as he did in *Twelfth Night*.

The play gathers force from the foreboding created at the beginning by the bond. And so the play can drift along on its pleasant dialogue and poetry,

> He is a proper man's picture, but alas ! who can
> converse with a dumb-show ?

> And let us make incision for your love,
> To prove whose blood is reddest, his or mine,

without our feeling it is getting nowhere. And when at last

one's worst fears are only prevented as by a miracle from being realized, the gay dance of Venetian life can continue for another Act at least.

But its strains are heartless, says Sir Arthur Quiller-Couch, ' every one of the Venetian *dramatis personæ* is either a " waster " or a " rotter " or both, and cold-hearted at that.'   But we cannot feel that the man, to whom Portia says,

> You see me, Lord Bassanio, where I stand,
> Such as I am : though for myself alone
> I would not be ambitious in my wish,
> To wish myself much better ; yet, for you
> I would be trebled twenty times myself,

is altogether without grace ; nor are we surprised that Jessica preferred the company of the lover who says,

> Sit Jessica : look, how the floor of heaven
> Is thick inlaid with patines of bright gold

to what Shylock calls his sober house.   It is true that when one looks into the private affairs of these gentlemen one can discover no visible means by which they support their bravery, and they clearly will have to depend on the money they marry.   But Bassanio passes the test devised by Portia's father, the death-bed inspiration (I, ii, 24) of an ever virtuous and holy man who loved his daughter, and was thus guided to safeguard her happiness.

Those who are provoked by Bassanio's idleness and borrowing must allow Portia's prophetic father to have known better. Nor could anyone trust Jessica's father, for all his virtues, to have picked for her a more promising young fellow than Lorenzo, who, in the moonlight, surely discovers enough music in his soul for salvation.

But · the character in whom Shakespeare's mind became engrossed was Shylock ; and round him there surged up in his mind a host of thoughts that can find no proper expression in such a plot as that of the *Merchant of Venice*, without disturbing the whole keeping of the piece.

> Hath not a Jew eyes ? hath not a Jew hands, organs,
> dimensions, senses, affections, passions ?

If a Jew wrong a Christian, what is his humility?
Revenge. If a Christian wrong a Jew, what should his
sufferance be by Christian example? Why, revenge.
The villany you teach me I will execute ; and it shall go
hard but I will better the instruction.

Shakespeare tries to have it both ways. Shylock has to
play the part demanded of him by the plot ; but Shakespeare's
thoughts go far beyond the mere business in hand, and we have
a picture of the Jew at bay that both Jews and Gentiles can
admire. He takes up the challenge,

> this money, lend it not
> As to thy friends, . . .
> But lend it rather to thine enemy,

and there is a kind of wild justice in his attempt at revenge.


## ROMEO AND JULIET

S.R. 22nd January, 1607. Burby transferred this play along
with *Love's Labour's Lost* and *The Taming of the Shrew* to Ling,
who transferred them with *Hamlet* to Smethwick in November
of the same year.

Q1 1597, which Burby had issued without entry in the
Register, ten years before the transfer, is a Bad Quarto, put
together from memory, though with the help here and there of
manuscript material, especially in the Nurse's part, which is
marked off in places from the surrounding material by being
printed in italics.

Q2 1599, *Newly corrected, augmented, and amended*, according to the title-page, was issued no doubt to remove the injury
the earlier version had done the author's art, though Shakespeare had to content himself with employing the publisher
who issued Q1. The printer of Q2 seems to have consulted
Q1 from time to time, but he had a manuscript in Shakespeare's
hand before him.

At I, iii, 24 the Nurse says, ' 'Tis since the earthquake **now**
eleven years.' *The* earthquake was that of 1580, and the **play**

has consequently been dated 1591 ; but somewhere about 1595, it is generally agreed, seems more probable from general considerations of style and characterization.

Shakespeare's principal source was *Romeus and Juliet*, a poem by Arthur Brooke, who was drowned in 1563, the year of its publication, while still a young man.   He used a French version of the story by Boisteau, who used an Italian version by Bandello. There are some features which connect Shakespeare's work with an Italian play, *La Hadriana*, by Luigi Groto.

Though Brooke shows in his poem both youth and enthusiasm, declaring as he contemplates the lovers,

> I grant that I envy the bliss they lived in,

he is more circumspect in his preface, where he commends his story to the reader as an encouragement ' to honest restraint of wild affections,' since he describes for us, he declares,

> a couple of unfortunate lovers, thralling themselves to unhonest desire ; neglecting the authority and advice of parents and friends ; conferring their principal counsels with drunken gossips and superstitious friars (the naturally fit instruments of unchastity) ; attempting all adventures of peril for the attaining of their wicked lust ; using auricular confession, the key of whoredom and treason, for furtherance of their purpose ; abusing the honourable name of lawful marriage to cloak the shame of stolen contracts ; finally by all means of unhonest life hasting to most unhappy death.

There is nothing of all this in the poem, and it shows how poets may, when they turn to criticism, take refuge in an inadequate formula.   And in our own day Mr. Masefield, anxious to fit the play to Bradley's theory of tragedy, has said much the same as Brooke :

> The play differs slightly from the other plays, which deal, as we have said, with the treacheries caused by obsessions.   The subject of this play is not so much the treachery as the obsession that causes it.   The obsession is the blind and raging one of sudden, gratified youthful

love. . . . It brings to an end in two hearts filial affection
and that perhaps stronger thing, attachment to family.
It makes the charming young man a frantic madman,
careless of everything but his love.  It makes the sweet-
natured girl a deceitful, scheming liar, less frantic, but
not less devoted than her lover.  It results almost at once
in five violent deaths, and a legacy of broken-heartedness
not easily told.  The only apparent good of the disease
is that it destroys its victims swiftly.

   It is unfair, perhaps, to take these sentences from a work
full of poetic observation and suggestion, but unless we take
them as an ironic version of Blake's lines,

> Children of the future Age
> Reading this indignant page,
> Know that in a former time,
> Love ! sweet Love ! was thought a crime,

they do violence to Shakespeare's inspiration.

   To represent as ' a deceitful scheming liar ' the child who
tried to circumvent the father who calls her ' you green sick-
ness carrion,' ' you tallow face,' and threatens to drag her to
church on a hurdle, is to reduce the theory that there must be
some moral fault in the victim of tragedy to absurdity.  And
Shakespeare is careful to show us the ' frantic madman ' be-
having with exemplary composure and forbearance, though
insulted by a quarrelsome bully in the presence of his friends.
If ever a provoked man turned the other cheek Romeo did,
and who can blame him if he has done with the fellow who
strikes that too ?  In Brooke's poem Mercutio has no part in
the episode where Romeo kills Tybalt ; but with Shakespeare,
the wonderful and truly tragic scene in which this gentleman is
killed grows from his design to show us that the act that ruined
the lover's chances was one of pure goodwill.  Some moralize
here on the vanity of good intentions ; but if Hell were paved
with good intentions such as Romeo's, its halls would be indistinguishable from Heaven.  Romeo's is no idle dream of
virtue, but an active endeavour to do the right, and if it ends in
disaster the blame is clearly not his.

This at least is how it seemed at the end to the Prince, who speaks with something of the authority of a chorus ; and to him it is the strife of the parents that is so unnatural as to have made even love fatal to their children.

## RICHARD II

**S.R. 29th August, 1597.** *Andrew Wise. Entred for his Copie by appoyntment from master Warden man The Tragedye of Richard the Second.*

**Q1 1597** and the two following reprints omit the so-called deposition scene (IV, i, 154–318). Elizabeth looked upon the deposing of Richard as a dangerous precedent, and certainly some of the followers of Essex thought they saw warrant in it for their own proceedings. They persuaded the Chamberlain's men to play *Richard II* on Saturday, 7th February, 1601, the day before that fixed for the rising in the City, and attended the Globe in the afternoon, after dining at Gunter's. They had to promise xls extra to the players, who feared the piece would not attract a good house being ' so old and so long out of use.' This came out in the subsequent trial, when the players were interrogated about their part in this proceeding. They were not, however, implicated in any way in the treason.

**Q4 1608,** the first reprint in the reign of James, added the deposition scene.

Shakespeare wrote *Richard II* in 1595 : he drew on Daniel's poem *The Civil Wars between the two houses of Lancaster and Yorke* (S.R. 11th October, 1594) published early in 1595 ; and the play was performed on 9th December, 1595, at the house of Sir Edward Hoby (Chambers' *Shakespeare*, II, 320).[1]

*Richard II* is a companion portrait to *Richard III*, Shakespeare working in a very different style in his endeavour to obtain a

[1] See Professor Dover Wilson's *Introduction* (which I have had the privilege of reading in manuscript) to his forthcoming text of *Richard II* in the New Cambridge Shakespeare. Students should also read there his admirable account of the borrowings from certain French Chronicles found in *Richard II*. The argument, however, by which he would rule out Shakespeare's first-hand knowledge of these Chronicles does not seem to me conclusive.

tragic effect.  For in *Richard III*, where open and fastened villainy
is the driving power in the character, Shakespeare had to introduce too much of the comic in his endeavour to preserve a
human likeness and gain the sympathy for his character necessary
in tragedy.  In *Richard II* wanton irresponsibility replaces
deliberate crime, and Shakespeare now makes a frontal assault
on the sympathy of his audience on behalf of the fallen king.
The love of his royal wife, the poor groom's loyalty, the picture
of the people as proud of their new master as Richard's favourite
charger under Bolingbroke's skilled hand, and, above all,
Richard's own appeals in a throng of Biblical references for
Christian compassion, are among the elements in this attack.

But Shakespeare tries to get the tragic pity by insisting on
the world's hard heart rather than by making us feel a virtue
that forces us to cry out against its indifference.  And the fallen
king's insistence on his own position, however much it may
touch the Judases and Pilates around him, is incompatible with
the self-forgetfulness which is as essential to the tragic as to the
Christian hero.  For this is not the waking as from a dream of
some disinterested heart to the self-seeking of society, but the
long lament of one who gave short shrift to a dying Gaunt ;
and this contrast between Richard's indifference to others and
exquisite sensibility for himself makes tragedy impossible.

It is clear from the Biblical allusions that Shakespeare had
in mind the whole problem of charity and pity, which lies at
the heart of literature no less than of religion, and its dramatic
treatment.  But those who see in Richard an early Hamlet have
not understood the great advance in Shakespeare's art and
thought that made possible the later masterpieces.  Shakespeare
has drawn Hamlet on lines the very opposite to those he employed
for Richard.  Instead of the open appeal, with Richard's
likening of himself to the central figure in Christian story,
there are a few reticent references to the scriptures—the comparison of man's fate and the sparrow's, the question of our
deserts—revealing an art whose restraint and force are in keeping
with what Shakespeare had now come to see as the tragic in
character.

## 1 AND 2 HENRY IV

**S.R. 25th February, 1598.** *Andrew Wyse. Entred for his Copie under thandes of Master Dix : and master Warden man a booke intituled The historye of Henry the IIIIth with his battaile of Shrews- burye against Henry Hottspurre of the Northe with the conceipted mirthe of Sir John Falstoff.*

Both parts must have been written by this date, for in the second, as in the first part, the original name of the Prince's boon companion was Sir John Oldcastle, *Old* for *Fal* being found as the speech-heading at I, 2, 137 in the Quarto of 2 *Henry IV.* Complaints from the Cobham family, into which Oldcastle had married, led Shakespeare to disclaim any intention of offering in his comic character a portrait of the historical knight. The Epilogue to 2 *Henry IV* says ' Oldcastle died a martyr and this is not the man.' This, however, as the Quarto text shows, is an addition to the original Epilogue. The first part Shake- speare may have spoken himself at the first performance, ' For what I have to say is of mine own making ' ; then an addition was made so that the epilogue could be given to a dancer. Then follows the disclaimer, possibly a further addition, where Shakespeare announces that ' our humble author ' hopes to continue his story in *Henry V.*

The reference in the lines, 2 *Henry IV*, V, ii, 48-9,

> Not Amurath an Amurath succeeds,
> But Harry Harry,

is to the slaughter in February 1596 by Amurath III of his brothers soon after his accession. Thus 2 *Henry IV* is fixed between February 1596 and February 1598. And if we accept Hotson's date for *The Merry Wives of Windsor* (*see* page 125) it must be before April 1597. It was entered three years later.

**S.R. 23rd August, 1600.** *Andrewe Wyse William Aspley. Entred for their copies under the handes of the wardens Two bookes. the one called Muche a Doo about Nothinge. Thother the second parte of the history of kinge Henry the IIIIth with the humours of Sir John Fallstaff : Wrytten by master Shakespere.*

**Q1 1598** of I *Henry IV* and **Q1 1600** of 2 *Henry IV* followed
their respective entries, the latter giving a version severely cut
by the censor, who removed all reference to the deposition of
*Richard II* (*see* page 116).[1]

In planning the series of plays that were to have Henry V,
first as prince and then as king, for their protagonist, Shakespeare
intended to take advantage of the popular tradition which
represents the younger years of his hero as wild and unpromising ;
for the public have this in common with the angels that they
rejoice over the reformed prodigal.   And he could count not
merely on this common touch of nature, but on that national
and patriotic enthusiasm which made Henry V twice a hero to
the Elizabethan public.   That Shakespeare strongly sympathized
with these feelings is shown in many passages where no ambiguity
can arise from the dramatic situation ; but this interest, though
it gives coherence to Shakespeare's whole treatment of the victor
of Agincourt, suffers eclipse in most unpredictable circumstances.

Falstaff is one of the satellites who is to add a reflected glory
to the splendour of Henry's rising ; yet he destroys any chance
Henry ever had of carrying off the magnificent part in which,
with no little self-satisfaction, he sees himself from the start.
Shakespeare leaves his hero after his first encounter with Falstaff
to soliloquize for our benefit, so that our minds may be easy
about his role :

> I know you all, and will awhile uphold
> The unyok'd humour of your idleness :
> Yet herein will I imitate the sun,
> Who doth permit the base contagious clouds
> To smother up his beauty from the world,
> That when he please again to be himself
> Being wanted, he may be more wonder'd at.

Though the soliloquy is a legitimate convention, it must be used
dramatically if it is to carry conviction.   The character must not
merely tell us how his creator means us to understand him ;
he must speak for himself as Hamlet does in his soliloquies,

[1] See *Shakespeare and the Homilies*, by Alfred Hart, 154-218.

where the unconscious character of the revelation is essential to its completeness and credibility. Should it be considered that in this soliloquy the Prince's words are in dramatic keeping since he is, for all his high spirits, a particularly detached and self-controlled nature, the question then arises as to his right to turn without warning on his companions, when it suits him to cast them off, and to point to Falstaff as ' the tutor and the feeder of my riots,' and to talk of the other poor fry as the ' rest of my misleaders.'

Shakespeare sympathized with the patriotic enthusiasm of his age, and shared the general admiration for such a conqueror as Henry V, a man who promised less than he meant to perform, as brave as Hotspur without his petulance, popular not because he played a part before the people like his father, but because the more familiarly he stood among them, the more they felt the ascendancy of the born leader. Yet he is not a Shakespearean character like Hamlet or Macbeth. Shakespeare has been content to reproduce the conventional portrait of him in his own heightened colours, but this more vivid presentment emphasizes inconsistencies that pass unnoticed in the earlier and cruder version. Shakespeare has not re-created him from the inside ; he is not the offspring of the poet's reflection and passion, and so he does not stand in the midst of human inconsistencies, like the tragic heroes, a single soul.

Even Hotspur has more dramatic life. Though he is a foil to show the Prince's soldiership, and though the business requires him to be overcome before our eyes, his few words to the king, or the conspirators, or his wife, show why

> Speaking thick, which nature made his blemish,
> Became the accents of the valiant,

and death cannot rob him of any of his additions. The love-making of King Harry and fair Katherine of France is a poor pendant to the picture of Harry Hotspur and his wife.

But it is beside the third of the group in this study of the military character that the prince's dramatic insufficiency is most obvious. Falstaff is that indispensable member of any company with pretensions to experience in the wars, rightly described by Maurice Morgann as the old soldier.

Morgann's essay on Falstaff is first, with the rest nowhere, among the appreciations which this remarkable portrait has drawn from its many admirers. But the essay has raised the question why it should be necessary to have Falstaff explained to us at all. Could not the author, it has been asked, have made clear his purpose, here or in *Hamlet*, by inserting some unequivocal statement of his intentions? But such an open declaration of the author's drift is found in Henry's opening soliloquy, and so far is it from carrying conviction that it destroys real belief in the character. The moment the author steps out of the circle prescribed by his art, his words have no further power over us. It is not his business to explain his characters to our intelligence, but to impress them on our imagination. They have to be experienced and enjoyed before they can be understood. But even our common experience, the moment it becomes the subject of intellectual inquiry, takes on an embarrassing complexity. 'The analysis of what we all agree to be true' is a recent definition of Philosophy. Few experiences can appear simpler and more instinctive than those involving sight; and the form of perception known as Imagination, without which Falstaff cannot be seen at all, is no less instantaneous in its operations than physical sight; but a critical account of what is thus seen may be as laborious as in the physical sphere. It is the task of the critic, in literature as in other spheres, to 'unite our understandings to our instinct.' These are the words in which Morgann explains his own purpose, and we need not, therefore, wonder that what we can see and enjoy in the very moment of its passing cannot be laid open to our understanding without much after reflection.

And criticism is especially difficult here, because an open contradiction usually divides the instinctive and the reflective attitude maintained towards Falstaff, even by his admirers. By universal consent he is the most humorous figure in English literature, a literature pre-eminent for comic types. But though all are content to enjoy his presence, too many dismiss him when his back is turned, as nothing more than a cowardly, immoral old rascal.

It is true he ran before the Prince and Poins at Gadshill, but it was no remarkable exhibition of cowardice. As Morgann says,

> In the present instance, *Falstaff* had done an illegalact ; the exertion was over ; and he had unbent his mind in security. The spirit of enterprise, and the animating principle of hope were withdrawn :—In this situation, he is unexpectedly attacked ; he has no time to recall his thoughts, or bend his mind to the action. He is not now acting in the Profession and in the Habits of a Soldier ; he is associated with known Cowards ; his assailants are vigorous sudden and bold ; he is conscious of guilt ; he has dangers to dread of every form, present and future ; prisons and gibbets, as well as sword and fire ; he is surrounded with darkness, and the Sheriff, the Hangman, and the whole *Posse Comitatus* may be at his heels.

Of course he tries to cover up his defeat ; but his story of the two rogues in buckram who became eleven is a humorous rodomontade, making admirable play with a weakness in human nature that Falstaff himself never exhibits except in conscious jest. He is not the victim of his own story ; and if others are simple enough to believe it, that is but an added jest. The lie is not in his soul.

Then there is the incident at Shrewsbury. That a man so advanced in years, and so little in training as Falstaff, should be expected to meet the champion who held ' from all soldiers chief majority ' seems only proper to some critics ; and they fancy that the laughter, as he adroitly declines the combat, is at his cowardice. But those more conversant with human weakness can regard it as an exhibition of presence of mind apiece with his handing the Prince, in the heat of the action, the bottle of sack instead of a pistol. Danger has no more power than drink to deprive him of his humorous detachment.

It is unnecessary to follow Morgann in examining other incidents, such as his leading at Shrewsbury, that tell in favour of his courage.  No one doubts his humour, and humour implies character as well as intelligence.  And his habit of making his fears into a jest is a trick he shares with his countrymen.  It is not on record that the Higher Command in the recent war, however sensitive to weakness of morale in the rank and file, ever found it necessary to forbid the troops to sing,

O ! my ! I don't want to die,
I want to go home.

Nor would a lecturer on discipline from Headquarters have made much impression on the fellow who, when asked if he had heard that shell, replied, 'Twice : once when it passed me, and then when I passed it.'  Such alacrity of spirit overtakes fear long before it grows to cowardice, and easily outruns it for possession of the soul.

And Falstaff had need of a double portion of this spirit. For it is not only the burden of fear he shares with ordinary humanity.  He has to carry as well nearly every encumbrance with which the flesh can weigh men down.  'Eight yards of uneven ground is three score and ten miles a foot with me ' he says, as he pants up Gadshill.  His carcass is indeed a trunk of humours ; so that the gaiety he shows on all occasions has about it something heroic ; though there are moralists who dislike gaiety with grey hairs, and who, like Regan and Goneril, would have age know its place—a place to men of spirit like Lear or Falstaff indistinguishable from the grave.

Falstaff is the embodiment of that spirit of laughter that preserves our carnal nature from putrefaction ; his humour is an antiseptic to cleanse the sores that are inseparable from a body and its vanities.  When cakes and ale are forsworn for good, and mankind is possessed with the ardour that enables the hero and saint to burst the bonds of the flesh, like a thread of tow touched with fire, they will not need to learn from Falstaff how to laugh at themselves and their weaknesses if they are to escape the prison of their own self-complacency.  But till that time Falstaff will remain, for all his vices, among the liberators of the human spirit.

9

For with Falstaff men laugh not merely at their fears, but at all the mortal longings of their self-love. ' I would it were bed time Hal and all well. . . . We have heard the chimes at midnight Master Shallow. . . . When I was about thy years, Hal, I was not an eagle's talon in the waist,' these are sallies that put heart into poor humanity on the march, groaning under a pack of like infirmities. No wonder Falstaff, for all his old soldier's tricks, is popular in the ranks.

## THE MERRY WIVES OF WINDSOR

**S.R. 18th January, 1602.** *John Busby. Entred for his copie under the hand of master Seton A booke called An excellent and pleasant conceited commedie of Sir John Faulstof and the merry wyves of Windesor.*

*Arthure Johnson. Entred for his Copye by assignement from John Busbye, A booke Called an excellent and pleasant conceyted Comedie of Sir John Faulstafe and the merye wyves of Windsor.*

Q1 1602 gives a defective and pirated version of the play, and the double entry in the register suggests that Johnson was leaving to Busby the responsibility of explaining the venture, should it be called in question.

Rowe recorded the tradition that Queen Elizabeth ' was so well pleas'd with that admirable character of Falstaff, that she commanded him to continue it for one play more and to show him in love.' Dennis, who had told the same story in the *Epistle* to his adaptation of *The Merry Wives of Windsor*, added ' she commanded it to be finished in fourteen days,' though elsewhere he says ten.

In the final scene the Fairy Queen orders her minions to see that the hearths and fires of Windsor Castle are swept and raked, and to prepare the Garter Chapel.

> The several chairs of order look you scour
> With juice of balm and every precious flower.
> . . . .

And nightly, meadow-fairies, look you sing,
Like to the Garter's compass, in a ring :
And *Honi soit qui mal y pense* write
In emerald tufts, flowers purple, blue, and white.

This makes probable the suggestion that the play was performed
at a Garter Feast to celebrate the election of the new knights,
prior to their installation at Windsor.   The Bad Quarto gives
an alternative ending, a mutilated report of that performed on
the public stage as a substitute for the more ceremonious conclusion of the original performance.   And the following
considerations point to the Garter Feast on St. George's day at
Greenwich, 23rd April, 1597, as a very likely occasion for the
first performance of the piece.

The play begins with Justice Shallow's complaint that Sir
John Falstaff has broken into his deer park.   He enlarges on the
insult to one of his standing, and Cousin Slender intervenes with
some details of the family coat of arms :

All his successors gone before him hath done't ; and
all his ancestors that come after him may : they may
give the dozen white luces in their coat.

The inevitable pun on 'louses' and old coats follows.   On
the strength of this jest, Justice Shallow has been identified with
Sir Thomas Lucy of Charlecote, near Stratford, whose coat of
arms showed three luces haurient (three pike rising to the
surface).   And since the tradition recorded by Davies and
Rowe represents this gentleman as having prosecuted Shakespeare for deer-stealing, we are asked to believe that Shakespeare
was trying to pay off old scores.   But as Sir Thomas Lucy
had no deer park at Stratford for Shakespeare to rob, the tradition
no doubt arose from the passage it pretends to explain.

In 1596 and 1597, however, Shakespeare was actually concerned in a dispute with one who had luces in his coat of arms.
On 29th November, 1596, a certain William Wayte took out
a writ of surety against William Shakespeare, Francis Langley,
Dorothy Soer, and Ann Lee, alleging that he went in fear of his
life.   Wayte, as Professor Hotson,[1] the discoverer of the whole

---

[1] In his *Shakespeare versus Shallow* (1931).

affair, has shown, was the step-son and creature of a Justice of the Peace for Surrey called William Gardiner. This man, whom Langley openly stigmatized as a false, forsworn and perjured knave, had used his position quite unscrupulously for his own ends, and was the real adversary of Langley, the owner of the Swan Theatre on the Bankside, and of Shakespeare. Having married as his first wife Frances Lucy, Gardiner could show her arms with his, as, indeed, he did; and the white luces still stand on the silver communion cup in Bermondsey Church, to purchase which he left by will ten marks.[1]

As Gardiner died on 26th November, 1597, the luce jest, if suggested by this Justice of the Peace, would hardly be in season after that date. It leaves, however, 23rd April, 1597, as a likely date for the allusion.

Further, Shakespeare and his company may well have been in duty bound to perform on that occasion. Their patron, George Carey, the second Lord Hunsdon, had become Lord Chamberlain on the death of Lord Cobham, who held the post from July 1596 to March 1597 as successor to the first Lord Hunsdon. The new Lord Chamberlain now became a knight of the Garter; and his Company, reinforced by his singing boys, as the Fairy scene in *Merry Wives* suggests, may have helped in the entertainment that St. George's day.

Among those elected on this occasion was the Duke of Württemberg, who, when still Count of Mömpelgart, had visited Windsor in 1592 to beg from his cousin, Elizabeth, the honour of the Garter. But though the Queen now granted his request, she did not invite him to the feast, and he obtained his insignia only from her successor. In the play we hear of a Duke who is coming in secret, but Dr. Caius informs the worried Host

> it is tella me that you make grand preparation for a duke
> *de Jarmany* : by my trot dere is no duke dat de court is
> know to come.

[1] See *Shakespeare versus Shallow.*

This and the phrase ' cozen garmombles ' in the bad Quarto have always been taken as a clear reference to the Duke and the title he bore on his former visit ; especially as Charles Knight in 1840, misunderstanding the terms on which the government was entitled to authorize the use of post-horses, held that the horse-stealing by the ' three couzin germans ' also pointed directly to him.   Professor Crofts,[1] however, finds here a reference to a liberty taken with the Queen's warrant for the use of post-horses, at Chard on 17th November, 1597, by some of the Howard family, as well as to an earlier trouble over horses in September 1596 that also came before the Privy Council. While Professor Crofts does not deny that there was a version of the play in existence by April 1597, he argues for later and extensive revision.

The traces of one other dispute may be noticed in the play. As the Bad Quarto and the context show, Ford originally assumed the name of Brooke when in disguise.   In the Folio it is Broome, perhaps because Brooke was the family name of the Cobhams : the name Oldcastle had been given up because it was taken for an attack on an ancestor of the Cobhams, and it was no doubt considered advisable to remove anything that might be represented, however mistakenly, as an insult to that family.

The play itself needs little comment.   If we see Falstaff in this piece, it is only Falstaff acting a part in a play to please the Queen.   He aggravates his voice so as not to frighten the ladies, and condoles at the conclusion in this measure,

> See now how wit may be made a Jack-a-lent, when
> 'tis upon ill employment.

Falstaff is capable when occasion requires, as Morgann reminds us, of much accommodation and flattery.   His performance in *The Merry Wives of Windsor* is indeed a sustained piece of courtly accommodation.

---

[1] *Shakespeare and the Post Horses*, 1937.

## HENRY V

**S.R. 4th August, 1600.**

> As you like yt, a booke
> Henry the Fift, a booke
> Every man in his humour, a booke          } to be staied
> The commedie of 'muche A doo about nothing' a booke

Though the Chamberlain's men had this entry made in the Register (*see* page 34) to secure themselves against pirates, **Q1 1600,** printed by Thomas Creede for Thomas Millington and John Busby, is a piracy. Millington no doubt felt protected against the entry, because Creede had entered for himself, on 14th May, 1594, *The famous victories of Henrye the Fyfth* and printed it in Quarto as recently as 1598. Millington took the precaution, however, of adding on the title page the name of John Busby, who had no doubt procured the text for him, as he had procured that of *The Merry Wives of Windsor* for Johnson.

The style of *Henry V* and its relation to *Henry IV* fit in with the date fixed for it by the lines in the fifth Chorus,

> Were now the general of our gracious empress—
> As in good time he may—from Ireland coming,
> Bringing rebellion broached on his sword.

Essex sailed for Ireland in March 1599 to deal with the rebellious Tyrone. After an inglorious campaign he returned the following September. The production of *Henry V* may therefore be dated between March and September 1599.

Though Shakespeare now shows Henry making good his promise to prove better than his word, and taking his leave of the public as the victor of Agincourt and heir to all France, the piece itself is a thing of shreds and patches, held together by the Choruses.

As Johnson observed, not even Shakespeare can write well without a proper subject, and Shakespeare himself keeps reminding us, in the Choruses, that the stage is unfitted for the mere presentation of battles and sieges, however bravely contested or celebrated in story. In *Julius Cæsar* or *Lear* the fighting is no more than a kind of dumb show to introduce the passions the author would have us hear speak.  There the strife is for more than victory, and the prearranged defeat of one side or the other merely the cue that brings in the real interest.  But Agincourt, here, must try to be itself.  Yet it must be remembered that to the Elizabethans the deeds of a Henry or a John of Gaunt had a symbolic value, and were an example and encouragement to them in their own fight for national independence and civil liberty.  The piece, therefore, is not so much a play as a pageant, with the all-conquering Henry passing in triumph from scene to scene, and like most pageants it requires local sympathies and some historical knowledge for its proper enjoyment.  Yet that these local sympathies for all their imperfections are not incompatible with the widest human outlook, and that they are the steps by which the mind may rise to a conception of human heroism without respect of place or person, are propositions suggested by the course of Shakespeare's work, and the public's reception of his greatest tragedies.

Shakespeare made what he could of Agincourt, especially in the Chorus where night and the expectancy of battle create the dark and ominous background against which the real captain is at once apparent.  The magic touch of leadership is here, and in the scenes that follow, associated by Shakespeare with the comradeship of the wars.  And whether this is true or not of the historic Henry it is a poetic truth with its own appeal, and with its justification in ' the band of brothers ' who, in later times, once more made England invincible.  But scenes such as Henry's wooing of Catherine, and his leading on the traitors to doom themselves, can only pass when the principal character is raised by some historic association above the judgments of drama.

In his difficulties Shakespeare found it necessary to provide a great deal of what is called comic relief.  Here and there are touches worthy of the master, as when Henry's

Once more into the breach, dear friends, once more

is followed by Fluellen's

Up to the breech, you dogs !  avaunt, you cullions.

But much of it is the weakest that even Shakespeare, who, like Molière and Aristophanes, retained a relish for primitive forms of fun, ever admitted to his plays. What Shakespeare, however, could do in that supreme form of comedy that is hardly to be distinguished from tragedy itself is also to be seen in the few lines that tell us about Falstaff's death.

## MUCH ADO ABOUT NOTHING

**S.R. 4th August, 1600.** *Much Ado* was entered with three other plays belonging to the Chamberlain's men *to be staied* (*see* page 128). Permission was given for its publication soon after.

S.R. 23rd August, 1600. *Andrewe Wyse William Aspley. Entred for their copies under the handes of the wardens Two bookes. the one called Muche a Doo about nothinge. Thother the second parte of the history of kinge Henry the IIIIth with the humours of Sir John Fallstaff: Wrytten by master Shakespere.*

The Folio text is practically a reprint of Q1 1600. This had been compared, however, with a copy in use in the theatre, for at II, iii, 33 the Quarto S.D. *Enter prince, Leonato, Claudio, Musicke* becomes *Enter Prince, Leonato, Claudio, and Iacke Wilson*, where Jacke Wilson is the name of the actor who was to sing ' Sigh no more Ladies.' The Quarto text was set up from Shakespeare's own draft, as in IV, ii, the constables Dogberry and Verges are regularly described in the speech headings as Kempe and Cowley. ' Dogberry and Verges were so life-like because they were not merely a constable and a watch-man in the abstract, but actually Kempe and Cowley whose every accent and gesture Shakespeare must have known, *playing a constable and a watchman,*' says Dr. McKerrow.[1] Through-out the Quarto such casually familiar touches indicate that it is very closely connected with Shakespeare's manuscript, and they are to be distinguished from the particular notes of a stage-manager assigning some piece of business, such as the song in II, iii, to one of the company.

The play is not mentioned by Meres, and had it been on the

---

[1] *The Elizabethan Printer and Dramatic Manuscripts.*

stage by 1597 he could hardly have omitted it ; for as Leonard Digges,[1] in the lines printed in the 1640 edition of Shakespeare's poems, indicates, Beatrice and Benedick ranked with their author's most popular characters.   It must, however, have been written before Kempe left the company in 1599, as he was to have a part.   In the lease of 21st February, 1599, in which Brend granted the ground for the Globe to the actors, Kempe is named ; but Heminge and Condell informed the court, in a suit brought in 1619 about the property, that Kempe ' about the time of the building ' of the Globe, or ' shortly after,' gave up this interest.

The Claudio and Hero story is in Bandello's collection, and was translated by Belleforest in his *Histoires Tragiques*.    Shakespeare took from the Italian or the French the names Peter of Arragon for the prince, and Leonato for the wronged lady's father, as well as Messina for the place of the action.   But it is Shakespeare's own additions to the plot, Benedick and Beatrice, Dogberry and Verges, that give the play its immortality.

Nowhere are Shakespeare's comic characters more clearly the expression of delight in the humours of men.   As the iron-worker reveals the strength of the metal he fashions in the pliant delicacy of the shapes into which he draws it out, so Shakespeare, in the very fantasy and lightness of the jesting, discovers the true spirit and pride of youth unalloyed by any false sentiment. Only in the heat of a passionate sympathy could he have wrought this arabesque of love.   The petulance of youth that betrays the tenderness it would conceal is as natural in that season of life as daffodils in March or roses in June.   But nowhere does this proud humility flourish more gallantly, at least in the garden of literature, than in the comedy of Beatrice and Benedick.

*Benedick.*—Thou and I are too wise to woo peaceably.

*Beatrice.*—It appears not in this confession ; there's not one wise man among twenty that will praise himself.

---

[1] Digges wrote these lines for the First Folio, but substituted a shorter set for them (*see* pages 137 and 226).

> *Benedick.*—An old, an old instance, Beatrice, that
> lived in the time of good neighbours.  If a man do
> not erect in this age his own tomb ere he dies, he
> shall live no longer in monument than the bell rings
> and the widow weeps.

Beatrice has, perhaps, on the whole, the best of it ; even the
wretched business of Hero's rejection is turned to fine account
in the blast of her anger :

> O God, that I were a man !   I would eat his heart in
> the market place,

and in the sudden passion of her ' Kill Claudio.'  But Benedick
is a proper bachelor, and his surrender something of a triumph
even for Beatrice.  And we see him long enough after his
recantation to consider him as another illustration of the rule
laid down by Keats ' that the man who ridicules romance is
the most romantic of men—and he who abuses women and
slights them loves them most—and above all, that they are
very shallow people who take everything literally.'  Benedick
promises well as he silences his future wife, who must still be
arguing, with a kiss, and he goes to his fate as to a ball,

> Prince, thou are sad ; get thee a wife, get thee a wife.
> Strike up, pipers.

To complain after this that the Hero–Claudio story is un-
satisfactory at many points is a form of ingratitude.  The titles
Shakespeare gave this series of comedies, *Much Ado about Nothing,*
*What you Will, As You Like It,* show that he himself has anticipated such criticism.  To take his word for it, however, that
these pieces are about nothing, or only attached to reality by
the slender substance of the main plots, is to be blind to the
modesty of his art.

## AS YOU LIKE IT

**S.R. 4th August, 1600.**  *As You Like It* was entered with three
other plays belonging to the Chamberlain's men *to be staied*
(*see* page 128) ; first printed in the **First Folio.**  The couplet
III, v, 81-2.

> Dead shepherd, now I find thy saw of might ;
> ' Who ever lov'd that lov'd not at first sight ? '

refers to Marlowe, and the second line is from his *Hero and Leander*, not published till 1598. Meres does not mention *As You Like It*. It may be dated between 1598 and 1600.

*As You Like It* is in general outline little more than a dramatic version of Thomas Lodge's novel *Rosalynde*. Lodge wrote it, his preface informs us, on a voyage to the Canaries, ' when every line was wet with surge.' And he seems to have turned his mind all the more willingly to pastoral charms, and to painting an Arcadian background for innocent love. Here the banished princesses find ' such cates as country state did allow them, sawst with such content, and such sweet prattle, as it seemed farre more sweet than all their courtly junkets.'

Shakespeare strengthens this contrast between court and country by giving the banished Duke and his followers a much more important place in the story ; they introduce a Sherwood forest note of independence and natural justice that protects, as it were, the pastoral peace of the shepherds. And Shakespeare avoids any insipidity in this feast of nature by the piquant commentary he provides to it in Jaques and Touchstone. Jaques reminds us that the struggle in society has its counterpart in nature ; he sees in Arden what he saw at court, ' a careless herd, full of the pasture,' shunning the stricken deer, and he knows that in forest as in town, ' misery doth part the flux of company.' Yet nature's unkindness, whether seen in herd or inclement sky, only emphasizes the human comradeship and joy in the forest. There is no return to the life of beasts ; a human art adds to nature, yet this art is felt to be quickened in men by nature itself. Jaques, after deploring the heartlessness of nature, may turn with more acrimony than consistency to call the Duke and his foresters

> mere usurpers, tyrants and what's worse,
> To fright the animals and to kill them up.

Yet the Duke is no thoughtless sportsman :

Come, shall we go and kill us venison ?
And yet it irks me, the poor dappled fools, . . .
Should in their own confines . . .
Have their round haunches gor'd.

He might have answered Jaques with the lines of Blake, could
he have known them,

The wild deer wandering here and there
Keep the human soul from care :
The lamb misused breeds public strife,
And yet forgives the butcher's knife.

In the encounters between Jaques or Touchstone and the
original actors in the story, Shakespeare allows to come to the
surface a profounder conception of pastoralism than anything
in Lodge.  But for the most part he is content to carry along
the story in a whirl of songs and ' flytings.'  Characters often
meet only to sing or exchange a few witty words : it is full of
trills and ornaments, like the descant of Jaques upon the seven
ages of man, or Touchstone's lecture concerning the seventh
cause, or the quartette, Rosalind, Orlando, Phebe and Silvius
(V, ii).  The tempo of the piece is that of ' It was a lover and
his lass.'  The beautiful Elizabethan setting of this song is by
Thomas Morley, and its happy vigour and speed are characteristic of the play in which it forms so attractive an interlude.


## TWELFTH NIGHT

**S.R. 8th November, 1623.**  First printed in the **First Folio.**

*Twelfth Night* must have been written before 2nd February,
1602, when John Manningham, according to his diary, saw it
performed at the Middle Temple,

At our feast wee had a play called ' Twelue Night, or
What You Will,' much like the Commedy of Errores,
or Menechmi in Plautus, but most like and neere to that
in Italian called *Inganni.*

A Don Valentino Orsino, Duke of Bracciano, visited the
Queen in January 1601, and it is a reasonable conjecture that
Shakespeare borrowed his name for the piece he had in hand,
and that *Twelfth Night* was composed in 1601.  Other references

seem to point to this date. In II, v, 161, there is mention of 'a pension of thousands to be paid from the Sophy' : the wealth and munificence of the Sophy, the Shah of Persia, had just been advertised in an account printed in 1600 of the adventures at his court of the three brothers Shirley. The Dutchman's beard (III, ii, 26) and the 'new map with the augmentation of the Indies' refer to recent geographical discoveries and their embodiment in a map, probably that issued in 1599-1600 with an edition of Hakluyt's *Voyages*. Finally, the snatches of song at II, iii, are found in Robert Jones's *First Book of Songs and Airs* (1600).

Joseph Hunter, who with Collier discovered the entry in Manningham's diary, followed up the reference, and his conclusions are interesting as throwing light on the curiosity and system that marked Shakespeare's reading when he took a subject in hand.

The main plot is borrowed from a comedy written, and performed at Siena in 1531 during the carnival, by a society of amateurs who called themselves the Academici Intronati (The Thunderstruck). Their play, *Gl'Ingannati* (The Cheated), was printed with the title *Il Sacrificio*, for prefixed to the play is an account of a sacrifice of love-tokens by members of the society. It had an international success, and was imitated and adapted in several languages under many titles. Though Shakespeare used the plot in a modified form he had glanced over the original, for his title *Twelfth Night* seems to have been suggested by a passage in the Introduction.

> The story is new, never seen nor read, and only dipped for and taken out of their own industrious noddles as your prize-tickets are dipped for and taken out on Twelfth Night (la Notte di Beffana).

Malvolio is an adaptation of the name of one of the sacrificing Academicians, Malevolti. Fabian may have been suggested by the name, Fabio, which the Italian heroine, Lelia, assumes in disguise.

Should these resemblances be dismissed as merely strange

coincidences, there is yet another to make them stranger still. Among the Italian imitations of this play were two called *Gl'Inganni* (The Cheats), the first by Nicolo Secchi, printed in 1562, the second by Curzio Gonzaga, printed in 1592. In Gonzaga's play the disguised heroine calls herself Cesare, while Shakespeare's Viola becomes Cesario.

In 1543 there was a French translation of *Gl'Ingannati* by Charles Estienne called *Les Abusez*.

The play was made into a story by Bandello in 1554, which was translated by Belleforest (1571) ; and it is retold by Rich in *Apolonius and Silla*, one of the stories in his *Farewell to Militarie Profession*. In this last version there is a shipwreck among the incidents, a device not so far associated with the plot.

In England the plot had been used in *The Buggbears*, produced about 1564, and again in a Latin play, presented at Cambridge before Essex in 1595, called *Laelia*.

In whatever version Shakespeare first became acquainted with the story he must have traced it back to its early Italian forms, as the names he borrowed in his apparently casual manner from both *Gl'Ingannati* and *Gl'Inganni* admit of no other explanation.[1]

Though Shakespeare seems to have considered the many versions of the story before adapting it to his own stage, the strength of *Twelfth Night* does not lie in the main plot. As in his best comedies there is always a combination of the poetical (*Midsummer Night's Dream*) or the romantic (*As You Like It*) or the heroic (*Henry IV*), with the humorous and realistic, and as both the poetry and prose gain by this happy marriage, so in *Twelfth Night* Viola's tenderness for the lovelorn Orsino, and the fantasy of the imperious Olivia, provide a perfect excuse and contrast for the ongoings of Sir Toby and his cronies and their

---

[1] Hunter came on a volume containing these two plays and others, some including *Il Viluppo*, which has among its dramatis personæ *Orsino inamorato*. ' I could almost persuade myself,' wrote Hunter, as he noted this, ' that the very volume in which the *Sacrificio* was first found by me had once been Shakespeare's.' The sight of the name Orsino in an Italian comedy may well have prompted Shakespeare to use that of the Duke of Bracciano in the plot of *Gl'Ingannati*.

feud with Malvolio. Shakespeare gives the love intrigue the necessary remoteness, by the poetic charm with which he invests it, and the delicate irony with which he touches it. Viola must have her Orsino, and Olivia finds a substitute for her Cesario ; and this Shakespeare achieves without provoking criticism by any realistic treatment of the story's improbabilities. But if the lovers are in themselves no more than ' creatures dear to half belief,' they seem less phantasmal from their association with ' that half Falstaff,' Sir Toby, or with Malvolio. ' There is a solidity of wit,' as Lamb observed, in the jests of Sir Toby and ' a kind of tragic interest ' in the fate of Malvolio unknown in dreamland. Feste and Maria help to give Illyria a familiar air.

The earliest references to *Twelfth Night* show that from the first Malvolio was recognized as the protagonist of the piece,

> The Cockpit Galleries, Boxes, all are full
> To hear *Malvoglio* that crosse garter'd gull.

No doubt the majority of the spectators laughed at his predicament in the manner of the mischievous Maria, or of the full-blooded Sir Toby, or even of the foolish Sir Andrew, rather than in the spirit of Lamb, who felt when the character gave full play to his bent that

> you had no room for laughter ! if an unseasonable reflection of morality obtruded itself, it was a deep sense of the pitiable infirmity of man's nature, that can lay him open to such frenzies—but in truth you rather admired than pitied the lunacy while it lasted.

The depth of Shakespeare's art is not to be estimated by the length of line required for a happy day's fishing on its waters ; thousands may enjoy the dramas without our being required to suppose they have fathomed their mystery, or that their profundities are non-existent because they are beyond what we choose to allow to the conscious reach of the Elizabethan spectator. Lamb's Malvolio may not be that of Digges, but it need not, therefore, be less Shakespeare's.

Malvolio is not essentially ludicrous. He becomes comic but by accident. He is cold, austere, repelling ; but dignified, consistent, and, from what appears, rather of an overstretched morality. Maria describes him as a sort of Puritan ; and he might have worn his gold chain with honour in one of our old round-head families, in the service of a Lambert, or a Lady Fairfax. But his morality and his manners are misplaced in Illyria. (*On Some of the Old Actors.*)

# V. THE THIRD PERIOD

THE Globe Theatre seems to have been occupied some
time before 16th May, 1599, the date of an inquisition
of the estate of Sir Thomas Brend, the father of Sir Nicholas
Brend, from whom the ground was leased for 31 years,
from 25th December, 1598. In this inquisition the Globe
is called *una domus de novo edificata . . . in occupacione
Willelmi Shakespeare et aliorum.* This was the sole theatre
regularly used by the Chamberlain's men till 1608. In
that year the Children of the Queen's Revels (an aery of
children, little eyases : *Hamlet* II, ii, 335), who had been
playing at the Blackfriars, were suppressed. Their manager,
Evans, who was responsible for opening the Blackfriars as
a private theatre (where the prices excluded the humbler
playgoer) with the singing boys of the Queen's chapel as
actors, had now on his hands a large part of the twenty-
one years' lease he had secured on 2nd September, 1600,
from Burbage. He was glad, therefore, to dispose of the
remainder of the lease on 9th August, 1608, to a company
of householders which included Richard and Cuthbert
Burbage, Shakespeare, Heminge, Condell, and Slye.

That no objection would now be entertained to the
playing of the actors in the Blackfriars was made certain by
the official recognition they had obtained since going to the
Globe. After the death of Elizabeth, and immediately on
the arrival of James in London in May 1603, the Chamberlain's men were taken under the king's own patronage,
and known from that time as the King's men. The patent

names the leading actors in this order : Shakespeare, Burbage, Phillips, Heminge, Condell, Slye, Armin, Cowley. The king joined with them a certain Lawrence Fletcher, who had acted before him in Scotland, and though Fletcher had not been a Chamberlain's man his name stands first in the list, no doubt because of the king's previous patronage. He soon drops out of their history. The leading actors were also appointed Grooms of the Royal Chamber, and in that capacity Shakespeare and eleven of his fellows attended on the Spanish Ambassador at Somerset House from 9th-27th August, 1604, when he came in state to negotiate a treaty between England and Spain.

The King's men, on taking over the Blackfriars, used it during the winter months, November to April, instead of the Globe, to the great increase of their winter drawings, which were calculated to be £1,000 more than formerly.[1]

Between 1599 and 1608 a number of important events in Shakespeare's family life fall to be recorded. His father died near the beginning of the period in September 1601, and his mother at its close in September 1608, not however without seeing one of her great-grandchildren; for Elizabeth Hall, the only child of Shakespeare's elder daughter and John Hall, the physician, who were married in June 1607, was born in February 1608. About this time there also died Shakespeare's youngest brother, Edmund, who was, like himself, an actor ; on December 1607 he was buried within the chancel of St. Saviour's, Southwark. Shakespeare's two surviving brothers were to die not long after, Gilbert in February 1612, and Richard in February 1613, both being buried at Stratford.

On Shakespeare's father we have an interesting note in a manuscript written by Thomas Plume about 1657 : [2]

---

[1] See Chambers' *Shakespeare*, II, 69.

[2] Chambers' *Shakespeare*, II, 247.

He (Shakespeare) was a glover's son—Sir John Mennis
saw once his old Father in his shop—a merry Cheeked
old man—that said—Will was a good Honest Fellow, but
he durst have crackt a jest with him at any time.

There seems to be a mistake here in attributing the
information to Sir John Mennis, but Plume could hardly
have known about the glover's shop except from someone
who had been there.   There was no work he could consult
for his information, and the gossip which found its way
into the early life is wrong about John's trade.   Plume's
informant who could report so accurately on the matter
at that time may well have spoken to the owner, and so
preserved an authentic and, for all its brevity, an illuminating
glimpse of father and son.

Shakespeare's continued prosperity is amply attested.
In May 1602 he purchased for £320 from his friends
the Combes some 107 acres of arable land beside Stratford ;
and in September of the same year a cottage and ground
in Chapel Lane beside New Place.   In July 1605 he ex-
pended £440 on certain Stratford tithes, which were
held in 1611 to give an annual return of £60.

Shakespeare's London residence during a considerable
part of this period has been established by Professor Wallace
from the records of a case that came before the courts in
1612.   A Huguenot tire-maker named Mountjoy (who
may have supplied the actors with wigs and head-dresses)
residing and trading in Silver Street, had a daughter Mary,
who married on 19th November, 1604, Stephen Belott,
at one time apprentice to her father.   In 1612 Belott, like
his father-in-law of French descent, claimed a dowry of
£60 which, he said, had been promised him, and asked for
some assurance that a legacy of £200, which, he declared,
had been included in the bargain, would also be paid.
For Mountjoy's wife had died in 1606, and he had become,

so it was alleged, extravagant.  Shakespeare was called as a witness, because he had lodged in the house.  He deposed that he had, at the request of the girl's mother, approached Belott concerning the match, but that he was unable to remember the financial details of the proposal.  He further declared he had known the parties to the suit for ten years or so ;  but as he speaks of Belott's good character with his master throughout his apprenticeship, and as this began in 1598, Shakespeare may have been with the Mountjoys when he amused himself by writing the French scenes in *Henry V*.  This happy glimpse of the king of poets, moving familiarly among the humbler subjects of his art, not only confirms the reports of his humane urbanity, but suggests that Shakespeare, so far from being afflicted with the invincible repugnance to acquire any language but his own, imagined for him by Farmer and others, may have gone to the Mountjoys partly to improve his French.

Shakespeare's most important achievement in these years is the succession of great tragedies, seven in number, that stretch across the decade.  In the first year comes *Julius Cæsar* (1599), then follow *Hamlet* (1600), *Othello* (1602), *Lear* (1605), *Macbeth* (1606), *Antony and Cleopatra* (1607), and in the closing year, *Coriolanus* (1608).

That Shakespeare did not enter on this part of his life disillusioned, or with any loss of that alacrity of spirit so conspicuous in *Henry IV*, is made plain by *Twelfth Night*, to some judges the most perfect of his comedies ;  for it is almost certain that it must be dated a year, or perhaps two, later than *Hamlet*.  If *Hamlet*, then, is taken as a cry of disillusion or disgust with life, Shakespeare must have been very much in love with life not long afterwards.  But any view of *Hamlet*, or of tragedy in general, which represents it as the outcome of some distaste for existence, or inspired by misery and despair, misses the artist's intention and distorts Shakespeare's story. The tragedies of Aeschylus and Sophocles are not the works of world-weary or disenchanted spirits ; and no one supposes that the men of Marathon and Salamis received their stories of old ill-fortune from a heroic past in any other spirit but that in which the author of *A Shropshire Lad* would school us.

> What evil luck soever
> For me remains in store,
> 'Tis sure much finer fellows
> Have fared much worse before.
>
> So here are things to think on
> That ought to make me brave,
> As I strap on for fighting
> My sword that will not save.

Shakespeare also wrote for a heroic age. The captains, gentlemen, and soldiers, who formed, as Nash tells us, so regular a part of the Elizabethan audience, were not behind the men of Athens in action or the appreciation of noble conduct. And Shakespeare's tragedies, like those of his Greek predecessors, deal with the high actions and high passions that naturally interested what was, for all its jesting and bravery, a resolute and serious generation. Like the Greek dramatists he took his material from a heroic past ; instead of their myths of demigods and eponymous heroes he had the story of Rome or tales of ancient Britain and Denmark. But if his tragic action is thus laid like Greek tragedy in the past, it is only that the appeal to the living may be the more direct, and unobscured by the thousand ephemeral considerations that play round the present, and distract from the essential.

The adequate treatment, by the dramatist, of themes already epic in their outline makes the utmost demand on the shaping spirit of his imagination. But this power is, as Coleridge's lines remind us, the gift of joy. What then is the source of the poet's joy as he deals with a world where it seems at times as if chaos itself had come again ?

It has been argued that Tragedy exhibits a mysterious moral force ruling the destinies of men. The rule of life, we learn, is nothing too much, for the tragic characters overstep in their wilfulness these limits, and perish in their pride. They contribute by some fatal imperfection or error to their own destruction. However strong, therefore, the sense of loss of individual value, the imperfection discovered in the character allows such critics as Professor Bradley to insist that the cosmos sacrifices its most glorious offspring only in its passion for perfection ; it reacts against their failure to conform to its moral demands, and their death arises from collision not with a fate or blank power, but with a moral power in whose decrees we acquiesce.

But such a view is contrary to common experience as well as to the intuitions of religion. The Christian does not regard earthly misfortune and disaster as the evidence of wickedness, though this is what every perverse generation is only too ready to take as a sign of guilt or sin. The friends of Job argued thus, and the argument that failure to survive in the struggle for existence necessarily reveals some defect in the victim is only the old materialism in modern guise. But we should need no Socrates to remind us that a man's very virtues may provoke the envy and slander of the multitude.[1] Nor are the observations of Thucydides on the plague at Athens unsupported by modern

---

[1] Mr. Rankine of the *Indus* was by far the best engineer I ever sailed with, and he taught me more about my business than all the others put together. I thought he would one day fill a great position but he never did. I have known many men his inferiors in every way who easily outstripped him. I think his hatred of deceit and humbug hindered him more than anything. He was not a prig, and he rarely expressed his dislike for trickery, but mean men felt uncomfortable in his presence, and I was often surprised to find how much he was hated by humbugs who hardly knew him.— *Adventures of an Obscure Victorian*, by W. J. Riddell.

instances. It took its toll from good and bad alike, but in greater measure from the good, since they exposed themselves fatally in their friends' behalf, while the others were not ashamed to let the sufferers die in solitude.

If to die in tragic circumstances is to be at fault, the best and bravest are among the world's greatest offenders. A world wise after the event can always point to some action that precipitated the fatal end. But it is precisely this slander the poet protests against, and the challenge to the verdict of such a tribunal in Sir Henry Newbolt's lines on *The Volunteer* shows in small compass what may be called the cross currents of feeling that contend in the tragic argument.

> He leapt to arms unbidden,
>   Unneeded, overbold ;
> His face by earth is hidden,
>   His heart in earth is cold.
>
> Curse on the reckless daring
>   That would not wait the call,
> The proud fantastic bearing
>   That would be first to fall !
>
> O tears of human passion
>   Blur not the image true ;
> This was not folly's fashion,
>   This was the man we knew.

A proud, fantastic bearing seems to some critics the undoing of all Shakespeare's tragic heroes. But as living or historical characters may appeal to literature to justify their conduct—since literature is first and last an imitation or criticism of life—so the creations of the poet's imagination refer us to reality for their interpretation. It was to the poet at whose feet Greece had grown to greatness that Socrates turned, when he told his judges of his determination not to humble himself by any appeal to their sentiment, or by any promise of change of conduct. He reminded them of a famous situation in the *Iliad,* a situation on which depends the whole significance of Homer's story. After the death of Patroclus, the mother of Achilles entreats her son to hold his hand against the slayer of his friend ; for, as she reminds him, fate has fixed that his own death shall follow hard on Hector's. Thetis makes her appeal in vain ; but Socrates did not offer Achilles as an example of a man who wilfully courts death, or as a warning against pride, but as one who will not turn aside from what he takes to be his duty for destiny itself—a man, therefore, who naturally commands our sympathy in this terrible situation. And Socrates insisted that he was like Achilles in this, that he could not give up his god-given mission whatever the consequences, and that in fact he was entitled to appeal to those very feelings in which Homer had so nobly instructed them in fiction. To some the attitude of Socrates seemed rather foolish and his pride his undoing ; they would have had him gratify the tyrant in his democratic judges by producing a weeping wife and children, and by appealing to what they called their mercy. Those, however, who would read Homer with something of the spirit of Socrates, or look on Socrates with some of Plato's understanding, cannot but attribute the verdict to a state of savage torpor —induced by personal and political prejudice—in which literature and life alike lose their meaning. Such readers will regularly find in what are regarded as the faults of Shakespeare's tragic characters the real grounds of their admiration and interest.

For it is the paradox at the centre of tragedy, that what we admire most in the man undoes him. He may, like Achilles, be driven to the fatal situation by his own fury and contriving, or be guided there by his duty, like Socrates ; but once there, even though the man has a thousand faults, it is what is noble in him that makes him a tragic figure.

And though this may be as different in various men as the savage virtue of Achilles and the courageous humanity of Socrates, it is always the expression of man's free will and of a loyalty conscious or unconscious to something beyond the rebuke of the ignorant present. For the more the epic poet or tragic dramatist stresses the fateful in the situation, the more he thereby emphasizes this human element. ' The character of Achilles seems to me,' wrote Wordsworth, ' one of the grandest ever conceived. There is something awful in it, particularly in the circumstances of his acting under an abiding foresight of his own death.' But the awe comes from the choice the man makes with the consequences in full view.

Tragedy is no more than an extreme instance of the exercise of that self-determination which gives men bounded in the nutshell of their material existence the infinite space their souls desire. Here it is unaccompanied by the flattering chances that so often attend on the exertions of the brave and free ; a worldly wisdom may now withhold the approval it would in happier circumstances be the first to bestow. Those who still admire it must choose it for its own sake with all its dangers thick upon it. And the tragic poet accepts the challenge of the situation to make clear not merely his preference for what is human and noble ' but the degree of preference ; the passionate and pure choice, the inward sense of absolute and unchangeable devotion.'

More than this the poet cannot tell us without assuming the mantle or authority of the prophet or priest ; but Shakespeare never professes more than what Socrates called a human wisdom ; though doubtless the ironic reserve he maintains to what are described as religious convictions is itself an artistic device that gives an added force to the evidence his work affords us about the ultimate nature of things and the grounds of religion itself. For even if the preferences and loyalties which find so universal an expression and acceptance in his drama may not seem to all the surest intimations of immortality, they are certainly among the profoundest of those communings with our internal Being with which, as Wordsworth reminds us, ' revelation coincides, and has through that coincidence alone (for otherwise it could not possess it) a power to affect us.'

## JULIUS CÆSAR

**S.R. 8th November, 1623.** First printed in the **First Folio.**

A Swiss traveller, Thomas Platter, recorded in his diary a performance of this play, which he saw ' in the straw-thatched house ' across the river—the Globe—on 21st September, 1599. The play, he notes, was followed by a Jig, the customary conclusion even to the most moving tragedies ; and into the dancing of this, as it now seems, strange afterpiece, the actors did not fail, he informs us, to put their acknowledged skill and grace.

Phrases in Jonson's *Every Man out of his Humour,* ' Et tu Brute ' and ' Reason long since is fled to animals you know ' (cf. *Julius Cæsar,* III, ii, 104), were doubtless suggested by Shakespeare's play. If Jonson's play was performed about the opening of the Globe, *Julius Cæsar* can be dated late 1598 or early 1599. The absence of any mention by Meres and the style of the play fit in with such a date.

References to Cæsar and his fortunes are frequent in the plays, and range from the boyish admiration of Prince Edward's ' That Julius Cæsar was a famous man,' to Falstaff's familiar reference to ' the hook-nosed fellow of Rome.' It is not surprising, therefore, that Shakespeare should have dramatized some part of his life ; but that Cæsar, when he does appear on Shakespeare's stage, should be only the shadow of his imperial self is certainly unexpected, and has provoked much adverse criticism.

Those who think that Shakespeare's work as a dramatist implies no remarkable powers of thought or reflection argue that *Julius Cæsar* reveals his deficiency in that historical sense on which the present age prides itself.  Mr. Shaw complains that Shakespeare has glorified a political blunder of the first magnitude, misunderstood the state of Rome at this time, and missed the real tragedy of the situation for Rome itself.  To this, however, it might be answered, that, like the contemporary philosopher who, according to Plutarch, wrote an excellent book on the death of Julius Cæsar and called it *Brutus*, Shakespeare found his chief interest in the connection between character and action, deed and motive, which underlies all history ; and that Shakespeare, if he felt that Brutus provided the most interesting problem on these lines, could hardly have chosen better than he did.  And to the charge that Shakespeare showed himself destitute of political insight in glorifying Brutus, the obvious answer is that his whole treatment of Brutus comes entirely from his recognition that the  assassination was a grievous political blunder.

Shakespeare follows Plutarch in representing the conspirators as opposed to the irresistible current of affairs in Rome.  Plutarch's sympathies are republican, but he recognized that the Republic was at an end, and he tells us how

> men of deep judgment and discretion, seeing such madness and fury of the people, thought themselves happy if the commonwealth were no worse troubled than with the absolute state of a monarch and sovereign lord to govern them.

This is from the life of *Julius Cæsar*, and in his *Marcus Brutus* he speaks in his own person :

> Howbeit the state of Rome (in my opinion) being now brought to that pass, that it could no more abide to be governed by many lords, but required one only absolute governor : God, to prevent Brutus that it should not come to his government, kept this victory from his knowledge.

What is, perhaps, the one weakness of the play, the one-sided portrait of the dictator, actually comes from the need the dramatist felt to emphasize the tendency in the times that had set towards a Cæsar. For though Shakespeare may have had warrant in his source for all the great man's infirmities, yet they are emphasized to show that, as far as flesh and blood went, the conspirators had no insuperable antagonist ; and that what mocked their daggers was an impersonal power attaching to the man, later embodied in the ghost of Cæsar. This Brutus himself recognizes at the end :

> O Julius Cæsar, thou art mighty yet !
> Thy spirit walks abroad.

The futility of the attempt to save the Romans from themselves is obvious at every turn. First, Brutus is isolated from the people whose liberty he would preserve. As he explains to them how he has slain his best friend for the sake of the Republic, there is a shout ' Let him be Cæsar, Cæsar's better parts shall be crown'd in Brutus.' However human such feelings may be, there is here none of the temper necessary to retain the edge Brutus seeks to give them. Then he stands apart even from the inner circle of the conspirators, however resolute their spirit, in the integrity of his purpose. And Shakespeare is only giving Antony the sentiments that Plutarch gave to him, and to many others who saw the events for themselves, when he makes him say,

> All the conspirators, save only he,
> Did what they did in envy of great Cæsar ;
> He only in a general honest thought
> And common good to all, made one of them.

Brutus stands alone. And this gives him his ascendancy with the people, who feel the honesty of his purpose, and his power to inspire the conspirators.

Nor is he found wanting in action. At the moment when all seems discovered, and Cassius in the confusion is for killing himself, Brutus alone keeps the ranks of the conspirators steady. Yet bookish commentators represent him as a student unfitted by his philosophical studies for active affairs. And it is true that the integrity which holds the conspiracy so firmly together till success is achieved is in the sequel its undoing. For if to be consistent in motive and scrupulous in act is an academic failing, then Brutus is indeed pedantic in his observance of honourable limits. He refuses to kill Antony, and readily allows him to praise the dead Cæsar. And had the multitude been worthy of the sacrifice of his best friend, Antony would have spoken in vain. Though had perfect wisdom been given Brutus, he would no doubt have seen that the necessity of the sacrifice was sufficient evidence of its futility.

At the very moment when the doubts of the spectator about the motives of Brutus are roused by the success of the conspiracy, and by the natural reaction at the sight of the victim, Shakespeare throws into the action the character whom, as Mr. Granville-Barker has observed, he has kept in reserve for this decisive moment. It is impossible not to yield for a time to Antony's brilliant pleading, and to share his misgivings about the ' honourable ' men and their more honourable leader. Yet Antony has to take advantage of the weaker side of the multitude, luring them on with Cæsar's will as with a bait, caring not how much of the ignoble and senseless may be in a fury that can destroy poor Cinna the poet only for his name, provided it serves his turn. And beside the doings of the triumvirs with their cold-blooded murders—Lepidus bartering away his brother's life for that of the son of Antony's sister—the murder of Cæsar becomes a heroic enterprise.

The reaction having spent itself in this waste of shame, we are prepared to listen again to the one man who at least means honestly. But once more he is insisting on honesty when surrounded by unscrupulous foes and inexorable circumstances. Those who stoop to murder need not strain, one feels, at peculation or bribery. But he who could not put honour a little to the side to spare his friend should not put it aside for money even to ransom himself, or he stands a confessed murderer. His refusal to buy his own safety at such a price distinguishes Brutus even from his fellows. And as Brutus stands before us somewhat awkwardly in his inflexibility, Shakespeare reminds us that the source of his strength is not inhumanity. The death of

Portia brings back the tenderness that all his stoicism could not conceal,

> You are my true and honourable wife,
> As dear to me as are the ruddy drops
> That visit my sad heart.

If he has sacrificed his friend, he has also given up the wife he loved.  But he would try to bear all with constancy :

> Speak no more of her.  Give me a bowl of wine.
> In this I bury all unkindness, Cassius.

And as Cassius pledges him his admiration overflows in the loyal resignation and devotion that give so noble a touch to the last acts of this shrewd and unashamed contriver.

No work can speak more clearly than *Julius Cæsar* of the futility of honourable assassinations.  Yet nothing could show the disinterested nature of the man's action more than the attempt to keep such a deed free from dishonourable circumstances.  And if this only makes more obvious the madness of such a hope, yet

> in the blind and awful lair
> Of such a madness, reason did lie couched.
> Enow there are on earth to take in charge
> Their wives, their children, and their virgin loves,
> Or whatsoever else the heart holds dear.

Brutus would no doubt have been wiser to stay at home with his wife and books, and leave his fellows to endure the inevitable servitude ; yet his conduct has been felt as an everlasting reproof to such counsels of a not altogether ignoble ease by many of the world's rarer spirits, whether poets, artists, statesmen, or humbler lovers of their country, and not least by Shakespeare.

## HAMLET

**S.R. 26th July, 1602.**  *James Robertes.  Entred for his Copie under the handes of master Pasfeild and master waterson warden A booke called ' the Revenge of Hamlett Prince Denmarke' as yt was latelie Acted by the Lord Chamberleyne his servantes.*

This was a ' blocking ' entry made for the Company by

Roberts to prevent any printer forestalling their desire to print their own piece. But in spite of the precaution a pirated version, **Q1 1603**, appeared, purporting to give the piece as it had been played *in the Cittie of London : as also in the two Universities of Cambridge and Oxford and elsewhere.* In replacing this by a version **Q2 1605** (1604 on some copies) *Newly imprinted and enlarged to almost as much againe as it was according to the true and perfect Copy*, the Company seems to have had to compromise so far as to allow Nicholas Ling, one of the offending publishers, to vend the work, now printed by Roberts himself instead of by Valentine Simmes.

Gabriel Harvey's note in his edition of Speght's *Chaucer* (1598) seems to fix a date about 1600 for the piece.

> The Earle of Essex much commendes Albions England . . .
> The younger sort takes much delight in Shakespeare's Venus, and Adonis : but his Lucrece, & his tragedie of Hamlet, Prince of Denmarke, have it in them, to please the wiser sort.

Essex must surely have been alive when Harvey wrote ' commendes ' ; he started his rebellion on 8th February and was executed on 25th February, 1601. Meres makes no mention of the play.

An older version of the piece must have existed, however, in 1589, when Nash in his *Epistle* to Greene's *Menaphon* attacks English imitators of Seneca :

> English *Seneca* read by Candlelight yeelds many good sentences . . . and if you intreate him faire in a frostie morning, hee will affoord you whole *Hamlets*, I should say handfuls of Tragicall speeches. . . . *Seneca*, let blood line by line and page by page, at length must needes die to our Stage ; which makes his famished followers to imitate the Kid in *Æsop*, who, enamoured with the Foxes newfangles, forsooke all hopes of life to leape into a newe occupation.

Kyd was certainly an imitator of Seneca, and is here glanced at by Nash ; but it does not follow from this that Kyd was the only dramatist indicated, or the author of a *Hamlet*. And a *Hamlet* passed with a group of Shakespeare's plays to the Chamberlain's men, being played with *the Shrew* and *Titus Andronicus* in June 1594 at Newington Butts. That it continued in their repertory is shown by the allusion in Lodge's *Wits Miserie* (1596) to a devil as pale 'as the Visard of the ghost which cried so miserably at the Theatre (the house used by the Chamberlain's men), like an oister wife, Hamlet, revenge.'

This ur-Hamlet, as it has been named by some, has tempted writers to explain away what seem to them irreconcilable elements, especially in the character of the hero. The English dramatist took his plot from Belleforest's *Histoires Tragiques*, who retold the adventures set forth from traditional and other sources in the *Historia Danica* (about 1200) by Saxo Grammaticus. In the transformation of the bare and saga-like story of the earlier avenger into the tragedy of *Hamlet* several minds played a part, and we must expect to find, it is argued, in the final work incongruous and contradictory elements.

'One of the hardest things,' says Lamb, in the finest piece of criticism ever written on *Hamlet*, 'is to reconcile Hamlet's love for Ophelia with his bitter words to her.' But Sir Arthur Quiller-Couch, betrayed for a moment by the little learning about the sources denied to Lamb, finds it easy to explain away. In the early tale Hamlet's uncle puts a woman in the young man's way to beguile his secret from him : here is the original of Ophelia, and we are asked to believe that while Shakespeare in his wisdom changed this woman of the world into the innocent Ophelia, he yet retained for his hero a style of address in keeping, so we are told, with the earlier conception of the part. But a dramatist capable of such a palpable contradiction would not deserve the care and time Sir Arthur Quiller-Couch has given to his craftsmanship. The real explanation was given by Lamb himself when he wrote :

> The truth is, that in all such deep affections as had subsisted between Hamlet and Ophelia, there is a stock of *supererogatory love*, (if I may venture to use the expression) which in any great grief of heart, especially where that

which preys upon the mind cannot be communicated, confers a kind of indulgence upon the grieved party to express itself, even to its heart's dearest object, in the language of temporary alienation.

And Shakespeare, when he represents Hamlet as sitting down in the play-scene by the side of Ophelia, and choosing this affectionate heart in a wilderness of courtiers on which to vent his cynicism, has but dramatized the experience, familiar to many less subtly organized minds than we are to imagine in Hamlet—the mood expressed by Coleridge in the lines that tell how

> he at last
> Must needs express his love's excess
> With words of unmeant bitterness.

A work such as *Hamlet*

> Universally crowned with highest praises

that seems to grow in power and meaning from generation to generation must be in all essentials a perfect whole. Nothing less could so satisfy the imagination. Those who think otherwise would, if consistent, have to reverse the finding of the great critics from Aristotle downwards on the nature of Art. And any view which imputes the defects of our interpretation to the work itself, by pronouncing it an artistic failure, or a piece of deliberate mystification to deceive the thoughtless Elizabethans, must either deny the very principles on which criticism rests, or ignore the play's universal appeal.

In *Hamlet*, as in other works of Shakespeare's maturity, the structure of the piece provides the clue to its interpretation ; for the form is no arbitrary framework, but the counterpart of the poet's idea. Here the most remarkable feature in the construction is the interlude-like nature of so many of the most famous scenes and speeches. It does not seem necessary for the conduct of the action that Hamlet should discourse at such length with the players, or among the graves, or on the army of Fortinbras ; but how much is lost by their curtailment is often only too evident on the stage. Yet the soliloquies that

II

frequently terminate such episodes—and it is very much in keeping with the deeply introspective nature of Hamlet's mind that he should be, as Oscar Wilde has said, the spectator of his own tragedy—are felt to be so essential to a proper understanding of the story, that it is Hamlet himself who is responsible for the common report that he is a dreamer with just enough sense of reality to be ashamed of his own conduct. And accepting this admission as proved the critics proceed to pass judgment according to their temper. The athletic Furnivall calls Hamlet a shirker, and finds our sympathy with him explicable only because we are all in some way miserable shirkers ; while Coleridge had almost in self-defence to find this very fault a virtue. He was himself so unwilling at times to face the realities of his own unhappy situation that he would delay for months to open letters from his family and friends. But he found a formula that made all well : ' the moral obligation is to me so strong a stimulant that in nine cases out of ten it acts as a narcotic. The blow that should rouse *stuns* me.' And he shared his own excuse with Hamlet : the Prince delayed because he felt his duty too powerfully to be able to perform it. Dowden and Bradley, in modifying this picture, made it more like the real Coleridge, in so far as they found the equivalent for the drug that numbed the poet's will in Hamlet's disgust at his mother's marriage.

Yet Hamlet, if he did suffer from anything like Coleridge's paralysis of will, had none of his ingenuity in self-justification. Here at least their symptoms are very different ; for Hamlet declares himself not more but less responsive than ordinary men. The soliloquies, however, where with a most princely generosity he praises a virtue in human nature he denies himself, are not to be understood except as part of the whole field of discourse in which his mind moves. For he is admiring, as he contemplates the actor or the soldier, an aspect of the glory of the world and that angelic action and godlike apprehension he discovers in man. And he sees through his trivial or almost insensate doings to ' the soul of sensibility in the heart of man ' that in all quarrels, in all contests, in all delights, in all employments which are either sought by men or thrust upon them, so immeasurably transcends its objects. Like Wordsworth, Hamlet stands amazed at the lack of correspondence between the trivial nature of the outward stimulus and the intensity of the response within. This is the point of the question,

> What's Hecuba to him, or he to Hecuba,
> That he should weep for her ?

and of his exclamation at men,

> Exposing what is mortal and unsure
> To all that fortune, death, and danger dare,
> Even for an egg-shell.

But this wonder opens his eyes to the source of man's greatness, and he sees the spring of moral effort rise of its own divine energy from the depths of human nature—

> Rightly to be great
> Is not to stir without great argument,
> But greatly to find quarrel in a straw
> When honour's at the stake.

For he looks as did Wordsworth when he wrote ' wars—why and wherefore ? Yet with courage, with perseverance, with self-sacrifice, with enthusiasm,' on a being whose very follies testify to an immeasurable power for good.

Yet the actor and the soldier are but humble types of that sensibility in the soul of man of which Hamlet is himself the exemplar. For if we are to believe the critics, Hamlet's obsession, beside which the passion of the actor and the emulation of the soldier are tame and ordinary, is itself about nothing. All he has to do is to drive his sword through a defenceless enemy. Shakespeare shows us the king unprotected and on his knees with Hamlet a sword's length behind him. This is the central scene of the central act, the very keystone of the action, that holds together the fabric of the play ; and here Shakespeare has reduced almost to visual terms the whole of Hamlet's problem. And Claudius is not spared because Hamlet is un-nerved at the prospect of blood : Shakespeare has taken special pains to make us realize his natural alacrity amidst danger and bloodshed. Nor is he saved, because Hamlet really means to stab him when he is drunk or in bed. Those who cannot see this from what goes before are told so by the ghost some minutes later. Hamlet's purpose has been blunted by nothing more than the natural reluctance in a man of proved nerve, courage, and resolution, to stab a defenceless man. For this is his only resource. He cannot challenge the king ; if the deed is to be done, it must be done in cold blood, in circumstances such as the prayer-scene does no more than set out in extreme form. And the more helpless the murderer the more reluctant the avenger. Hamlet's adversary must strike the first blow. Not that Hamlet can admit to himself, even for a moment, that this is what holds his hand. So unconscious is he of any virtue in this noble compunction that he cannot find words shameful enough to characterize it or blasphemous enough to excuse it.

Such a contradiction between the real nature of a character and the appearance it assumes in words is an essential resource of the dramatist who would instruct us in the realities of life as he shows us its illusions. Since often,

> Below the surface-stream, shallow and light
> Of what we say we feel—below the stream,
> As light, of what we think we feel—there flows
> With noiseless current strong, obscure and deep,
> The central stream of what we feel indeed.

What may be called this three-dimensional quality in Shakespeare's art is not confined to *Hamlet*. The dying Desdemona, asked by Emilia ' Who hath done this deed ? ' replies,

> Nobody ; I myself ; farewell :
> Commend me to my kind lord. O ! farewell !

There are commentators who call this a lie, and regard it as the final instance of the natural deceit which they find to be the fatal flaw in Desdemona's character. It is true Othello turns on Emilia in his distress to say,

> She's like a liar gone to burning hell ;
> 'Twas I that kill'd her.

For him, however, there is some excuse, since he must try to

believe in her treachery, though the very vehemence of his
assertion suggests that he feels already that liars are innocent
of such untruths. And if it were a mortal sin to misinterpret
Shakespeare, those who repeat in cold blood Othello's rash
assertion would have to find their answer in Emilia's reply,

> O ! the more angel she,
> And you the blacker devil.

No truth could show the honesty and loyalty of Desdemona
so plainly as this lie. Nor could Shakespeare have so surely
brought home to us Hamlet's courage and humanity, had he
not given him, as he puts up his sword, the words Johnson
declared too horrible to be read or uttered.

Such contradictions are so firmly grounded in human nature
that generous feeling tends to assume even in lighter matters a
similar form. And when we read of the aged Daumier, unable
to earn a living by his art and threatened with eviction, we do
not know whether to admire more Corot's kindness in buying
the house for him, or his way of explaining himself to his old
friend : ' I have not done this for you, but just to annoy your
landlord.' And how a man may shrink from acknowledging
an unfashionable compunction is well illustrated in Mr. Sassoon's
account of his horror at hearing himself, when he saw his first
fox breaking cover, cry out to a fellow member of the hunt,
who had uttered a professional view halloo, ' Don't do that ;
they'll catch him.' It needs no imagination to understand how
' It was too awful to dwell on.'

It is Hamlet's own complete understanding of this paradox in
human behaviour that forms a principal element in his intellectual
charm, and contributes most powerfully to the impression of
genius all acknowledge. In him the heroism of ordinary men
finds a voice, since ' their victories,' as a later champion declared,
' are to themselves known only imperfectly ; for it is inseparable from virtue in the pure sense of the word, to be unconscious
of the might of her own prowess.' And Wordsworth continues
in words that lead us directly to Hamlet himself, ' This is true
of minds the most enlightened by reflection ; who have forecast

what they may have to endure, and prepared themselves accordingly. It is true even of these, when they are called into action, that they necessarily lose sight of their own accomplishments and support their conflicts in self-forgetfulness and humility.'

It is one of the supreme achievements of Shakespeare's art, and the justification of the peculiarly discursive nature of the play, that he has been able to show us ' a mind the most enlightened by reflection ' in its ' self-forgetfulness and humility.'[1] This is the secret of the life-like quality of the character. Hamlet, though the spectator of his own tragedy, is unconscious of the true part he is playing. To regard this happy ignorance, which is the consequence of his noble qualities, as a plain proof of weakness is a tribute to the dramatic perspective by which Shakespeare has preserved the illusion of life, in which we are naturally slow to do a justice to others they cannot do themselves.

But it has been argued that, since Shakespeare shows us the whole fatal train of disasters following straight upon Hamlet's sparing the king, we must be meant to regard it as a folly or even a crime. Yet that

> We may not think the justness of each act
> Such and no other than event doth form it

is as true in tragedy as in life, since the tragic poet does not

[1] The general law laid down by Wordsworth is well illustrated in two particular instances from Proust's *Le Temps Retrouvé*. At the outbreak of war in 1914 Saint-Loup, though doing all he can to get to the front, cannot bring himself to express the bellicose sentiments that many who had no intention of fighting uttered freely. He even speaks like a defeatist.

Mais ces déclarations, Saint-Loup eût été incapable de les faire ; d'abord par une espèce de délicatesse morale qui empêche d'exprimer les sentiments trop profonds et qu'on trouve tout naturels. Ma mère autrefois non seulement n'eût pas hésité une seconde à mourir pour ma grand'mère, mais aurait horriblement souffert si on l'avait empêchée de le faire. Néanmoins, il m'est impossible d'imaginer rétrospectivement dans sa bouche une phrase telle que : ' Je donnerais ma vie pour ma mère.' . . . . . .

De même que toutes les actions de maman reposaient jadis sur le sentiment qu'elle eût donné sa vie pour sa mère, comme elle ne s'était jamais formulé ce sentiment à elle-même, en tout cas elle eût trouvé non pas seulement inutile et ridicule, mais choquant et honteux de l'exprimer aux autres ; de même il m'était impossible d'imaginer Saint-Loup prononçant une des phrases les plus éloquentes que peut dire le Ministre le plus sympathique aux députés debout et enthousiastes.

shrink from making plain the dangers of greatness. This is the source of what is called tragic fear, which is not fear of punishment for wrong-doing, but the more dreadful thought that virtue may entail consequences we are incapable of supporting. 'This therefore lay with great trouble upon me,' wrote the heroic Bunyan, speaking of the time when he was in prison wondering whether he would be able to face with proper courage the sentence of hanging that he expected, 'for methought I was ashamed to die with a pale Face, and tottering Knees, for such a cause as this.' It is the imitation of such scenes that Tragedy offers us. To drive out this fear by an idea of virtue that obliterates all cowardly considerations is the catharsis at which tragedy aims. To be open and generous, of a free and uncontriving nature, may well prove as dangerous in this world as in Denmark, to use men not after their deserts but after your own honour and dignity as fatal. But what reader of *Hamlet* does not believe, at least for the moment while the virtue of the play works in him, that it is also to be that wonder of the world, a gentleman?

Mr. Bernard Shaw has put on record an instructive story of how he once consulted an oculist, and was much taken aback when assured that his eyesight was normal; nor was his self-esteem restored till he discovered that the average man's eyesight is far below this standard. Hamlet is the most normal of Shakespeare's heroes, the man of unimpaired vision with an equally true discernment whatever side of our nature is in question. Few are beset with the passions of an Othello, or a Macbeth, but Hamlet's dilemma seems to grow more apparent as men's moral vision develops a strength comparable to that of their passions. To decide what becomes a man, where ruthlessness rather than courage is what the situation seems to demand, is in the conduct of the affairs of individuals or empires more and more perplexing. For Shakespeare secured the dilemma by no false conjunction, as some have argued, of savage and civilized. The appeal from beyond the grave must still be heard. As long as murder and violence survive, so long will this visitant continue to come before men with its imperious but sorrowful countenance. To neglect it is to forswear the loyalties of man's blood. Yet if men have found revenge too wild a kind of justice, the justice they have to substitute for it is so often like cold-blooded revenge as to give them pause. The play presents us with a type of this eternal struggle ; but from its baffling confusions and contradictions Shakespeare has created an action that brings before us a perfection of courage, intellect, and heart, ' the instinctive wisdom of antiquity and her heroic passions uniting,' in the soul of the hero, ' with the meditative wisdom of later ages '—a perfection so difficult of realization as to place its creator among the supreme artists of the world ; and yet a perfection so central to human nature, that the world, however it may continue to dispute about the rights and wrongs of Hamlet's situation, will always agree to wear him in its heart of heart.

## OTHELLO

**S.R. 6th October, 1621.** *Thomas Walkley. Entred for his copie under the handes of Sir George Buck, and Master Swinhoe warden, The Tragedie of Othello, the moore of Venice.*

Walkley issued QI 1622. The text is from a version in which the advanced stage-directions reveal the bookholder's hand. He is no doubt also responsible for certain cuts including the Willow Song, removed possibly because the voice of the boy who was to play the part had broken.[1] The version must have been prepared before the Act of Abuses took effect on 27th May, 1606, as all the oaths are retained. The Folio is from the full original text, with the oaths softened down.

The Revels Accounts show that *Othello* was acted at Court on 1st November, 1604. The Bad Quarto of *Hamlet* (1603), however, incorporates phrases from it, so that it cannot be later than 1603.[2]

It must have been written about the same time as *Measure*

---

[1] *Shakespeare's Use of Song,* R. Noble. The boy who played Desdemona had no doubt played Ophelia and already shown his skill in this type of song.

[2] A. Hart, Letter to *T. L. S.,* 10th October, 1935.

*for Measure*. The crude material for *Othello* is found in Giraldi Cinzio's *Ecatommiti*, which also contains the story retold in Whetstone's *Promos and Cassandra* and in *Measure for Measure*.

Although *Othello* has always been felt to be the most painful of the tragedies, and almost unendurable as a stage spectacle, the image of Othello and Desdemona that remains in the mind is one of the most gracious and vivid that comes even from Shakespeare's living page.

There is a romantic beauty in their union that their fate only intensifies. He comes as a stranger to Venetian society from the deserts of his race and home, after a life of soldiering that has left him unacquainted with the world he enters on his marriage. The imagery and sentiments through which Shakespeare re-creates him in our mind—the antres vast and deserts idle, the handkerchief the sybil gave his mother, the Turk at Aleppo, the Arabian tree—suggest a remote and romantic being. And the gulf Othello crosses to marry the Venetian senator's daughter opens before us as he says,

> for know, Iago,
> But that I love the gentle Desdemona,
> I would not my unhoused free condition
> Put into circumscription and confine
> For the sea's worth.

To this the reluctant pangs of abdicating bachelorhood in a Benedick or a Berowne are the merest growing pains ; and the power that subdues Othello so much the greater. And Desdemona on her side has come as far or further to meet him, not dazzled by the glamour of a stranger, but lighted on her path by the heroic ardour that gives a brightness to the least of his words and gestures. She cannot always understand him, for the circumstances of their birth and breeding make this impossible ; but she always, as Coleridge so finely observed, feels with him. Her helpless sympathy with him, even when overwhelmed in her own distress, her loyalty and self-forget-fulness in her utmost need, are truly heroic traits that may contribute to her own undoing ; but they give her a tragic greatness even beside the Moor himself.

Their disparity in age seems to give the last romantic touch to their union—the man

> declined
> Into the vale of years—yet that's not much—

his wife still in her earliest May. But this provides the last impediment to those explanations that become so necessary when they are entangled in the social maze to which the Moor has no clue.

Othello is far from jealous by nature.

> The Moor is of a free and open nature,
> That thinks men honest that but seem to be so,

says Iago, whose plot depends entirely on this credulity. And the malignity of the world, drawn to a head in Iago, makes a breach in the Moor's confidence where it is most manly and modest.

> Not to affect many proposed matches
> Of her own clime, complexion, and degree,
> Whereto we see in all things nature tends—
> Foh ! one may smell in such a will most rank,
> Foul disproportion, thoughts unnatural.

Othello, because he fears his fortune in marriage is too good to be true, allows the most signal proof of Desdemona's faith to be made the very basis of his doubts.

' The difference of high Sensations,' wrote Keats, ' with and without knowledge appears to me this : in the latter case we are falling continually ten thousand fathoms deep and being blown up again, without wings, and with all the horror of a bare-shouldered creature—in the former case, our shoulders are fledged, and we go through the same air and space without fear.' The man who knew how to rule the fight is in this emergency a bare-shouldered creature, perplexed in the extreme. The strength of his nature only makes the gusts of passion more violent and horrible. His love was as a conserve of his whole nature ; and it is as if his own heart had offended and must be plucked out. And the proof of this lies in the contrast between the slow and oppressive agony that forces him to the murder of his wife, and the swift and sure movements of his mind when he knows the truth and has only his own life to take.

The construction of the piece, with the gradual but irresistible progress of the action, has often been praised ; yet *Othello* depends no more than the finest Greek tragedy on surprise or mere plot. For like the Greeks, Shakespeare is master of a tragic irony that searches the situation to the quick. What could one expect, it might be said, of such a match ? An inexperienced girl breaks her father's heart by marrying an adventurous Moor of mature years ; and the doubts and fears of the world are naturally justified. The play may be cited, if one likes, as another proof of Shakespeare's sanity : ' Is he not jealous ? ' says Emilia, as she offers a prosaic explanation of a husband's conduct, and the reply of the true believer,

> Who, he ? I think the sun where he was born
> Drew all such humours from him,

seems to discover a terrifying blindness as of one walking in sleep towards an abyss. To feel that the vulgar ignorance of Emilia [1] is apparently to be justified at every turn, and the faith of Desdemona so cruelly rebuked, is an experience that familiarity with the play only intensifies.

But Shakespeare's irony does not stop with the contrast between the swift drift of events that the spectators can see has set for disaster and the lack of prescience in those it carries with it. There is the stranger contrast between the pitiful events and the dignity and intensity of the hearts that endured them. And now Desdemona's ignorance becomes a kind of heavenly wisdom from which neither the accident of Othello's countenance nor conduct could conceal his love.

But though *Othello* is in every respect a masterpiece, it contains, when considered not as a drama but as a material

---

[1] Emilia, of course, more than wins her pardon. The being who can say to the roused Othello,
> Thou hast not half that power to do me harm
> As I have to be hurt,

though she dies as she has lived knowing only half the truth, has earned a place in the story.

record of events, a glaring impossibility. According to a reckoning of time that can be extracted from the play, there was no opportunity for the intrigue between Cassio and Desdemona that Iago invents, and his story would have been so obviously an invention that he could never have ventured to hint at it to Othello. But Shakespeare had set before himself a much more 'philosophical' end than the realization of historical probability. He has to reveal the heart of a human situation, a situation in which, he makes clear to us, the seeds of suspicion and jealousy might easily take root. To create an elaborate replica in material terms to satisfy the intelligence, when the imagination can gather all it needs of the situation from what Shakespeare can spare for mere exposition, would be a breach of artistic economy, and would distract attention from the inner train of events. It is not merely that the liberties Shakespeare takes with time pass unnoticed in the heat of representation ; they are the means he employs, as legitimate or necessary as perspective or foreshortening, for no art has all the dimensions of reality, to concentrate attention on the essentials of what was to him a story of the innocence of love.

## KING LEAR

**S.R. 26th November, 1607.** *Nathanael Butter John Busby. Entred for their Copie under thandes of Sir George Buck knight and Thwardens A booke called. Master William Shakespeare his ' historye of Kinge Lear' as yt was played before the kinges maiestie at Whitehall uppon Sainct Stephens night at Christmas Last by his maiesties servantes playinge usually at the ' Globe' on the Banksyde.*

*King Lear* must have been written between the performance on 26th December, 1606, here recorded, and the publication of Harsnet's *Declaration of Popish Impostures* (S.R. 16th March, 1603), from which Shakespeare borrowed or adapted the names of the devils, Frateretto, Fliberdigibet, Hoberdidance, Smolkin, Maho, and Modu. There was a notable eclipse of the sun on October 1605, and earlier in September one of the moon :

these may have suggested the late eclipses (I. ii, 99) as they were associated in men's minds with the treason of the Gunpowder Plot, discovered on 5th November, 1605.

Butter dated **Q1 1608.** This gives an earlier draft than that in the Folio. The irregularities of the text are many, verse often being printed as prose. This has suggested to some that it was printed from a shorthand report ; but the Folio text of the contemporary *Timon* shows how irregular an early Shakespearean draft might be. We need not be surprised that Shakespeare did not write *Lear* in perfectly regular blank verse, but in powerfully rhythmic phrase that could later be given a smoother outline.

The story had been dramatised by 14th May, 1594, when *The True Chronicle History of King Leir and his three daughters— Gonorill, Ragan, and Cordella* was entered in the Register. It was re-entered and published in 1605.

Shakespeare consulted a number of versions of the Leir story, including Holinshed's, and Spenser's from whom he took the spelling Cordelia ; he added the sub-plot of Gloster and his sons, an adaptation of the story of *The Paphlagonian unkind King and his kind son* from Sidney's *Arcadia* ; and he gave the story its tragic ending.

' No principle,' says Lamb, commenting on a performance of this play, ' can be more clear, than that cruelty and ingratitude are black in proportion to the weakness and helplessness of the objects on which they are exercised. The great master of the human heart accordingly makes this good old king represent himself as a man standing upon the last verge of life—a man " eighty years old and upwards." It is from turning such a man as this out of doors, and by his ungrateful children, too, to bide the pelting of the pitiless storm, that the interest principally arises.'

Lamb was here writing in extreme haste, content to make one point at a time where he had no leisure for his distilled prose with its quintessential truth ; and what he says must be corrected from his own *Essay* on the tragedies. For Lear's weakness though a truth is not the whole truth, nor indeed its most important aspect; otherwise how should the caged lion be a more tragic spectacle than a mouse or a canary in the same plight? It is not Lear's weakness but his strength that makes his story a tragedy—the grandeur which baffles the malice of his daughters and the elements, and, when the blast and lightning are over and the rage of his defiance is gone, the yet more impressive stillness of his reconciliation with Cordelia.

The story might have ended there had Shakespeare not felt he must make clear to us that this sovereign shame and tenderness are not the weakness of a spent man, but a passion as deep as it is still, a passion that only such a heart as Lear's can hold. And it so overflows even his capacity that there is room for nothing more, and the once irresistible swordsman does not ask or care whether the field is lost or won. But the power that sleeps in his love for Cordelia is unconfinable when disturbed, and neither age nor infirmity can stay his arm against the murderer of his child; and Lear dies in an ecstasy of joy, which even his frame cannot support, at the thought his daughter lives:

> Look on her, look, her lips,
> Look there, look there!

This principle then is as clear as Lamb's, that courage and humanity are heroic in proportion to the frailty and need of the agent that shows them. Great strength reduced to impotence was the definition of the tragic situation given by Crawley in *The Last Chronicle of Barset*, as he comments from the depth of his own affliction on the Samson of Milton's tragedy; but he was himself an unconscious example of the constancy that gives to such a situation the dignity of tragedy. The ground in *Lear* is from the first prepared on these lines. By a device sanctioned by folk story, Shakespeare shows us an absolute and imperious monarch placing himself in his old age at the mercy of ungrateful children. There is nothing, however, improbable in what may be called the psychology of the plot. He has but given the pomp of circumstance to a situation not unknown in ordinary life. The child that respects her father too much to play a part in the humiliating family scene his wilful fancy has designed for them is cast off, and those who take full advantage of their father's folly are empowered to cast his age into an unregarded corner. The requirements for which they have greedily allowed him to pay a thousandfold they now deny him as unnecessary, and they would treat him as once again a child. Great strength is reduced to impotence.

But the monarch to whom authority was as natural as breath cannot accept life on such base terms. Denied the relief of instant and conclusive action his mind can only turn inward, and Shakespeare by a supreme dramatic stroke makes of the storm a device to lay bare the inner structure and workings of the king's mind. The debate he cannot sustain against his own flesh and blood he maintains against the elements themselves ; and a shameful family wrong becomes before the bar of heaven a plea in the name not only of age but of all other helpless conditions against ruthless power. He does not plead that age is faultless, but only asks for it the charity that all states need, not least official righteousness. For it is Lear's glory that the greater his own need grows, the more he comes forward as the champion of others.

In his *Simon Lee* Wordsworth, like Shakespeare, contrasts the vigour and strength of the huntsman's prime with his helpless age—for if to be weak is to be miserable such a man has a double portion of affliction—so that we may admire the more the heroism of the heart such misery cannot make unkind. And Shakespeare's theme is, like Wordsworth's, not the cruelty or indifference of the world, or man's weakness, but the more tragic theme of his gratitude and strength. In *Lear* as in *Simon Lee* we see the triumph of the spirit not merely over neglect, or injustice and wrong, but over the last infirmity of our own nature, for

> Nature, as it grows again towards earth,
> Is fashion'd for the journey dull and heavy.

Lear's spirit feels no such retiring ebb : gathering strength with age it breaks through the too contracted bounds of our mortality in an irresistible current of gratitude and joy.

## MACBETH

**S.R. 8th November, 1623.** First printed in the **First Folio.**

Simon Forman, the astrologer, recorded in his Diary a performance at the Globe on 20th April, 1611, and gave a summary of the plot. The versification points to an earlier date for its composition. It cannot be earlier than 1603, as the piece is in some ways a compliment to James, dealing with his ancestor Banquo and glancing at matters such as witchcraft and touching for the king's evil that interested James. The reference in the Porter scene to the doctrine of equivocation, which was offered as a justification for his evasions by Father Henry Garnet during his trial (March 1606) for complicity in the Gunpowder Plot, suggests a date when the allusion was still topical ; further, there was an expectation of pienty (that caused the farmer to hang himself, II, iii, 4) in 1606, corn being cheaper then than during the next 13 years. Plays of this or the following year allude to *Macbeth*. *The Puritan* (S.R. 6 August, 1607) recalls Banquo's ghost, ' instead of a Iester, weele ha the ghost ith white sheete sit at upper end a 'th Table.' The story of the witches and James's ancestor may have been recalled to Shakespeare by the ' tres Sibyllae ' who greeted James on his visit to Oxford in August 1605.

Maeterlinck has asked, in the fine preface to his translation of *Macbeth*, how the story of two murderers, neither of them remarkable for intellectual power or sympathetic qualities, should yet leave the impression of ' beauté sombre et souveraine, noblesse mysterieuse et comme immemoriale.' Yet his answer, that the poet has achieved his sublime effect by raising Macbeth and his wife to a height from which right and wrong are almost indistinguishable and much less important than mere existence itself, though at the other extreme from the view that sees in the events of this life clear and direct anticipations of God's final judgments, is no more satisfactory. For the inspiration and awe of the tragedy come from the struggle by Macbeth to maintain that there is no distinction between right and wrong, and the revelation of an indestructible rightness in his soul,

which, to use the words of Robert South, there is no fluxing
out of its immortality.

The depth of his tragedy is touched when Macbeth hears
of his wife's death, and feels that even this now matters nothing,
since

> To-morrow, and to-morrow, and to-morrow,
> Creeps in this petty pace from day to day,
> To the last syllable of recorded time ;
> And all our yesterdays have lighted fools
> The way to dusty death.

Mr. Bernard Shaw and others have considered this a proof of
Shakespeare's profound pessimism.  But had Shakespeare represented a murderer like Macbeth as a man of cheerful yesterdays
and confident to-morrows, he would indeed have despaired of
human nature.  Here are words bitter with the very dregs of
despair, but in the mouth of Macbeth they reveal in the dramatist
a faith in the rule of righteousness as firm as that graven in the
Aeschylean Chorus, which tells how memory of wrong-doing
becomes in sleep an agony to the heart, and how the unwise
become wise against their will.  Nothing could be more classic
than the revelation of this truth to Lady Macbeth :  the linking
of sleep and the deeper knowledge one would deny by day is
truly Aeschylean in its solemnity and power to move tragic fear.
Nor is it Macbeth's death at the hands of Macduff that makes
the play a tragedy, but his destruction by something in his own
nature, an imaginative power that appals and fascinates us, but
at the same time humanizes and redeems him.  ' What need we
fear who knows it, when none can call our power to account ? '
asks Lady Macbeth in her sleep, repeating the words with
which they must have tried to comfort themselves in their
villainy.  But they had reckoned without themselves ; and
Shakespeare brings the subsequent horror before us in words
that give to the profoundest moral wisdom the immediacy
of sensation and feeling, ' yet who would have thought the
old man to have so much blood in him.'  The forms that
torment their imaginations are different, but who shall say
which is in the lower circle of hell ?

12

It has been objected, by the late poet laureate among others, that a man of Macbeth's imaginative temperament would never have committed the dastardly murder which leads to the tragic situation ; and that the preordaining of the murder is a further blot on the probability of the plot. But the murder is not preordained, though Macbeth's rule as king may be ; and the prophecy is one of the incitements to the deed that contributes to its plausibility. It is impossible to tell whether Shakespeare believed in ghosts or witches. There are some who think *Macbeth* proves that he shared the credulities of his time, for we have, as Lafeu complained, ' our philosophical persons, to make modern and familiar, things supernatural and causeless. Hence it is we make trifles of terrors, ensconcing ourselves into seeming knowledge when we should submit ourselves to an unknown fear.' But the unknown fears remain, and Shakespeare's embodiment of them in supernatural agents is a legitimate poetic device. The weird sisters encounter the soul in every generation : in Shakespeare's play they come as witches, because that was the form his audience would best understand. What they stand for in the imaginative design is real enough, and whether Shakespeare believed in them, as did James VI, is an irrelevant question. It is part of their task to transport our minds almost to a time ' Ere humane statute purg'd the gentle weal,' when the temptation for a man like Macbeth, cousin to the king and with legitimate pretensions as the chroniclers insist to the succession, is such as we must use our imagination to comprehend. To represent *Macbeth* in modern costume, and dress the thane as a brigadier, is to add to our difficulties ; for the temptations to which the modern officer is exposed do not include, at least in Scotland, the murder of his sovereign. Each age has its own dangers, though Shakespeare does not make this an excuse for Macbeth. Duncan's meekness, which made the deed intelligible to the chroniclers, is only an added burden on the murderer's conscience. But it is clear that what would be impossible for a man of Macbeth's temperament to-day might very well be probable in the circumstances chosen by Shakespeare.

These circumstances are such that Macbeth's moral strength
—that imaginative recoil in a man who knows no physical fear
at the thought of crime and its consequences—is made to appear
to himself mere weakness. Here his wife's part is decisive.
She persuades him that his want of heart for the deed is cowardice.
His very strength is made a goad to drive him to the murder
and his undoing : the supernatural soliciting, the sudden opportunity, the helplessness of Duncan, would be let pass, so the
taunts of his wife suggest, only by a weakling. And once the
deed is done his pious cowardice destroys him.

Yet how should a fighter of Macbeth's power, one so
eminently suited for rule and homage, be so troubled by
Duncan's taking-off, as never again to be the man he was,
but for some profound rightness in his soul, an inexorable
goodness that will assert itself the more, the more it is denied ?
And he and his wife—to whom tragedy comes through her
husband—find death a merciful release from themselves.
' Fate,' said Arnold, thinking of the distractions man foolishly
pursues,

> That it might keep from his capricious play
> His genuine self, and force him to obey,
> Even in his own despite, his being's law,
> Bade through the deep recesses of our breast
> The unregarded River of our Life
> Pursue with indiscernible flow its way.

In *Macbeth* the unregarded River of man's Life is seen in its
irresistible flood and grandeur ; his being's law is presented
with a power and magnificence unsurpassed even by the first
and severest of the Greek tragedians. But though Macbeth
may stand somewhat apart from Shakespeare's other tragic
heroes (though, of course, his wife is at his side) ; for they were
at the worst honourable murderers ; yet he is in their company.
Shakespeare unfolds the crime in a manner that would satisfy
Rhadamanthus himself, yet brings home to us the truth in
Donne's Christian surmise, ' Thou knowest this man's fall,
but thou knowest not his wrastling ; which perchance was such
that almost his very fall is justified and accepted of God.'

## ANTONY AND CLEOPATRA

**S.R. 20th May, 1608.** *Edward Blount. Entred for his copie under thandes of Sir George Buck knight and Master Warden Seton A book called. The booke of Pericles prynce of Tyre.*

*Edward Blunt. Entred also for his copie by the lyke Aucthoritie. A booke Called. Anthony. and Cleopatra.*

*Antony and Cleopatra* was not printed however till 1623, in the **First Folio.** Nor did Blount print a text of *Pericles;* so that he no doubt made the above entries for the players (*see* page 35). He entered *Antony and Cleopatra* again on 8th November, 1623, in the general entry for the Folio.

In 1607 Daniel had reprinted among other poems his *Cleopatra* with alterations that seem suggested by Shakespeare's play. The metre of the play links it with those of the last period. Light and weak endings become numerous for the first time.

' *Feliciter audax* is the motto,' says Coleridge, ' for its style comparatively with his other works, even as it is the general motto of all his works compared with those of other poets '; and he continues, ' this happy valiancy of style is but the representative and result of all the material excellencies so exprest.'

The construction is as daring as the style, but here Shakespeare is usually censured for lack of discretion. The play contains some 42 scenes—two have four lines, one six, one nine, and two ten. What can be made, it is asked, of this shifting from place to place, from Rome to Egypt, this succession of episodes extending over years ? The answer must be that on the picture stage nothing can be made of it, that the pauses and changes of scenery would leave no time for the play itself. But Shakespeare's stage was the same for Rome or Parthia ; though the spectator need not have been in any doubt where the scene was laid, when this knowledge matters. The spectator is lifted above the undramatic limitations of place and time, for something of the amplification of the novel that Goethe observed in Shakespeare's drama was made possible by Shakespeare's stage. The play must be judged as a stage creation with reference to the theatre for which it was designed.

And the story of Antony and Cleopatra can show its most dramatic aspect only against the world-wide background Shakespeare chose for its setting. For the solitude to which their passion brings them cannot be made more absolute than by the fierce society in which they must play out their part ; and Antony cannot be more alone with Cleopatra than when, with the world divided in two and trembling for his weight to turn the scales of victory, ' he forgot, forsook, and betrayed them that fought for him ' to pursue her ' through the middst of them that were in fight.'

Plutarch marks the opening of the last phase of Antony's career, which provides the material for the play, with these words :

> Antonius being thus inclined, the last and extremist mischief of all other (to wit, the love of Cleopatra) lighted on him . . . and if any spark of goodness or hope of rising were left in him, Cleopatra quenched it straight.

And he closes their history by saying,

> Now Cæsar, though he was marvellous sorry for the death of Cleopatra, yet he wondered at her noble mind and courage, and therefore commanded she should be nobly buried, and laid by Antonius.

Between these points is ample scope for the fullest moralizing on what sensual indulgence may bring man to. And Shakespeare is not behind Plutarch in improving the occasion. Even Mr. Shaw, disguised for the moment as the uncompromising Puritan, approves of Shakespeare's ' faithful picture of the soldier broken down by debauchery, and the typical wanton in whose arms such men perish.'

But Shakespeare's play has another side to it that Mr. Shaw cannot reconcile with his interpretation ; and this he would explain away, declaring that ' Shakespeare finally strains all his huge command of rhetoric and stage pathos to give a theatrical sublimity to the wretched end of the business, and to persuade foolish spectators that the world was well lost by the twain.' Yet Octavius himself, to whom Mr. Shaw would allow a strong touch of realism, was a spectator of their fate, and foolish enough to wonder at Cleopatra's noble mind and courage. And the manly and moral Plutarch gives Shakespeare the material for his situations.

Though Mr. Shaw is a lover of paradox, the knot in which Shakespeare knits up the contrarieties of feeling that strain so hard one against the other in this theme is too intricate for his comprehension as long as he insists on playing the Puritan. For in Shakespeare's play the sensual Antony becomes the victim of a passion in its essence unsensual. In *Julius Cæsar* he is a foil to the serious-minded conspirators, gamesome, the lover of plays, the hearer of music. Since then he has had the world at his feet. 'In the manner of his life,' Plutarch tells us, ' he followed Bacchus, and therefore he was called the new Bacchus ' ; but he is also the descendant of Hercules, and unites in his person both their attributes. When, however, he appears for the second time a new turn has been given his nature. If there was something of Bacchus in him before, he is now drunk with a new fury beyond the grape. Having enjoyed all the world can give to unlimited power and the richest physical endowment, he finds in Cleopatra's company a joy beyond anything he has known. And the world, whatever it may say of those who sacrifice reputation and wealth for such a satisfaction, does not readily forget their story, guessing dimly no doubt at the truth with which Aristophanes entertained Socrates and his friends, when he told the fable of the creatures cut in half by Zeus and condemned to go as mere tallies till they find and unite with their counterpart. For the master of Attic Comedy, whatever licence he permitted himself in scourging the follies of men, was too great a poet to make this his final interest : ' for surely,' he concludes, ' it is not satisfaction of sensual appetite that all this great endeavour is after : nay, plainly, it is something other that the soul of each wisheth—something which she cannot tell, but, darkly divining, maketh her end.'

The picture of their companionship Shakespeare found in

Plutarch, who, for all his disapproval, describes with enthusiasm Cleopatra's charms and gifts and her ability to cope with and overgo Antony in his exercises and recreations. This is the weft that crosses the warp of the incidents in the play. Now it is Cleopatra recalling old days on the Nile and longing for her departed Roman, or it is Enobarbus in Rome recalling their eastern adventures. The caustic soldier is a kind of chorus to remind us of his captain's folly and withal of his greatness ; and Cleopatra's charms never appear more triumphant than in the anger and contempt of his narrative. The Romans, Plutarch tells us, did pity the deserted Octavia ' but much more Antonius, and those especially that had seen Cleopatra : who neither excelled Octavia in beauty nor yet in young years.' But how Cleopatra could dispense with youth and its advantages, we learn from Enobarbus, as he reveals what such cold-blooded assessors had overlooked, the infinite variety and grace that could make defect itself perfection.

Shakespeare, however, does not represent the lovers as transformed into ideal home companions. In his rage Antony is still the cave man, regarding her as a chattel, an object of appetite,

> I found you as a morsel cold upon
> Dead Cæsar's trencher ; nay you were a fragment
> Of Cneius Pompey.

And Cleopatra shows the feminine counterpart to this brutality —a cunning past man's thought, as it seemed to the high-handed Antony. The scenes actually presented on the stage between Antony and Cleopatra are almost all violent with their quarrels and reproaches. They are never in each other's arms except when some sharp grief or joy makes mere voluptuousness impossible. No doubt, since Shakespeare's Cleopatra was played by a boy, it would have been folly to try here to compete with nature, but Shakespeare turns this limitation to dramatic gain. The sensual part is there : Antony's very reproaches create for the imagination a way of life only too congenial to his nature. But it is there as the groundwork of a struggle that would not, certainly, have taken place had they not been creatures of the senses, but that could not have taken place had they been only this. The flame of their passion burns too fiercely to be extinguished even by the dross of their sensuality.

Antony dies while the play has still an act to run, but without this act his story would be incomplete. For Cleopatra has to vindicate her right to his devotion.

> Husband, I come :
> Now to that name my courage prove my title !

is her unregenerate prayer. No doubt she has cast longing, lingering looks behind to the land of the living since Antony has died ; but her death scene is the ritual that makes visible to the eye of sense the mystery of their union.

## CORIOLANUS

**S.R. 8th November, 1623.** First printed in the **First Folio.**

Jonson's *Silent Woman*, acted January 1610, seems to have a humorously critical reference to Shakespeare's line, II, ii, 99, ' He lurch'd all swords of the garland,' in Truewit's remark, ' Well, Dauphine, you have lurch'd your friends of the better half of the garland.' The story Menenius tells of the Belly (I, i, 94-153) owes some touches to Camden's version in his *Remaines* (1605). The phrase (I, i, 177) ' the coal of fire upon the ice ' may be a reminiscence of the burning of pans of coal on the frozen Thames during the great frost of 1607-8. It was forty years since the river had been icebound. The internal evidence agrees with the date 1608, the number of light and weak endings linking it with *Antony and Cleopatra* and the later plays.

Though the later Roman plays are both quarried from Plutarch, and belong to the same period, no two pieces could differ more in style and atmosphere. The courteous Antony is replaced by Coriolanus who was, in Plutarch's words, churlish, uncivil, and altogether unfit for any man's conversation ; but what Plutarch calls his temperancy was as much a marvel to men as Antony's intemperance. The language and imagery of the plays reflect the contrast in character and subject. Each has its own unity down to the very metaphors and figures employed, and this unity is the measure of the power with which Shakespeare has possessed, and been possessed by, his subject.

*Coriolanus* lacks the colour and warmth of its predecessor ; the hero's very virtues seem beside the faults of Antony to have less claim on our sympathies. Yet there is at the heart of it all a rare tenderness whose native quality is only enhanced by the rough wars and civil tumults on whose dangerous slopes it so shyly reveals itself.

The virtue of the man has on one side a strange impersonality ; for, though it does not take the form of the patriot's devotion, nothing could be further from the desire for individual aggrandizement. His readiness to take second rank, provided he has the foremost place in the fighting, is only made the more generous by the ignoble comments of the tribunes. His valour has indeed strains from the heroic age in its composition,

αἰὲν ἀριστεύειν καὶ ὑπείροχον ἔμμεναι ἄλλων [1]

without which he cannot respect himself. And, as in the heroic age, this feeling has its personal side in the bond between him and his family, μηδὲ γένος πατέρων αἰσχυνέμεν.[1] 'And as for others,' says Plutarch, 'the only respect that made them valiant, was that they hoped to have honour : but touching Marcius, the only thing that made him to love honour was the joy he saw his mother did take of him. For he thought nothing made him so happy and honourable, as that his mother might hear everybody praise and commend him . . . which desire they say Epaminondas did avow and confess to have been in him, as to think himself a most happy and blessed man, that his father and mother in their lifetime had seen the victory he won in the plain of Leuctres.'

This human side Shakespeare has emphasized by the creation of Virgilia, whom Plutarch only mentions in passing. She is essential to our proper understanding of the man's character, and Shakespeare introduces her with a masterly economy of

[1] To fight ever among the foremost and outvie my peers, so as not to shame the blood of my fathers. *Iliad* vi, 208-9. Butler's Translation.

design. 'My gracious silence' is her husband's greeting to her, and yet, though she utters scarcely a hundred words, her presence and the instant response of her husband's nature to hers are unmistakably felt. From the tender apprehensions yet firm expression of her first words, 'But had he died in the business, madam ; how then ? ' through her silence and tears of joy as she greets her returning husband, to the few phrases with which she seconds Volumnia in the camp of the Volsces, there shows a spirit as resolute as it is womanly. A match for her redoubtable mother-in-law, though her most effective foil, she gives the family circle in which the hero stands a tenderness that has found its way into her husband's heart and discovers itself in his few but exquisite exchanges with her. Add to this his prayer for a valiant future for his son, and we have a picture of the hero as son, husband, and father, only surpassed, though not in all respects, in the sixth book of the *Iliad*.

In his bearish exterior Marcius is only a remarkable example of a class of men that the charlatan and the vain find insufferable. It is not difficult for his friends to find some excuse for his plain dealing. Not that Shakespeare represents the ordinary man as unappreciative of this side of his character ; one of the officers laying the cushions in the Capitol calls it a ' noble carelessness,' contrasting it with the supple and courteous policy of the climbers into public favour. There is, however, a natural and not unmanly resentment in the populace of his open scorn of them, though this does not prevent their having

> pardons, being asked, as free
> As words to little purpose.

His merits are insupportable only to the Siciniuses of the world. The pride of Marcius may be such as destroyed the great archangel, but, beside it, the vanity of the unmeriting proud wealsmen, ambitious for poor knaves' caps and legs, is a darkness that obscures entirely the original brightness of human nature. When such prate of service no wonder he is speechless with rage. And he makes it easy for them to misrepresent him to the people, since he misrepresents himself, actually ' affecting the malice and displeasure of the people' in his hatred of 'the bewitchment of some popular man.' This is why in his conversation with the citizens over their votes, the ordinary men, acting like gentle-men, have the better of him ; and even when the tribunes urge them to resent what they only half understand there is still a voice to speak the truth, if not the whole truth,

> 'tis his kind of speech, he did not mock us.

No doubt the manners of Marcius are bad, but how much better than the moderation of his mother, who thinks it would have been wiser,

> if
> You had not show'd them how you were dispos'd,
> Ere they lack'd power to cross you.

For his wrongheadedness conceals a virtue whose price is beyond all reckoning.

> I will not do't,
> Lest I surcease to honour mine own truth,
> And by my body's action teach my mind
> A most inherent baseness.
>
> III, ii, 120-24.

This choice at the crisis of his fate takes the hero above the limits of self-respect to which the most aristocratic birth or breeding can raise a man. Into that austerer air only a dis-interested passion for honour and integrity can climb.

Those who pause here to discourse of the man's faults should remember the words of More : ' But if you live the time that no man will give you good counsel, nor no man will give you good example, when you see virtue punished and vice rewarded, if you will then stand fast and firmly stick to God, upon pain of my life, though you be but half good, God will allow you for a whole good.' Shakespeare's play is not the glorification of pride and pugnacity ; nor does he here discredit by implication such virtues as humility and love of peace. What is glorified in Coriolanus is heroic fidelity to an ideal, even when, as in this man's case, such fidelity could be paid for only at such a price [1]

---

[1] I owe some phrases here to Father R. H. J. Stewart, S.J., on Benedick Labre in *Diversity in Holiness*.

His words to the tribunes, or to the conspirators who stand round him later in Corioli, may be unwise but are not ignoble. Compared with his open dealing the mean schemes that bring him down make us feel with Menenius,

> His nature is too noble for the world :
> He would not flatter Neptune for his trident :

especially as at the end all the characters save Marcius are alive, and the meaner the survivors, the more they are indebted to Coriolanus for their lives.   For we do not find inhuman virtue on one side opposed to weak humanity on the other.   It is the man who declares

> I'll never
> Be such a gosling to obey instinct, but stand
> As if a man were author of himself
> And knew no other kin,

who dies that the others may live.   No doubt it is his own fury, kindled by folly and ingratitude, that thrusts the fatal choice upon him.   But the greater his rage, and the more uncontrollable the current of his revenge, the firmer must be the foundations on which his nature stands to resist them.   And he emerges from the tempest of his life, as from the lesser storms of the wars, like the great sea-mark of his own noble imagination, standing every flaw that the baseness of his countrymen and his own impatience and pride can cast upon him.


## TIMON OF ATHENS

**S.R. 8th November, 1623.**  First printed in the **First Folio.**

The manuscript supplied by Heminge and Condell gave a version of the play still rough-hewn in places, not unlike parts of the first Quarto of *King Lear*.   The printer, for lack of clear guidance, often printed verse as prose, and prose as verse ; and he had to set up long passages which though not in regular blank verse have a strongly marked rhythm.

When *Troilus and Cressida* was removed, in the course of printing, from among the Tragedies, *Timon of Athens* was inserted in its place. Apart from this accidental connection between the plays, there is a similarity in their construction. *Troilus*, as internal and external evidence suggests, was written for a special and no doubt an academic audience. In *Timon* the intellectual appeal is as slightly disguised. There is little here of the brilliant invention that masks the profound thought in the great tragedies, where there is nothing so uniform as the unbroken succession of interviews that make up the second part of *Timon*. But *Timon* stands beside them in the passionate power with which its idea is expressed.

The central scene in the play is an argument between Alcibiades and the senators of Athens concerning the sentence of death they have passed on one of his soldiers. This man has attacked and killed in hot blood an opponent who had defamed him. The senators do not deny that he displayed on this particular occasion what Alcibiades calls a 'noble fury and fair spirit'; they merely insist that the man is known to drink and is dangerous, that ' to revenge is no valour but to bear,' and that men must be taught to wear their wrongs as external as their raiment and not to prefer them to their heart. Alcibiades answers that, if there be such valour in bearing, the senators should offer their throats to their enemies rather than maintain an army in their defence ; and he appeals to them not to undo a soldier for showing on his own behalf the spirit they demand in their service as a duty. But the adamant of the self-preserving instinct is impervious to such pleading. In a cold passion for strict law, bred of their love of personal security, they condemn the soldier to death.

The Athenians treat Timon as they treated the soldier. Their gratitude to the man who has spent a fortune in the defence of the state, and in befriending his fellow citizens, turns to indignant censure the moment they are asked to repay a little of what they owe. What threatens their person or their purse is given short shrift.

Alcibiades turns in his anger and rends them. But the

fury of Timon is more inward. His tragedy is not that he is
reduced to poverty and cast off, but that the godlike image of
man in his heart is cast down, and his dreams of human fellowship destroyed. These gone, his life is only a burden to him ;
and he cries out at the insufferable sufficiency of breath,

> That nature being sick of man's unkindness
> Should yet be hungry.

This is the too too solid flesh of which only death can rid a
man.

To say that Timon took his trouble too much to heart is
just what the senators said of the soldier ; and the criticism
that finds in his untimely death a judgment on his ' kindly
self-indulgence ' or ' easy generosity ' is exactly in the sena-
torial vein. ' No doubt,' says Dowden, ' he who carefully
built up his worldly fortune could not approve of Timon's
magnificent prodigality.' But where is the easy-going folly
in the man to whom Alcibiades can say,

> I have heard, and griev'd,
> How cursed Athens, mindless of thy worth,
> Forgetting thy great deeds, when neighbour states,
> But for thy sword and fortune, trod upon them—

or in the man who can remind Apemantus that with the world
at his employment he had chosen to follow

> The icy precepts of respect.

And when Mr. John Bailey continues, ' we know well that
Lear would never have cared to go back to his old pomp and
vanities,' and asks, ' But do we feel sure that Apemantus is
wrong when he says to Timon :

> Thou'dst courtier be again,
> Wert thou not beggar ? '

the answer is that we know Apemantus is wrong, since Timon is
no longer a beggar, having discovered as he dug for roots
enough gold to call even from Athens, had he so desired it,
the spirits who once obeyed the magic of his bounty. Later
the senate's embassy comes in most abject humility to beg him

to return as dictator. Timon's misanthropy is the thing itself and not a form of vanity.

Apemantus with his raillery is created to emphasize what these incidents tell us. He is the needy hater of the world. who, owing to some deprivation, covers up with the vehemence of his contempt what is now known as an inferiority complex, On this sore Timon puts his finger,

> If thou had'st not been born the worst of men,
> Thou hadst been knave and flatterer.

The misanthropy of Apemantus is only the world's self-love inside out. But Timon's hate is from no such malice ; and his occupation is gone not because the citizens will not repay their borrowings, but because their refusal wakens him from his dream of restoring the golden age and all its charities in such a nest of vipers. Apemantus could see the world given over to beasts and remain a beast with them, but Timon will be a man or nothing ; and his misanthropy comes on him, as it does on the other great misanthrope of the stage, because it seems impossible to remain a man among his fellows.

Molière's Alceste is a true lover of his kind baffled at every turn by their betrayal of his hopes in them. The key in which the work is composed Molière establishes beyond doubt by the repetition of the verse Alceste recites to the sonneteering Marquis,

> Si le Roi m'avait donné
> Paris, sa grand 'ville,
> Et qu'il me fallût quitter
> L'amour de ma mie,
> Je dirais au roi Henri :
> Reprenez votre Paris,
> J'aime mieux ma mie, au gué,
> J'aime mieux ma mie.[1]

---

[1] A play attains artistic perfection just in proportion as it approaches that unity of lyrical effect, as if a song or ballad were still lying at the root of it, all the various expression of the conflict of character and circumstance falling at last into the compass of a single melody, or musical theme. As, historically, the earliest classic drama arose out of the chorus, from which this or that person, this or that episode, detached itself, so, into the unity

With this the charming Célimène, who will leave her Paris for no one, is out of tune, and Alceste has no art to bring her or the world into harmony with his tonic idea. Molière makes fine game of such ideal passions. And Rousseau and similar solemn moralists think he is speaking to us in the vein of Autolycus, 'what a fool Honesty is, and Trust, his sworn brother, a very simple gentleman.'

But the laughter in which Molière immerses Alceste, no less than the madness that engulfs Timon, is a resource employed by the poet to maintain that temperance in the midst of his passion without which it loses rhythm and power. His tragic story permits Shakespeare to pierce the pretences of the world with an invective beyond anything in Molière's sardonic smile. Timon can no longer endure that part of himself that makes him one of the conspiracy into which society so regularly resolves itself.

> Raise me this beggar, and deny't that lord ;
> The senator shall bear contempt hereditary,
> The beggar native honour.
> It is the pasture lards the rother's sides,
> The want that makes him lean.   Who dares, who dares,
> In purity of manhood stand upright,
> And say, ' This man's a flatterer ? '   If one be,
> So are they all ; for every grize of fortune
> Is smooth'd by that below : the learned pate
> Ducks to the golden fool : all is oblique ;
> There's nothing level in our cursed natures
> But direct villainy.   Therefore, be abhorr'd
> All feasts, societies, and throngs of men !
> His semblable, yea, himself, Timon disdains.

He turns in disgust from all that seems to nourish this monster in our natures.

of a choric song the perfect drama ever tends to return, its intellectual scope deepened, complicated, enlarged, but still with an unmistakable singleness, or identity, in its impression on the mind.   Just there, in that vivid single impression left on the mind when all is over, not in any mechanical limitation of time and place, is the secret of the ' unities '—the true imaginative unity— of the drama. *Appreciations*, by Walter Pater.

Oh ! a root ; dear thanks :
Dry up thy marrows, vines and plough-torn leas ;
Whereof ingrateful man, with liquorish draughts
And morsels unctuous, greases his pure mind,
That from it all consideration slips !

Lear expresses the same thought in his own characteristic imagery,
and in Timon's, as in Lear's injured mind the crime of man seems
to infect the universe of nature.

In these two plays, which cannot be far apart in date, Shakespeare uses the same device to maintain the balance of his piece.
Flavius, the steward, is a companion worthy of the faithful Kent,
and like Kent stands at the end unrecognized by his distracted
master. ' This,' says Lamb,

> is the magnanimity of authorship, when a writer, having
> a topic presented to him fruitful of beauties for common
> minds, waives his privilege, and trusts to the judicious
> few for understanding the reason of his abstinence.
> What a pudder would a common dramatist have raised
> here of a reconciliation scene. . . . The old dying king
> partially catching at the truth, and immediately lapsing
> into obliviousness, with the high-minded carelessness of
> the other to have his services appreciated, as one that
>
> —served not for gain
> Or follow'd out of form,
>
> are among the most judicious, not to say heart-touching,
> strokes in Shakespeare.

In *Timon* Shakespeare shows a similar reticence in handling
the parting of the servants that still wear Timon's livery in their
hearts, and in the last interview between Flavius and his master.

There is at the core of the play, as in Timon's own heart,
a rare humanity ; and the sense of the nobility in simple service
finds expression in these humbler figures. They reassure us of
the humanity in Timon himself, and that it was indeed his
goodness that undid him.

Poor honest lord ! brought low by his own heart,
Undone by goodness. Strange, unusual blood,
When man's worst sin is he does too much good !

13

Here Flavius is but their spokesman, and they are the only characters in the play, save Alcibiades, whose faith and service give any warrant for the truth of their words.

## MEASURE FOR MEASURE

**S.R. 8th November, 1623.** First printed in the **First Folio.**

*Measure for Measure* was acted at Court on 26th December, 1604 ; the following extract from the Revels Accounts refers to that date : *By his Maiesties plaiers. On St. Stivens night in the Hall A play Caled Mesur for Mesur.* In the column headed, *The poets which mayd the plaies* (for a number of plays [1] were performed during this season) stands the name *Shaxberd.*

The main plot is found in an Italian collection of stories, Cinzio's *Ecatommiti.* Whetstone, an adventurer and man of the world, borrowed it for his two-part play *Promos and Cassandra* (1579), adding to it a background of low life such as we find in Shakespeare. Whether Shakespeare went from Whetstone to Cinzio, or examined the English play after reading the Italian, is uncertain ; but that he used the Italian collection is proved by his taking from it the plot of *Othello,* which must have been composed about the same time as *Measure for Measure.* That he even looked through Cinzio's *Epitia,* a play on the same theme, is suggested by the name he gives his deputy ; for Angelo may be a reminiscence of Angela, in Cinzio, the deputy's sister. Similarly he may well have read Whetstone's prose version in his *Heptameron* (1582), for it is there 'reported by Madam Isabella.' Here, as for *Twelfth Night* and for *Lear,* we have evidence of Shakespeare's turning over a number of versions of the story he had in mind for dramatisation.

The passages at I. i, 67–72, and II, iv, 24–30, explain how a king who loves his people may yet disrelish the demonstrations of the multitude, and how the multitude in crowding with obsequious fondness to their ruler's presence may unwittingly give offence. These remind us of the dislike of crowds shown by

---

[1] See Chambers' *Shakespeare II,* 331.

James.   General considerations of style, and its relation to other plays, particularly *Othello*, suggest a date about 1603 or 1604.

The main plot is treated more realistically than in the preceding comedies, and the subsidiary comic business is correspondingly less light-hearted.   The jesting in Vienna is grimmer than in Illyria.   But to ignore, in interpreting this and the comedies that go with it, the conventions in which they are framed is to misunderstand the poet's intentions.   Robert Bridges was so offended with the hugger-mugger interment of Angelo's hypocrisy and Bertram's viciousness, in the happy endings Shakespeare gave *Measure for Measure* and *All's Well*, that he declared that only rank insensibility in the audience and lack of artistic conscience in the playwright could have permitted them. But the same objection might be made against some famous stories that have charmed not the least sensitive of mankind. The story of the sad courage of Griselda when tried by her husband, first with the loss of their children, and then of her place as wife, was given by Boccaccio the place of honour in his *Decameron*, as the tenth story of the tenth day.   Petrarch so approved his friend's choice that he translated it into Latin, and Chaucer in his turn put it back again into another vernacular. Yet if the husband be taken seriously, or regarded from outwith the convention of the story, the happy ending becomes a mockery and Griselda's heroism something worse than folly.   Shakespeare had to bring his story within the bounds of comedy, if he was not to shock the sensibilities of his audience ; unless he had been prepared to raise the whole action to the level of tragedy, and it is not of the kind he chooses for his tragedies. To make the story acceptable Shakespeare softened features already toned down by Whetstone.   Bernardine, whose head is to be substituted for that of Claudio, refuses to die ; and Shakespeare has to introduce the Mariana episode to enable his heroine to evade the deputy's bargain.   A good deal of manipulation was now required to bring this within the five acts, and Shakespeare has to use the Duke as a kind of ever-ready *deus ex machina*.

Though Shakespeare failed to convert much of the stage

business into drama, the power in the piece is remarkable. ' If
he had left not a record beside,' says Bridges,

> we should know him from Isabella's three great scenes
> to have been by far the most gifted dramatist of all time.
> Even the short scene between the Duke and Julietta—
> where the Duke, graciously playing the confessor's role,
> finds himself at every professional move baffled and
> checkmated by the briefest possible replies of a loving
> and true heart, till he is rebuffed into a Christ-like sym-
> pathy—appears to me a masterpiece which in its kind no
> other dramatist can have equalled.

And this creative energy peoples the suburbs of Vienna
with a wonderful crowd of sinners.  To regard them as merely
a dark background to set off the saintly Isabella is to reduce, as
Raleigh remarks, Shakespeare's picture to the level of some
Christmas cards. ' The wretches,' he insists, ' who inhabit
the purlieus of the city are live men pleasant to Shakespeare,'
and those who are offended with them should read Raleigh's
comments, especially on Bernardine, the Farinata of this other
underworld, who looks round on it all, executioner, gaoler,
and Duke, indifferently, with a disdain worthy of the great
Ghibbeline. ' Even Lucio,' he pleads for ; but there is no
need to make an exception of this scapegrace, though modern
critics have disliked him more than the others.  His superfluous
folly cannot conceal much sense and humanity ; and the Duke
might have taken more lightly the impossible slanders the young
reprobate insists on thrusting upon him.  The Duke might have
seen that his own mystery-mongering helped to provoke them,
and said with the Florentine lord who listens to the scared but
still ingenious Parolles, ' I begin to love him for this. . . . He
hath outvillained villainy so far that the rarity redeems it.'
The false emphasis on Isabella, produced by the undue
darkening of these loose-livers, provokes the opposite error of
those who denounce the heroine as cold and inhuman.  To
imagine that only the easy-going sinner is capable of sensibility
is as much an error as to deny him humanity.  A passionate

austerity may spring from unusual keenness of feeling, and the
famous lines,

> The impression of keen whips I'd wear as rubies,
> And strip myself to death, as to a bed
> That longing I've been sick for, ere I'd yield
> My body up to shame,

are no less quick with the delighted spirit and the sensible,
warm motion of living than the words of her brother, when he
shudders at the chill news of death. The charity of Shakespeare's art embraces the virtuous as well as the sinner.


## ALL'S WELL THAT ENDS WELL

**S.R. 8th November, 1623.**  First printed in the **First Folio.**
Some think this play the *Love's Labour's Won* referred to
by Meres in 1598 ; but the tone and style of the piece
link it with *Measure for Measure*, and it is generally taken as of
this period.
' The story of Bertram and Diana,' as Dr. Johnson observes,
' had been told before of Mariana and Angelo, and, to confess
the truth, scarcely merited to be heard a second time.'    Shakespeare here used Paynter's version, from his *Palace of Pleasure*, of
Boccaccio's ninth story of the third day.    The despised wife,
who by her courage and ingenuity recovers or gains her husband's
entire affection, is a popular figure in folk-story, and such a
vindication of a wife's right was not considered unbecoming
even in the nobly born.    Helena therefore comes of most
respectable ancestry, with the voice of ancient tradition in all
parts of the world in her favour.    Nor has Shakespeare, as some
have supposed, handled the story in a critical or ironical spirit.
She is a wife

> Whose beauty did astonish the survey
> Of richest eyes, whose words all ears took captive,
> Whose dear perfection hearts that scorn'd to serve
> Humbly called mistress.

This is not the language of convention or irony.

The difficulty in the theme, as the Griselda story shows, is with the husband : the worthier the heroine, the more despicable the man. Johnson has summed up well on this point :

> I cannot reconcile my heart to Bertram ; a man noble without generosity, and young without truth ; who marries Helen as a coward, and leaves her as a profligate : when she is dead by his unkindness, sneaks home to a second marriage, is accused by a woman whom he has wronged, defends himself by falsehood, and is dismissed to happiness.

Shakespeare frankly relied on the convention of the sudden conversion of such husbands, their social standing being assured. Stories however of this type can only reconcile us to this heavy borrowing on our credulity by paying back handsomely in some other way. And many critics find in the resolute but modest Helena ample compensation.

Modern criticism, however, tends to overlook the character who was no doubt at the time regarded as the attraction of the piece, and not merely by the vulgar spectator. Though we know that Shakespeare's were the plays ' that so did take Eliza and our James,' the first royal critic whose opinions are still extant in his own hand is Charles I. These unfortunately consist of no more than the substitution in his copy of the plays (a Second Folio now in the library at Windsor) of the name Malvolio for *Twelfth Night* and Parolles for *All's Well*. Charles was not content merely to enjoy the plays as stage productions ; they were the delight of his private hours, and in darker days were known to be, as Milton tells us, ' the closest companion of these his solitudes.' Charles was, for all his faults, of some judgment in the arts ; so that his opinion is important, coming from one who not only saw the plays performed before the stage tradition was broken by the civil war, but also viewed them with no vulgar apprehension.

Parolles is not just a common coward any more than Malvolio is a simple gull. He is no Falstaff, however, and Johnson's note on him is misleading, for lack of this necessary qualification.

Parolles has many of the lineaments of Falstaff, and seems to be the character which Shakespeare delighted to draw, a fellow that had more wit than virtue.  Though justice required that he should be detected and exposed, yet his *vices sit so fit in him* that he is not at last suffered to starve.

But his is not the heart to be ' fracted and corroborate' as long as ' competence of life ' was allowed him :

> if my heart were great
> 'Twould burst at this :  Captain I'll be no more,
> But I will eat, and drink, and sleep as soft
> As Captain shall.   Simply the thing I am
> Shall make me live.

Falstaff for all his vices belongs to another order of character.


## TROILUS AND CRESSIDA

**S.R. 7th February, 1603.**   *master Robertes.   Entred for his copie in full Court holden this day to print when he hath gotten sufficient aucthority for yt, The booke of Troilus and Cresseda as yt is acted by my lord Chamberlens Men.*

This entry, no doubt made for the players by Roberts to prevent piracy, gives the lower limit for the composition of *Troilus and Cressida*.   It must be later than 1601, the date of Jonson's *Poetaster ;* for the words of Shakespeare's Prologue,

> hither am I come,
> A Prologue arm'd, but not in confidence
> Of Author's pen, or Actor's voice ;  but suited
> In like conditions, as our Argument,

glance at Jonson's Prologue, who enters armed, not because the play to follow dealt with war, but to convey in dress as in words the author's defiance of his detractors.

Jonson in his *Every Man Out of his Humour*, played by the Chamberlain's men in the autumn of 1599, had parodied the style of Marston's *Histriomastix*.   This attack he continued in

1600 in his *Cynthia's Revels*, written for the Children of the Chapel Royal, to whom he had transferred his services for performance at the Blackfriars theatre. Dekker, a friend of Marston, replied in his *Satiromastix*, which was acted not only by the boys of St Paul's, for whom Marston had written his *Histriomastix* and *What You Will* (1600), a reply to *Cynthia's Revels*, but also by the Chamberlain's men ; for Jonson had in *Cynthia's Revels* reflected on what he called the ' common players ' and the ' common stages,' expressions taken up by Shakespeare, who lets Hamlet reply to these jibes in his conversation with Rosencrantz (II, ii, 338, 344) about the boy actors. So the ' Poetomachia ' led to the War of the Theatres.

In his *Poetaster* (1601) Jonson again attacked Marston, representing himself as Horace purging Marston of his ill-digested vocabulary with a pill ; and he now openly ridiculed the Chamberlain's men. That Shakespeare intervened decisively the academic play, *The Return from Parnassus*, Part II, played at Cambridge about Christmas 1601, makes plain. It is a sequel to the *The Pilgrimage to Parnassus* (1598) and *The Return*, Part I (1599), and describes the difficulties of young University men in finding employment in ordinary life after their journey to the land of the Muses. In their search they try the theatre, and Burbage and Kempe are introduced to give them what is now called an audition.

> *Kempe.* Few of the university men pen plaies well, they smell too much of that writer *Ovid*, and that writer *Metamorphosis*, and talke too much of *Proserpina* and *Juppiter*. Why heres our fellow *Shakespeare* puts them all downe, I and *Ben Jonson* too. O that *Ben Jonson* is a pestilent fellow, he brought up *Horace* giving the Poets a pill, but our fellow *Shakespeare* hath given him a purge that made him beray his credit.

> *Burbage.* Its a shrewd fellow indeed. I wonder these schollers stay so long, they appointed to be here presently that we might try them : oh, here they come.

Some see in the character of Ajax in *Troilus and Cressida* Shakespeare's answer to Jonson.

Q1 1609 did not appear till the play was again entered in the Register.

28th January, 1609. *Richard Bonion Henry Walleys. Entred for their Copy under thandes of Master Segar deputy to Sir George Bucke and master warden Lownes a booke called the history of Troylus and Cressida.*

It was first issued with the statement on the title page, *As it was acted by the Kings Maiesties servants at the Globe.* This was, however, cancelled, a new title page inserted, and a prefatory letter added calling it ' a new play, never stal'd with the Stage, never clapper-clawd with the palmes of the vulger,' and declaring it ' passing full of the palme comicall,' and as worthy of study ' as the best Commedy in *Terence* or *Plautus.*' This suggests that Shakespeare wrote the play for some private occasion, but not, as some think, for performance at Court before Elizabeth, since the whole tone of the piece makes this impossible. At one of the Inns of Court, however, its scurrilities would be in keeping with their tradition of ' lewd and lascivious plays' and wittily obscene speeches.

The writer of the epistle encourages readers to buy by telling them that the ' grand possessors,' presumably the actors, were unwilling to have their plays printed, and that only good fortune had given this one to the public. A piece written for a coterie would certainly have had to be copied for some of the many of worship who admired Shakespeare's art, and whom the actors would feel bound to please. Such a transcript may at last have reached a publisher. Heminge and Condell, however, had Shakespeare's manuscript in their possession, and though the Folio printers worked from the Quarto it was corrected from this manuscript. The corrector inserted mechanically a repetition that was not intended by the author to stand in the finished version. At V, x, 32–35 there stands in both versions,

> *Pan.*—But hear you, hear you !
> *Tro.*—Hence, broker-lackey, ignomy and shame
>     Pursue thy life, and live aye with thy name.

The Folio gives practically the same words at V, iii, 112–5, where, as the context shows, they must have stood originally. They were later transferred to the end to allow Pandar to make his only appearance on the battlefield, quite inappropriately as far as the action goes, to speak his characteristically scurrilous Epilogue.

The subject and its treatment support the evidence that can be drawn from the Epistle concerning the occasion of the piece. The reduction of Homer's heroic debate to a 'war for a placket' is not to be explained away as merely the mediæval attitude to the classical story. Chaucer's contribution is deliberately degraded. Much of this would be lost on an audience who were ignorant of their Chaucer and Homer. But if it was written for a group of worldly-wise young clerks, hardened, in theory at least, like the wife of Bath's fifth husband with his delight in reading of the wiles of women, then the cynicism of the piece need not be taken at its face value, but rather as a device to startle these simple worldlings out of their complacency.

The very language of the play is peculiar. In the Prologue, as in many of the important speeches, Shakespeare falls into the highly Latinized style he adopted when aiming at a powerful effect, while constrained by the situation as in the players' speech in *Hamlet*.

The chance that preserved the Prologue is worth noting as revealing the resources of Heminge and Condell's material. *Troilus* was first placed among the tragedies after *Romeo and Juliet*, but when three pages were set up it was removed, to be finally placed between the Histories and Tragedies. The last page of *Romeo and Juliet* (since *Troilus* began on the other side) had to be reprinted, and was then numbered 79 in error for 77. Pages 79 and 80 were transferred intact to their new position, but 78 had to be discarded as it had *Romeo and Juliet* on the back. It was reprinted, and the Prologue unearthed to fill the space left blank on the back by the omission of *Romeo and Juliet*. Till recently it was thought that this change of position was due to the ambiguous nature of the play, since, though it may well be regarded as a Tragedy, its first well-informed critic insists in his Epistle that it is a Comedy. But Mr. Willoughby's recent work on the Folio (*see* page 41) points rather to some trouble with the stationers, to whom the printing rights had been entered, as the explanation of the alteration.

The energy of thought that informs the political discourse of Ulysses has always attracted readers to this play ; but the power with which the passion of Troilus is realized is perhaps even more remarkable. Keats could talk of throwing his whole being into Troilus when he repeated the lines,

> I stalk about her door,
> Like a strange soul upon the Stygian banks
> Staying for waftage.

And every phase of the hero's passion, to its final incredulous despair,

> Sith there is yet a credence in my heart,
> An esperance so obstinately strong,
> That doth invert the attest of eyes and ears,

is made memorable by some fine excess of phrasing or rhythm.

As a whole, however, *Troilus* is to the great tragedies something like the antimasque to the masque, the satyric play to the tragedies it followed.

# VI. THE FINAL PERIOD

SHAKESPEARE'S work as a dramatist may be taken
as ending with the burning of the Globe theatre, for
there is no evidence of any literary composition during the
last three years of his life ; even his final work, *Henry VIII*,
produced in June 1613, was probably a return to the stage
in the interests of his Company. He had intended to close
his career as a dramatist two years earlier, in 1611, with
*The Tempest*.

In September 1609 Shakespeare's cousin, Thomas
Greene, the town clerk of Stratford, was residing at New
Place, and he recorded in his diary under that month that
he found, contrary to his expectations, that he could stay
on there another year. By June 1611 he had moved to
other quarters. His departure confirms the evidence of
the plays themselves, that some time in 1611 Shakespeare
retired to Stratford from his active work with his Company
in London.

But although we may regard Shakespeare as settled in
Stratford from this time, there is evidence that he was a
frequent visitor to London.

In May 1612 he was at Westminster, and was described
as of Stratford-on-Avon when he gave his evidence in the
Mountjoy case. In the following year his stay in London
must have been of some duration. In March 1613 the
poet was paid 44 shillings by the young Earl of Rutland,
for inventing the device his lordship carried on his shield
at the tournament on 24th March, 1613 to celebrate the

King's Accession Day. Just as at the joyous passage of arms at Ashby, described in *Ivanhoe*, the jousters bore devices, of which Front de Bœuf's black boar's head on a white shield with the motto *Cave Adsum* was an example singular only in its arrogance, so their Elizabethan successors exercised their fancy in the same way. Shakespeare's idea was executed by Burbage, who was well known for his skill as a painter, and for his work he received the same payment as Shakespeare. Earlier in this month Shakespeare's name is recorded in connection with what is, financially at least, a more important transaction. On 10th March, 1613, he purchased for £140 a house in Blackfriars, putting down £80 and mortgaging the property for the balance.[1] The Conveyance and the Mortgage both carry Shakespeare's signature. These two, and that of the previous year to his deposition in the Mountjoy suit, are the only three certain signatures from his hand outside his will, which also contains three signatures, one on each of its pages.

Shakespeare had no doubt leisure to see to this business in March, since only ill-health could have excused his absence from the festivities for the marriage of the King's daughter, Princess Elizabeth—the famous Elizabeth of Bohemia—to the Elector Palatine in February 1613. Shakespeare's Company were paid £153 6s. 8d. for some twenty performances at these celebrations, Shakespeare's pieces being produced on eight occasions. Whether he stayed on for the production of *Henry VIII* in June is uncertain. Tradition points to his having directed the rehearsals, since

---

[1] Professor Hotson has shown that the William Johnson, vintner, who with Heminge acted for Shakespeare in this transaction, was the host of the Mermaid tavern, made famous by the gatherings at which Jonson presided. For the activities of the Gunpowder Plot conspirators at the Mermaid and at this house, see *I, William Shakespeare*, 172 *seq.* Many were Warwickshire men. It may be noted here that Shakespeare in *Othello*, I, iii, 44 introduces the name of Marco Lucchese, proprietor of the Italian ordinary in London. *M.L.R.*, 1916, p. 339.

he is said to have instructed Lowin in the part of the king, and he may well have spoken the Prologue himself.[1] The production was recognized as an event of importance, the audience included men of rank and fashion, and the actors had spared no expense. At this first performance, however, the discharge of one of the two pieces of ordnance used for the royal salute in Act I, Scene iv, ignited the thatched roof, and while everyone was intent on the stage the fire gathered strength, and finally destroyed the whole fabric. It was rebuilt the following year in a more elaborate manner, with tiles instead of thatch on the roof over the galleries. The burning of the Globe, however, marks off the period of Shakespeare's theatrical activities.

The plays written during the final period are different in subject matter and style from those of the third period. Nor is the difference merely in a return to the convention of comedy with its happy ending ; for just as the comedies of the previous period have a gravity that distinguishes them from the earlier plays in this kind, so the final comedies have a peculiar ethos which has gained for them the title of Romances.

In this turn from tragedy to romance some see little more than a change in fashion to suit the taste of the Jacobean Court, more and more given over to sentiment and spectacle, and particularly delighting in the masque. This influence may have been reinforced by the tradition established at the Blackfriars by the Children of the Revels. Music naturally had an important place in the performances of singing boys, and the interior lighting might also encourage the introduction of scenic devices of a more elaborate kind. Beaumont and Fletcher have been regarded as showing the way to this new style of play, with their heroes and heroines playing their high-born parts as in a pageant. No one,

---

[1] See Chambers' *Shakespeare*, II, 264.

however, has dated *Philaster, Cymbeline* or *Pericles,* with the certainty that permits of our deciding who first staged these stories of lost princes and princesses with their Arcadian adventures.

It is also probable that the King's men, whose senior sharers were now advanced in years, welcomed plays that gave more scope and work to the younger actors ; and Shakespeare in planning his Romances may well have been deliberately turning to account special talent then at the disposal of the organization.

But such speculations, even did they rest on more secure foundations, are here beside the point. Shakespeare's Romances have been raised by the genius of their author far above any temporary conditions that may have suggested them, for they are clearly the expression of something he had very much at heart. The only question of importance concerns the nature of the vision informing them, and its place in the whole story of his work.

This inward change to the final manner has seemed to one commentator at least so sudden and unexpected as to be in the nature of ' a revolution rather than an evolution.' For he finds a Christian note in the forgiveness and recon- ciliation of the Romances he cannot hear in the Tragedies. And critics have naturally been glad to dwell on the serenity and beauty of this close as adding the final perfection to Shakespeare's work. Like the last utterance of some classic tragedy it dismisses the spectator, given over for a space to pity and fear, with some calm and sententious precept that brings to the mind spent with passion, consolation and peace.

But the late Lytton Strachey, provoked no doubt by a certain materialism and sentimentality in the popular picture of the dramatist, writing serenely at last in the com- fortable afternoon of his worldly prosperity and domestic peace, insisted that the Romances are indeed a development from the Tragedies, that they are even less serene than the latter, or that their serenity is more disturbing than tragic confusion and storm. What he would have us regard as the pessimism and disgust of the Tragedies only deepened, as they succeeded one another, sinking at last to Timon's furious denunciation of mankind ; till the poet, no longer able to contemplate the world with the composure necessary for sanity, abandoned reality for good and turned to fairy tales, creating by the magic of his style an artistic world remote from reality and its disgusting sights ; yet not remote enough to exclude all sound of its unpleasing voices, for we still hear jealous and misshapen monsters disturbing with their clamour the peace of the Arcadian retreat. Instead then of the serene Olympian we are asked to imagine Shakespeare, at the end, as a man 'bored with people, bored with real life, bored with drama, bored, in fact, with everything except poetry and poetical dreams.' Beauty is there ' but it is a presentment of decoration not of life.'

But if tragedy is the expression of despair, it is a divine despair at the heroism of humanity ; and this unreal art described by Lytton Strachey is his own invention, not that of the poets. Criticism is with one voice against him. 'In the poet,' says Charles Lamb, speaking of Spenser's great work, which is more remote from reality than the Romances,

> We have names which announce fiction ; and we have absolutely no place at all, for the things and persons of the Fairy Queen prate not of their ' whereabout.' But in their inner nature, and the law of their speech and actions, we are at home and upon acquainted ground. The one (the common run of fiction) turns life into a dream ; the other (the poet) to the wildest dreams gives the sobrieties of everyday occurrences. By what subtle art of tracing the mental processes it is effected, we are not philosophers enough to explain.

But of the connection between Art and Reality, Lamb is as sure as are Aristotle, Coleridge, and Johnson. The last, indeed, has declared the business of criticism to lie precisely in that tracing of the mental processes which Lamb, with a becoming irony, has declared beyond him ; for Johnson said of one work, ' there is no criticism in it : nothing which shows the beauty of the poet's thought as founded on the workings of the human heart.' And certainly, if, as Wordsworth has said, ' poetry is the history or science of feeling,' an organisation of our imaginative life, criticism which ignores the principles on which poetry gives coherence and therefore beauty to our experience, by insisting that art can be a mere denial of reality, will not help us to an understanding of Shakespeare.

The voice of authority apart, common experience tells us that it is not the disillusioned who delight in fairy tales, but the most hopeful part of mankind. Shakespeare may appear to ascend through tragedy and chaos, like Milton's heroic figure,

Upborne on indefatigable wing,

to look into the Paradise of the Romances ; but if he had come only to escape the hell of his own thoughts, how could he have avoided all jealousy or envy of the inhabitants of this happier Eden, or put by the thought, which saddened even Satan himself, that the coming years will deliver youth

to woe,
More woe, the more your taste is now of joy ?

This, at least, is how that great but disillusioned writer, Tolstoi, felt in his closing years about such stories of romantic love :

I feel afraid of such tender feelings, and I have been unfortunate enough in my life never to have seen a single spark of truth in that kind of love, nothing but falsehood,

14

in which the senses, conjugal ties, money, the desire to bind or unbind one's self had so complicated the feeling itself that there was no making anything out of it.

Such sobering sentiments find an appropriate place and voice in the Romances. They are heard at the crisis of *A Winter's Tale.* Camillo, whose worldly experience and unspoilt nature give him some claim to the philosophic mind, feels bound to warn Florizel of the dangers of defying his father, and to tell the lovers of the folly of

> a wild dedication of yourselves
> To unpath'd waters, undream'd shores, most certain
> To miseries enough,

and he adds,

> Besides, you know
> Prosperity's the very bond of love,
> Whose fresh complexion and whose heart together
> Affliction alters.

But to this familiar wisdom that passes current with more than merely talking men Perdita replies,

> One of these is true :
> I think affliction may subdue the cheek,
> But not take in the mind.

And the old man is surprised into confessing the faith he has concealed even from himself,

> Yea, say you so ?
> There shall not in your father's house these seven years
> Be born another such.

This theme is not new to the poet,

> If this be error and upon me proved,
> I never writ, nor no man ever loved.

But it is enriched with the insight that has remained from the high passions of the tragedies. Shakespeare now sees the daily beauty in the life of an Imogen, or a Perdita, as a conquest of the world that reveals a power comparable to that in the tragic passions of an Antony or a Coriolanus. Out of this strength comes the sweetness of the Romances. This is the touch that disarms the worldly-wise Camillo, and makes him stop, with an enthusiasm for the education of nature worthy of Wordsworth himself, all apologies for her ignorance of the conventions of fashionable life,

> I cannot say 'tis pity
> She lacks instructions, for she seems a mistress
> To most that teach.

This reconciliation of the wisdom of experience with what are truly the tragic enthusiasms and instincts of humanity, here dramatized in the encounter of Perdita and Camillo, is further developed in the relation of father and daughter in *The Tempest*.

Of all Shakespeare's characters who are represented as standing on the threshold of age, Prospero is most blessed with the sweet hope which Pindar declared the kind nurse of old age. Delivered from the savage mastery of the passions, though not without such scars of the struggle as his impatience and absentmindedness still upon him, Prospero looks through the insubstantial fabric of earthly existence with something of prophetic vision. But though he knows the world for what it is, what most sustains his heart is his sympathy with the spirit that goes out to it in hope and love,

> How beautous mankind is ! O brave new world,
> That has such people in't.

Here no less than in tragedy is that sensibility in the heart of man that so transcends its objects. Here are the seeds of the flame that may kindle into the phœnix-like blaze in which the heart is tragically self-consumed, or that, in happier circumstances, may touch the ordinary concerns of life ' with something of angelic light.' In the story of Prospero and Miranda, Shakespeare has shown us that union of man's thought and instincts in which alone he can realize his strength.

If sweet hope in old age is indeed the reward of the just life, and if justice lies, as Plato taught, in the harmony or proportion among the sides of man's nature, *The Tempest* makes it clear to us that Shakespeare looked upon the charities between youth and age as indeed the fulfilment of this law.

And this reconciliation of the very different hopes of youth and age is the final episode in the struggle between man's reason and instinct, his thought and action, which is the theme of Shakespeare's work ; a conclusion possible only to one who, thanks to the honesty of his outlook and the integrity of his art, found at the end that ' Sweet hope was still his companion cheering his heart.'


## CYMBELINE

**S.R. 8th November, 1623.** First printed in the **First Folio.**

Simon Forman gave an account of *Cymbeline* in his *Notes*, and although this entry is not dated it may be attached by reference to its context to April 1611.

The verse shows the free use of light and weak endings, first developed in *Antony and Cleopatra* ; the romantic tone connects it with *The Winter's Tale* and *The Tempest*. It was composed, therefore, before *The Tempest*, and probably some time after *Antony and Cleopatra* and *Coriolanus*.

The story of Cymbeline Shakespeare found in Holinshed's romantic histories of the early British kings and their dealings with the Romans. In the final battle-piece, he adapted the same historian's account of how a Scotsman and his two sons decided a battle against the Danes by their unexpected and resolute intervention. To this Shakespeare added an Italianate intrigue from the *Decameron* (II, 9), which he consulted in the original, as the conclusion of Boccaccio's story, turned to comic use in *The Winter's Tale*, does not appear in *Frederick of Jennen*, the only known available version in English.[1]

Judged from the historical or realistic standpoint the result merits Johnson's censure :

> To remark the folly of the fiction, the absurdity of the conduct, the confusion of the names and manners of different times, and the impossibility of the events in any system of life, were to waste criticism upon unresisting imbecility, upon faults too evident for detection, and too gross for aggravation.

But as Shakespeare was not writing a history but a play, the only relevant question is how all this affects the imagination. And the prevalence of the fabulous over the real in the Romances, a characteristic mark, according to Longinus, of the work of a great genius that has passed its intensest phase, is felt to correspond to a state of mind in Shakespeare that has far-reaching parallels in the development of other great artists.

What gives unity to Shakespeare's last works is the atmosphere in which he has steeped them.    Turner at the end painted light, and his final inspirations rise like some miraculous dome on the sure foundations of his earlier science.    Shakespeare became preoccupied with a comparable radiance in the inner world of drama.    Lytton Strachey talks of his style as now everything, as one might talk of Turner's or Rembrandt's colour being everything in their final masterpieces.    But no one supposes that this is a sign of boredom in the painters, or anything but a transformation and intensification of certain life-long interests.

The golden haze of *Cymbeline* naturally captivated such an artist as Tennyson, but it was still his favourite play when he knew he had done with art.    For though Shakespeare in the

---

[1] *Winter's Tale*, IV. iv, 773.  He has a son, who shall be flayed alive ; then 'nointed over with honey, set on the head of a wasp's nest . . . the sun looking with a southward eye upon him where he is to behold him with flies blown to death.

*Decameron* II. 9.  Ambrogiuolo il dì medesimo che legato fu al palo et unto di mèle, con sua grandissima angoscia dalle mosche e dalle vespe e da' tafani . . . . fu non solamente ucciso, ma infino all'ossa divorato.

setting of his days seems like the poet gazing westward in the afterglow, his thoughts

> sunk far
> Leagues beyond the sunset bar,

though his longings are like Imogen's ' beyond beyond,' he looks towards the gulfs of evening over no strand forlorn.   It is as if the human voice to which he had been so responsive still sounded in his ears, making what was already unearthly into ' a kind of heavenly destiny.'   For the Romances give sustained and dramatic expression to the vision that finds momentary expression in the lines,

> and while my eye
> Was fixed upon the glowing Sky,
> The echo of the voice enwrought
> A human sweetness with the thought
> Of travelling through the world that lay
> Before me in my endless way.

It is, of course, the voice of Imogen that gives its meaning to this play, as it is the voices of Hamlet and Lear that give significance to their tragedies.

Imogen, the last of Shakespeare's long line of heroines who have to masquerade as boys, is, though a married woman, in some ways the most romantic of them all.   On this point Hazlitt, as strong an admirer of the play as Tennyson, in his own different way, wrote :

> No one ever hit the true perfection of the female character, the sense of weakness leaning on the strength of its affections for support, so well as Shakespeare— no one else ever so well painted natural tenderness free from affectation and disguise—no one else ever so well showed how delicacy and timidity, when driven to extremity, grow romantic and extravagant ; for the romance of his heroines (in which they abound) is only an excess of the habitual prejudices of their sex, scrupulous of being false to their vows, truant to their affections and taught by the force of feeling when to forego the forms of propriety for the essence of it.

Hers is the heavenly alchemy that gilds to some tinct of

brightness even the basest characters in the story. ' I am distressed in the *Cymbeline*,' wrote Bridges, ' by the contact of Iachimo with Imogen, and its great unpleasantness is evidently due to the exquisite beauty of Shakespeare's creation.' But part of that beauty had escaped us but for the subtle Italian's contribution to its sum. Iachimo no less than Cloten or the simple mountaineers is a mirror to reflect the heroine. Each shows an image in accord with its quality and kind. ' How angel-like he sings,' says the enthusiastic Arviragus of the disguised Imogen, and his older and more prosaic brother adds, ' But his neat cookery.' The scenes between Imogen and Iachimo are an essential part of the portrait, and Iachimo's soliloquy in her bedchamber one of the triumphs of the play. And without his gross talk with Posthumus, and the outspoken fury to which this drives his dupe, how much reality and life would be wanting in the portrait ?

Though Shakespeare may have been quite indifferent to historic probability he was, as Hazlitt noted, careful to adapt his material for the stage :

> The last act is crowded with decisive events brought about by natural and striking means. . . . The fate of almost every person in the drama is made to depend on the solution of a single circumstance—the answer of Iachimo to the question of Imogen respecting the obtaining of the ring from Posthumus.

When Shakespeare comes to what demands careful treatment he can still show his old craft.


## THE WINTER'S TALE

**S.R. 8th November, 1623.** First printed in the **First Folio.**

*The Winter's Tale* was performed at Court 5 November, 1611, and had been seen by Forman on 15 May, 1611. The versification and outlook place it among the Romances. It stands last among the Comedies in the First Folio, and was added, as the signatures and other bibliographical details prove, after some headway had been made with the Histories. Heminge and Condell may have wished before printing to find the official copy of the play. This was still missing on 19th August, 1623, as the following entry under that date in the Office Book of the Master of the Revels shows :—

> For the king's players. An olde playe called Winter's Tale, formerly allowed of by Sir George Bucke, and likewyse by mee on Mr. Hemmings his worde that there was nothing prophane added or reformed, thogh the allowed booke was missinge ; and therefore I returned it without a fee, this 19 of August, 1623.

If Mr. Willoughby's reckoning is right (see page 40), the players had by this time printed it from a transcript put together either from the author's original papers or the assembled actors' parts. The use here in the Folio of brackets, the apostrophe, and the hyphen, have suggested to Mr. R. C. Bald[1] that the transcript was the work of a professional copyist, Ralph Crane, who is known to have worked for the King's men at this time.

Shakespeare borrowed the plot from Greene's *Pandosto, The Triumph of Time*, first printed in 1588, and reprinted in 1607. He took the names, Leontes, Antigonus, Cleomenes, Archidamus [2] and Mopsa, from Sidney's *Arcadia* ; Florizel may come from *Amadis de Gaul*, and Autolycus though in the *Odyssey* is also in Ovid and Golding.

The reunion of Hermione and Leontes, which is not in Greene, has been censured by Robert Bridges on moral as well as material grounds:

> We are diverted and delighted by Autolycus and Perdita ; our interests are magically shifted,—the relief of the contrast almost justifies the uncomfortable distress of the earlier acts,—and we are gratified to find Hermione alive at the end. But how are Leontes and Hermione to meet ? It is a situation worthy of Labiche ; yet we are expected both to take it seriously and to overlook it.

But the affairs of Leontes are only a frame for the maying

---

[1] *Middleton : A Game at Chesse*, edited by R. C. Bald, p. 42.

[2] Moorman in the Arden edition shows how Shakespeare took Greek names to help towards his creation of a Greek setting.

of Florizel and Perdita, and the frame must match the picture. The rhythm of the main theme makes the distortion, if one will, in the subsidiary matter, essential and natural.    This has to provide the colouring and contrast that gives a sense of reality to the heroism of romantic youth, but it must not conflict with it.    What we are to take seriously and what we are to overlook in the Leontes story is dictated by the requirements of the main theme.    The accommodation demanded of the imagination in *The Winter's Tale* is less than that needed in many acknowledged masterpieces, particularly in the art of painting.

Even what might have proved the somewhat stagey device of the descent from the pedestal is carried beyond the merely theatrical by the presence of a powerful current of feeling ; for Leontes gives life to the statue before him like another Pygmalion, animating it, however, not by dreams of the future but by the passionate recollection of the past ; and Hermione steps down from her pedestal after we have seen her brought to life in her husband's memory and repentance.    Those who cannot keep from dwelling on the historical and material side of the situation may comfort themselves with the observation of Longinus on the improbabilities of Homer, ' But what else can we term these things than the veritable dreams of Zeus ? '

## THE TEMPEST

**S.R. 8th November, 1623.**    First printed in the **First Folio.**
The date of composition is fixed between the performance on 1st November, 1611, recorded in the Revels Accounts :

> *By the Kings players    Hallomas nyght was presented att*
> *Whithall before the kinges Maiestie*
> *a play Called the Tempest.*

and the late autumn of 1610, when Sylvester Jourdan had returned from America with the story he published in *A Discovery of the Barmudas, Otherwise Called The Isle of Devils* (the dedication is dated 13th October).    Jourdan set out in 1609 with Sir George Summers, Sir Thomas Gates, William Strachey, and others, for

Virginia. Their ship was separated from her consorts in a tempest and driven on the Bermudas, where they had a miraculous escape. The island, though the air was temperate and the country abundantly fruitful, seemed to them, owing to strange noises, enchanted and ' given over to devils and wicked spirits.' Here they had to spend ten months, but at last they set out again in two boats they had built, and reached Virginia in May 1610. Jourdan set out again for England on 15th July, bringing with him Strachey's *A True Reportory of the Wracke and Redemption of Sir Thomas Gates, Knight* [1] (the title when printed later in *Purchas his Pilgrimes*, 1625). This was circulated to the London Council of Virginia. Among the various accounts of this remarkable adventure Shakespeare knew at least those of Strachey and Jourdan.

How Shakespeare could have seen Strachey's account, which was treated as confidential and only privately circulated at first, has been shown by Professor Hotson.[2] Amongst the council of the Virginia Company, which included the Earl of Southampton, was Sir Dudley Digges, son of Thomas Digges, the distinguished mathematician and astronomer.[3] Sir Dudley's mother married in 1600, as her second husband, the widower Thomas Russell, owner of the manor of Alderminster, near Stratford, and Shakespeare's intimate friend. Shakespeare lodged for some time in Silver Street near the town house occupied by Digges, and must have known the family well. It was no doubt Sir Dudley, who had taken a great interest in the Virginia venture, who showed Shakespeare Strachey's letter, either in town or on his visit to Alderminster in November

---

[1] Part of which was incorporated for publication in the *True Declaration of the estate of the Colonie in Virginia* (S.R., 8th Nov. 1610).

[2] *I, William Shakespeare*, p. 225.

[3] He had been muster-master general of the army with Leicester in the low countries, and written on the art of war to prove that ' the ancient discipline' of the Greeks and Romans was not out of date. Fluellen in *Henry V* echoes many of his dicta. Digges also possessed the engraved portrait of Tycho Brahe with the names of that astronomer's noble ancestors, who included Rosenkrans and Guldensteren. *I, William Shakespeare*, pp. 116, 124.

1610.  It may be noted in passing that the merchant venturer selected by the Virginia Company to raise the money for their scheme was William Leveson, who was well known to the actors and to Shakespeare, having acted for them as trustee when they took over a half interest in the Globe Theatre from the Burbages.

The Tempest is more of a piece than the other romances ; and this superiority is not merely one of construction.  It indeed observes the Unities of Place and Time as does no other of Shakespeare's pieces except The Comedy of Errors.  But such a work as Antony and Cleopatra is quite independent of place and time, and yet is clearly seen as a whole.  The unities are, therefore, not the secret of this or any action's superiority, which must come from some inward reference in the story that enables the poet to give blameless vent to his most intimate feelings, and from the completeness with which this reference informs the various parts.  Stories that trace in outline the events of the poet's own life are not necessarily the best calculated to produce a frank and unimpeded utterance of mind.  As a man may speak out more strongly and unequivocally for another than he can for himself, so a poet may find in the impersonal themes of drama the best opportunity of unburdening his heart.  To make the inwardness of Hamlet or Antony and Cleopatra depend directly on events in Shakespeare's own life is to ignore this obvious truth.  But The Tempest may be different, and it would not be uncharacteristic of Shakespeare if he never introduced his own person into his drama till he was about to quit the stage himself.  For we can hardly suppose he was unconscious of all resemblance between Prospero's renunciation of his rough magic and his own intention to withdraw from the theatre.  Nor is Lytton Strachey's remark that Shakespeare could never have seen himself as the somewhat testy Prospero a real objection.  One might as well say that Chaucer would not introduce himself among his pilgrims as the stout and long-winded gentleman that tells The Tale of Melibeus.  Your humorist knows better than to offer himself as a model character.  Prospero as an absent-minded recluse and a dealer in magic, though of the white kind, is a figure so ambiguous to the literally minded that he shelters Shakespeare sufficiently from prosaic inquirers not satisfied with the partial illuminations of art.

It is true that the poet Campbell seems to have been the first to say, Shakespeare is Prospero. But the chronological order of the plays was not established even approximately till late in the 18th century, and before this was done it was hardly possible to relate *The Tempest* to Shakespeare's own story.

Nor is it necessary to allow Campbell's suggestion to harden into the theory that *The Tempest* is an esoteric history of the dramatist's career, showing us the stage held at his arrival in London by pieces as misshapen as Caliban, till he liberated the spirit of Poetry, as Prospero frees Ariel, and concluding with his return to Stratford and the company of his married daughter.

The character of Prospero, however, enabled Shakespeare to give expression, more fully than was possible in pieces with such fathers as Cymbeline and Leontes, to thoughts that must, as all the Romances show, have been constantly present to him at this time ; and particularly to his sense of the bond between the generations of men that unites the hopes, however diverse, of the young and the gracious of every age. For the forgiveness that has been dwelt on as peculiarly characteristic of the final period is only an aspect of this larger justice, which, provided the wheat is allowed to grow, can suffer the tares to await the final threshing.

And the sense of infinity that all feel in *The Tempest* is heightened by Shakespeare's treatment of the sub-plot. On the surface the man-monster, Caliban, and his first encounter with drunken sailors, may seem no more than some much-needed—but obvious—comic relief, for a play whose scene is laid on a desert island. But reflection shows that here, in embryo, is the complexity that confronts the historian, or baffles the philanthropist, as he contemplates or assists at the meeting of men on different levels of civilization. Not that Shakespeare makes an allegory of the meeting of savage and civilized, master and man ; but in the very simple cross purposes of the enchanted island, Shakespeare has reduced to their lowest and most intelligible terms the incommensurables that cannot be cancelled out of the social equation.

Here indeed is the Shakespearean world as it has been characterized for us by Signor Croce—a world of unresolved opposites warring in the characters themselves, no less than in the contrary purposes of one to another. For Caliban is at once a beast and a visionary, speaking a poetical language his sailor friends have long forgotten, and yet for all the music in his soul more apt than they for stratagems and spoils. And Stephano is an equally incongruous mixture, sinking at times as far below the savage as he rises above him in the fuddled rightness of the famous order (' the last word ' as Sir Arthur Quiller-Couch has called it ' of our mercantile marine ') :

> Every man shift for all the rest, and let no man take care for himself ; for all is but fortune.

That Shakespeare knew he was handling in his own way the elements to which the statesman strives to give form is suggested by the famous quotation about the ideal commonwealth, from Florio's translation of Montaigne's essay *Of the Canniballes*. This is no mere expedient to fill out a scene, but a living branch on the main trunk of the work.

In *The Tempest*, no less than in *Hamlet*, Shakespeare makes us aware of the puzzles arising from the contrarieties of human nature that perplex a fair-dealing humanity ; and in Caliban and his mates they assume a less deadly but, perhaps, even a more baffling form than in Hamlet's stepfather.

But this sense of unreconciled opposites, though an important feature in Shakespeare's dialectic, is not its final note. This ' umorismo,' a term that suggests itself to Signor Croce as hinting at its real nature, this admission of human ignorance, is like the Socratic irony not the end but the means. To awaken men to the obvious contradictions of the world, and the insufficiency of all merely formal explanations of its mysteries, is its first business, and then to force them back on the convictions of the heart on which Socrates himself stood his ground against his own ignorance and the even deeper ignorance of his self-satisfied fellow-citizens. The paradoxes of Shakespeare's art, like those of the heroic Athenian, remind us of the antagonisms which from the very nature of things the affections of our nature must encounter. But beside the mere paradox-monger Shakespeare stands like Socrates before the forward Euthyphro, when that youthful moralist told him of how he was about to prosecute his father on a charge of murder, although, as his account of the circumstances of the case showed, the empanelled wisdom of the world could not have resolved the affair into its rights and wrongs. To those who love to parade the singularity of their virtue in such calculated unconventionalities and inhuman charities, whose pertness stands unabashed in the presence of noble and humane tradition, Shakespeare turns the face of old loyalties and time-honoured loves, as surely as he confounds those who think the letter of law and custom provides a text in which men can read the limits of their nature and its aspirations.

*The Tempest* shows Shakespeare more conscious than ever of the strange tangle of earthly existence, but surer than ever of what gives beauty, worth, and humanity to the lives of men.

## HENRY VIII

**S.R. 8th November, 1623.** First printed in the **First Folio.**
The date of the first performance, 29th June, 1613, has been recorded for us because during that performance the Globe was burnt to the ground. Of several accounts of the event, including one added to Stow's *Annals*, the best is Sir Henry Wotton's in a letter to Sir Edmund Bacon :

> Now, to let matters of state sleep, I will entertain you at the present with what has happened this week at the Bank's side. The King's players had a new play, called *All is True*, representing some principal pieces of the reign of Henry VIII, which was set forth with many extraordinary circumstances of pomp and majesty, even to the matting of the stage ; the Knights of the Order with their Georges and garters, and Guards with their embroidered coats, and the like : sufficient in truth within a while to make greatness very familiar, if not

ridiculous.  Now, King Henry making a masque at the
Cardinal Wolsey's house, and certain chambers being shot
off at his entry, some of the paper, or other stuff, where-
with one of them was stopped, did light on the thatch,
where being thought at first but an idle smoke, and their
eyes more attentive to the show, it kindled inwardly, and
ran round like a train, consuming within less than an hour
the whole house to the very ground.  This was the fatal
period of that virtuous fabric, wherein yet nothing did
perish but wood and straw, and a few forsaken cloaks ;
only one man had his breeches set on fire, that would
perhaps have broiled him, if he had not by the benefit
of a provident wit put it out with bottle ale.

The Folio version was printed from a carefully prepared
manuscript in which the ordering of the elaborate pageants
is very fully indicated in the lengthy stage-directions.  The
Prologue spoken at the first performance, possibly by Shakespeare himself, is also given.  This apologizes for the absence
from the piece of the mirth that Shakespeare knew well was
expected from him :

> I come no more to make you laugh, Things now,
> That beare a Weighty, and a Serious Brow,
> Sad, high, and working, full of State and Woe :
> Such Noble Scœnes, as draw the Eye to flow
> We now present.

And after warning his audience that they are to see neither
Foole nor Fight, he concludes :

> Therefore, for Goodness sake, and as you are knowne
> The first and Happiest Hearers of the Towne,
> Be sad, as we would make ye.   Think ye see
> The very Persons of our Noble Story,
> As they were living : Thinke you see them Great,
> And follow'd with the generall throng, and sweat
> Of thousand Friends : Then in a moment see
> How soon this Mightinesse, meets Misery.[1]

---

[1] This quotation shows the style of punctuation and the use of capital
adopted by Jaggard in the First Folio.  Students who wish information
about Shakespeare's own spelling and punctuation should, as in all questions
of detail, consult *A Shakespeare Bibliography* and its *Supplement* by Ebisch
and Schücking.

On this Prologue Dr. Johnson observed :

> There is in *Shakespeare* so much of *fool and fight,*
> the fellow
> In a long motley coat guarded with yellow,
> appears so often in his drama, that I think it not very
> likely that he would have animadverted so severely on
> himself.

and he goes on to attribute it to ' the friendship or officiousness of Jonson.' But as this Prologue was not, as Johnson suggests, for a revival, but clearly for the first performance, we should have to suppose that the managers of the King's men, whose admiration for Shakespeare, as Jonson hinted, verged on idolatry, permitted such criticism from an outsider, and further, that Jonson had neither the sense nor taste to know what such an occasion required. Only the author himself could have ventured to introduce the play in the terms of this Prologue ; and in it Shakespeare gives us the key in which the piece is written.

The theme is the familiar one of the vanity of worldly place and greatness, with Buckingham, Wolsey, and Katherine as strongly contrasted variations. The very pomp and pageantry of the play are justified artistically as a foil to the sombre realities of the situation. On this scene appears the child Elizabeth, and Cranmer is represented as inspired to foretell her glorious future :

> She shall be lov'd and fear'd ; her own shall bless her ;
> Her foes shake like a field of beaten corn,
> And hang their heads with sorrow ; good grows with her.
> In her day every man shall eat in safety
> Under his own vine what he plants ; and sing
> The merry songs of peace to all his neighbours.
> God shall be truly known.

Many who see that the author of these lines was a representative Elizabethan in his love of national and religious liberty are unable to reconcile them with the sympathetic portrait of Katherine earlier in the play. Spedding argued that Shakespeare, if he had been the sole author, would have shown Henry reproved

for his ambition by the hand of God in the death of Anne
Boleyn's son, or, taking the other side, would have dwelt
more on the personal attractions of Anne Boleyn and Henry's
championship of the Protestant cause.

But these lines on Elizabeth at first suggested another manner
of dividing the play. Theobald and others were unable to
believe that they were not written for Elizabeth's own ears.
To them they seemed mere flattery, and, on such an interpretation, they could not have been written ten years after the Queen's
death, and in the reign of a successor who did not love to hear
her praises.   Working on this suggestion and some observations
on the metrical peculiarities of the play, Malone had the hazy
idea that it had been revised or rewritten after the coming of
James VI. Hickson and Spedding, following up the examination
of the verse, assigned passages with a high percentage of double
endings to Fletcher, leaving the others to Shakespeare. This
gave the lines on Elizabeth and the famous scene with Katherine,
that so took such different critics as Johnson and Swinburne,
to the same hand.   And this division between Shakespeare and
Fletcher cuts right across that proposed by Johnson, who held
that ' the genius of Shakespeare comes in and goes out with
Katherine,' as well as across Spedding's own division based on
religious and political grounds.

The metrical division, however, can carry no weight by
itself, since Shakespeare's later plays show an increase in the use
of double endings that might well have developed as in *Henry
VIII*. There is nothing in Fletcher comparable to the scenes
assigned to him from *Henry VIII*, nor would his participation
explain the contradiction between the strong Elizabethan tone
of the piece and the sympathy for Katherine.   But the presence
of such humane oppositions is characteristic of the work of
Shakespeare—superbly reconciled in his tragedies, though here,
and in some of the lesser plays, each pulling us its own way
—and the play as a whole has the compassionate outlook of
the Fourth Period. For Shakespeare, though his *King John*
and this play have left us in no doubt of his strong sympathy
with the national and religious feeling of his country, was

15

quite unable to cast the events of these times into any such narrow mould as Spedding suggested. Katherine was wronged, and Shakespeare does not fail to move our sympathies for her ; yet Elizabeth was a blessing to England, and Shakespeare rejoices in her almost miraculous appearance. Indeed, Shakespeare's treatment in *Henry VIII* of a subject matter inevitably controversial might be used to support Cardinal Newman's view of him as the most Catholic of the poets. But he was this, not as Newman seems to have thought, in spite of his times, but in part because England gave him the vantage ground from which alone such a Catholic outlook was possible. For the national fervour of Elizabethan England was no mere selfish family feeling, but the domestic aspect of a passion for liberty that reached far beyond its own doors. Writing to the Queen of the war in the Netherlands Sir Philip Sidney had said :

> If her Majesty were the fountain ; I would fear, considering what I daily find, that we should wax dry. But she is but a means whom God useth. And I know not whether I am deceived ; but I am fully persuaded, that, if she should withdraw herself, other springs would rise to help this action. For, methinks, I see the great work indeed in hand against the abusers of the world ; wherein it is no greater fault to have confidence in man's power, than it is too hastily to despair of God's work.

This is indeed the consecration of the national spirit in the service of what Milton calls the free and heaven-born spirit of man. And in Shakespeare, England's effort finds a universal voice in which all nations can rejoice ; and these days take their place among the great ages of the world as an example for ever to men. That Shakespeare should acknowledge so freely his debt to his own times, in what are among the very last lines he ever wrote, is one of those generous gestures that we recognize as coming naturally from the most magnanimous of the poets.

NOTE—The only real evidence for Fletcher's hand in *Henry VIII* is provided by *The Two Noble Kinsmen*, entered in the Register and published in 1634 as the joint work of Shakespeare and Fletcher, though later included in a Folio collection of plays by Beaumont and Fletcher. This play can be divided on metrical grounds into two sets of scenes similar to those that make up *Henry VIII*. But neither the metrical evidence, which admits of various interpretations, nor the attribution in 1634 of part of *T.N.K.* to Shakespeare, can weigh against the fact that Heminge and Condell included *Henry VIII* in the First Folio and omitted *T.N.K.*; for their knowledge and good faith are no longer open to question. See *New Shakespeare Society's Transactions*, 1874, Appendix, and *Essays and Studies for the English Association*, xvi, 99.

# PERICLES

**S.R. 20th May, 1608.** *Edward Blount. Entred for his copie under thandes of Sir George Buck knight and Master Warden Seton A booke called. The booke of Pericles prynce of Tyre.*

**Q1 1609** was issued by Gosson not Blount, and because of this and the irregularities of the text, verse being often printed as prose and prose as verse, it has been regarded as a Bad Quarto. But it gives, in spite of printer's errors, and the peculiarities transferred from the Copy, what seems a good text.

Heminge and Condell did not include *Pericles* in the First Folio, and since Blount's entry safeguarded the printing rights, they must have omitted it because it was not wholly by Shakespeare.

The First Folio was reprinted in 1632 (the Second Folio), and again in 1663 (F$_3$), and 1685 (F$_4$). In the second issue of the Third Folio (1664) the publishers added seven plays to the thirty-six already in the canon : *Pericles,. The London Prodigal, Thomas Lord Cromwell, Sir John Oldcastle, The Puritan Widow, A Yorkshire Tragedy*, and *Locrine*. No critical spirit guided their choice, for they included *The Life of Sir John Oldcastle, the Good Lord Cobham*, though the Prologue indicates that it was a counterblast to Shakespeare's *Henry IV*. The authors, Drayton, Munday, Wilson and Hathaway, to whom Henslowe paid £10 for the piece and another ten shillings at the first performance, compare their own picture of the hero with Shakespeare's Oldcastle, renamed Falstaff, when they say

It is no pamper'd glutton we present,
No aged Counsellor to youthful sin.

They offer what they call Truth in place of 'forg'd invention.'
The publishers of the Third Folio, therefore, merely added some
plays that had been attributed to Shakespeare, openly or under
cover of the initials W.S., by former booksellers. Critical
considerations have rejected from the canon all of these additions
except *Pericles*.[1]

Though the broken-backed character of the play bears out
Heminge and Condell's rejection of it from Shakespeare's
*Works*, few will doubt, from the opening of the third act—

> Thou God of this great vast, rebuke these surges,

with its sublime sea music, that they are listening to Shakespeare.
Even the much disputed brothel scenes cannot be denied to the
author of *Measure for Measure*.  Shakespeare's interest in Marina's
fate must have been roused by considerations that find expression
in the other romances ; and he has in this fragment created a
companion picture to those of Perdita and Miranda.  This
and the occasional magnificence of the poetry justify the inclusion
of *Pericles* with Shakespeare's works, where it has found a regular
place since the time of Malone.

It has been conjectured that George Wilkins was Shakespeare's collaborator.  In 1608 he published a prose version of
*Pericles*, derived, as Sir Edmund Chambers has argued (*Shakespeare* I, 523 *sqq*.), from the play.  Though he was connected
with the King's men, having written a play for them, the
evidence is too slight to make this more than a guess.

---

[1] Its pagination in the third Folio suggests that it was to be the only
addition, and that the others were added as an after-thought.

# VII. SHAKESPEARE'S LAST DAYS

THOMAS GREENE, the Stratford Town Clerk, was on Corporation business in London on 17th June, 1614, when he noted :

> At my Cosen Shakspeare commyng yesterday to towne I went to see him howe he did.

Greene's way of expressing himself, and the fact that Shakespeare was accompanied by his son-in-law, the physician Hall, have suggested to some that the poet was no longer in sound health. Instead, however, of giving the information we would so gladly have had about Shakespeare's interests and conversation in these last years, Greene records some details about the enclosure of common fields near Stratford that the Combes, who were acquainted with the poet, intended to proceed with. Shakespeare, as owner of certain tithes, was financially concerned in the business, but the Combes, we gather from other sources, had guaranteed him against any loss. The Corporation of Stratford, who were against the change, wrote officially to Shakespeare to secure his services on their side ; but we do not know how Shakespeare acted. He had, however, told Greene that in his opinion there would be nothing done at all ; and he proved right, for the courts, in the end, stopped the Combes.

No one acquainted with the doings of the world will think it strange that Greene should have recorded these trivial matters when there was so much to tell for which posterity might have thanked him. But the detachment from the strenuous business of living, without which such observation is impossible, is itself a sign of genius. To-day the imitation of this gift is common and abundant, but it only makes the clearer the genius of Walton, or Aubrey or Boswell. Unfortunately there is no real substitute for this living source of information, and the attempt to manufacture it from documents, sometimes only half understood, has not proved successful.

Shakespeare's will has provided material for experiments of this kind. The object of such a document is to dispose of the testator's property in a business-like and unambiguous manner. This Shakespeare's will does. His heir is his daughter Susanna, who was married to John Hall. To her Shakespeare left his main properties to be handed down from generation to generation as an entailed estate. To this he added his various investments such as the Stratford tithes. For his younger daughter, just married, he makes ample provision : she is to have £150, and the interest of another £150, which was to be paid to her husband when he made a corresponding settlement on her. To his sister he left the Henley Street house during her life and £20. His wife was not mentioned in the original draft of the will, but when it was revised an addition between the lines gave her the second-best bed. This has been held to prove that Shakespeare had been unhappy with his wife, and intended to insult her in his will. But the will could hardly have been drafted without her approval, for she was legally entitled to a third of her husband's estate—as is still the law in Scotland. She could, therefore, have broken the will had she so desired. But it is clear the arrangement was that she was to continue to live at New Place with her daughter, who was devoted to her mother, if the inscription she put on her tomb means anything. Shakespeare can have had no doubt that his dispositions would be acceptable to all : the will shows the understanding and harmony that must have prevailed in the home. Any explanation of the mention of the second-best bed that runs counter to the whole drift of the will ignores the main evidence for our interpretation of it.

While some have found in the will evidence of an unhappy home life, others regard it as a proof of the poet's illiteracy. There is no mention of books or manuscripts. There was, however, no need to mention books. The will is not an inventory of his possessions, any more than it is, as some would have liked it to be, a literary or philosophical testament for the delight and profit of after-times. What Shakespeare had to give to posterity he gave in his plays. Here he was concerned only with his worldly possessions ; and he made his arrangements like one who knew he was dealing with friends, ready to believe he had made the best possible arrangements for their temporal welfare.

The will was first drafted some time before 25th March, 1616, when it was finally shaped. The event that made the alterations necessary was the marriage of Shakespeare's younger daughter, Judith, on 10th February, 1616, to Thomas Quiney, a younger son of Richard Quiney, the Bailiff of Stratford and the poet's friend. Of the original three sheets the first had to be rewritten, but the others required only a few alterations and additions. That the final arrangements were made in haste is suggested by certain small errors and omissions in the wording, and, though Shakespeare did not die till 23rd April, it seems very likely that he was far from well at the end of March.[1]

A most valuable clue to one side of Shakespeare's social life has been found by Professor Hotson [2] in the name of the gentleman whom Shakespeare appointed to act with

---

[1] For an admirable analysis of the Will, see Professor Quincy Adam's *Life of Shakespeare*, p. 461 *seq.;* for a description of the tomb, 478 *seq.* As a part-owner of the tithes Shakespeare had the right of burial within the chancel of the Parish Church.

[2] *I, William Shakespeare.*

Francis Collins, his lawyer and Greene's successor as town clerk, in overseeing the execution of his will. This was Thomas Russell, Esquire.

Russell's mother was the second wife of Sir Thomas Russell of Strensham, near Stratford. On his father's death she married Sir Henry Berkeley of Bruton, in Somersetshire. Thomas Russell, though left in easy circumstances, and brought up with half-brothers who played distinguished parts as soldiers and courtiers, seems to have preferred the quieter life of a country gentleman. He was for a short time at the University of Oxford, and went on a venture with Sir George Gifford, well known for his fighting qualities and skill as a naval commander ; but he never tried to thrive at Court being, as he says himself, ' never acquainted with compliment,' and he declined the honour of knighthood. His stepfather, however, who was something of a fire-eater, liked him, and he was on the most intimate and friendly terms with men who were, like Endymion Porter, the favourites of kings, as well as with men like Sir Tobie Mathew, honoured for their learning and taste. If a man is known by the company he keeps, Thomas Russell was a friend worthy even of Shakespeare's regard, and might have sat for the portrait of Hamlet's Horatio. And Professor Hotson has been able to show how, through this connection, Shakespeare must have known his step-sons, Sir Dudley Digges, Master of the Rolls, and Leonard Digges, the Oxford scholar, whose verses in memory of Shakespeare, with those of his friend, James Mabbe, Fellow of Magdalen, were included in the First Folio. This and many other pieces of evidence pointing to Shakespeare's intercourse with a group of able and brilliant soldiers, scholars, and courtiers, Professor Hotson has discovered in his investigations, which show that Shakespeare could not have chosen a man better qualified than Russell by character, position, and experience, to discharge the duty entrusted to him.

In spite of this evidence of order in Shakespeare's affairs, and the probability of ill-health in the poet's last days, the favourite story of his death represents him as killing himself in a final frolic.  John Ward, who became vicar of Stratford in 1662, noted in his diary some time after that date,

> Shakespear, Drayton, and Ben Jhonson, had a merry meeting, and itt seems drank too hard, for Shakespear died of a feavour there contracted.

Unfortunately medical science, as Smart has observed, knows of no such fever, and none of Ward's entries suggests that he was in a position to hear authentic stories of the last days, or had the acuteness of mind to distinguish idle gossip from truth.  He was, indeed, so credulous as to believe that his contemporaries, Milton and Lambert, were Catholics in disguise.  The Catholic obsession seems to have been prevalent among Anglican clergymen at that time, and it did not fail to touch Shakespeare's name.  The Rev. Richard Davies, the first but incoherent recorder of the deer-stealing story, notes, ' He dyed a papist.'  And some have tried to find in the final plays, and especially in *The Tempest*, confirmation of Shakespeare's supposed change of faith.  Such an interpretation misses the real relation of the Romances to the Tragedies, and the essential unity of Shakespeare's work.  And it also ignores the view of the Reformation expressed in the line, ' God shall be truly known,' a view not surprising in the author of *King John ;* and *Henry VIII*, in which Cranmer delivers these ' inspired ' words, comes after *The Tempest*. It further conflicts with the very little we know of Shakespeare's home life at Stratford.  Certainly Shakespeare's daughter and her husband were good Protestants, and in 1614 there was entertained at New Place one of the visiting preachers invited by the Corporation to deliver some annual sermon. The Corporation, notoriously Puritan, would hardly have gone to the expense of twenty pence for a quart of sack and a quart of claret for one not of their own persuasion. But most of all it is contradicted by what we know of the poet from himself, for it attributes too childish a concern with mere outward forms of faith to one who is, even among the poets, pre-eminent for his catholicity. That he was familiar with the Bible in translations popular in the Reformed Churches, there can be no doubt, and his intimate knowledge of the Anglican Prayer Book has been demonstrated by Mr. Richmond Noble.[1] That Shakespeare conformed, outwardly at least, to the Established worship seems clear. To push the inquiry further on these lines, in an effort to determine the precise local use, whether Anglican or Roman, of the cult which he inwardly favoured, is to attempt to impose too parochial a form on the belief of one whose religion was that of 'all sensible men.'

[1] *Shakespeare's Biblical Knowledge*, by Richmond Noble, gives an excellent survey of Shakespeare's knowledge and use of the Bible, in the Genevan and the Bishops' translation, and of the Book of Common Prayer.

# APPENDIX

# TABLE A

| | ENTRY IN REGISTER IF PREVIOUS TO PUBLICATION | | DATE OF PUBLICATION | SOLD BY | PRINTED BY |
|---|---|---|---|---|---|
| | DATE | ENTERED TO | | | |
| 1. The Troublesome Raigne of King John | — | — | 1591 | Sampson Clarke | — |
| 2. Titus Andronicus | 6th Feb. 1594 | John Danter | 1594 | Thomas Millington, Edward White | John Danter |
| 3. The Contention *Bad Quarto of 2 H. vi* | 12th March 1594 | Thomas Millington | 1594 | Thomas Millington | Thomas Creede |
| 4. The True Tragedie *Bad Quarto of 3 H. vi* | — | — | 1595 | Thomas Millington | P(eter) S(hort) |
| 5. The Taming of a Shrew *Bad Quarto* | 2nd May 1594 | Peter Short | 1594 | Cuthbert Burby | Peter Short |
| 6. Love's Labour's Lost *Bad Quarto* | [No copy known : but conjectured from (a) analogy between title pages of L.L.L. and R. and J. (Q.2) ; (b) absence of entry in Register] | | | | |
| *ii Good Quarto* | — | — | 1598 | Cuthbert Burby | William White |
| 7. Romeo and Juliet *i Bad Quarto* | — | — | 1597 | — | John Danter |
| *ii Good Quarto* | — | — | 1599 | Cuthbert Burby | Thomas Creede |
| 8. Richard II | 29th Aug. 1597 | Andrew Wise | 1597 | Andrew Wise | Valentine Simmes |
| 9. Richard III | 20th Oct. 1597 | Andrew Wise | 1597 | Andrew Wise | Valentine Simmes |
| 10. 1 Henry IV | 25th Feb. 1598 | Andrew Wise | 1598 | Andrew Wise | P(eter) S(hort) |
| 11. Merchant of Venice | 22nd July 1598 *(Blocking entry)* | James Roberts | — | | |
| | 28th Oct. 1600 | Thomas Hayes | 1600 | Thomas Hayes | J(ames) R(oberts) |

## TABLE A—continued

| | | | | | |
|---|---|---|---|---|---|
| **12. Henry V** <br> *Bad Quarto* | 4th Aug. 1600 <br> *(Staying entry)* | — | 1600 | Thomas Millington and John Busby | *Thomas Creede* |
| **13. Much Ado About Nothing** | 4th Aug. 1600 <br> *(Staying entry)* <br> 23rd Aug. 1600 | — <br> *Andrew Wise, William Aspley* | — <br> 1600 | Andrew Wise and William Aspley | *Valentine Simmes* |
| **14. 2 Henry IV** | 23rd Aug. 1600 | *Andrew Wise, William Aspley* | 1600 | Andrew Wise and William Aspley | *Valentine Simmes* |
| **15. Midsummer Night's Dream** | 8th Oct. 1600 | *Thomas Fisher* | 1600 | Thomas Fisher | *[James Roberts]* |
| **16. Merry Wives of Windsor** <br> *Bad Quarto* | 18th Jan. 1602 <br> *(and transferred same day to)* <br> *[printed in spite of blocking entry]* | *John Busby* <br> *Arthur Johnson* | 1602 | Arthur Johnson | *T(homas) C(reede)* |
| **17. Hamlet** <br> i *Bad Quarto* <br> ii *Good Quarto* | 26th July 1602 <br> *(Blocking entry)* <br> 7th Feb. 1603 <br> *(Blocking entry)* | *James Roberts* <br> *James Roberts* | 1603 <br> 1604 | N(icholas) L(ing) and John Trundell <br> N(icholas) L(ing) | *(Valentine Simmes)* <br> *J(ames) R(oberts)* |
| **18. Troilus and Cressida** | 28th Jan. 1609 | *Bonian and Walley* | — <br> 1609 | — <br> Bonian and Walley | — <br> *G. Eld* |
| **19. King Lear** | 26th Nov. 1607 | *Nathaniel Butter,* <br> *John Busby* | 1608 | Nathaniel Butter | *(Nicholas Okes)* |
| **20. Othello** | 6th Oct. 1621 | *Thomas Walkley* | 1622 | Thomas Walkley | *N(icholas) O(kes)* |

## TABLE B

| | ENTRY IN REGISTER IF PREVIOUS TO PUBLICATION | | DATE OF PUBLICATION | SOLD BY | PRINTED BY |
|---|---|---|---|---|---|
| | DATE | ENTERED TO | | | |
| As You Like It | 4th Aug. 1600 (Staying entry) | — | — | — | — |
| Antony and Cleopatra | 20th May 1608 (Blocking entry) | Edward Blount | — | — | — |
| Pericles | 20th May 1608 (Blocking entry) | Edward Blount | 1609 | Henry Gosson | (William White) |

## TABLE C

| | DATE | ENTERED TO | DATE OF PUBLICATION | SOLD BY | PRINTED BY |
|---|---|---|---|---|---|
| The Famous Victories | 14th May 1594 [1] | Thomas Creede | 1598 | Thomas Creede | Thomas Creede |
| King Leir | 14th May 1594 [2] | Edward White | — | — | — |
| | 8th May 1605 [3] (and transferred same day to [4]) | Simon Stafford / John Wright | 1605 | John Wright | Simon Stafford |

## TABLE D

| | DATE | ENTERED TO | DATE OF PUBLICATION | SOLD BY | PRINTED BY |
|---|---|---|---|---|---|
| Venus and Adonis | 18th April 1593 | Richard Field | 1593 | John Harrison | Richard Field |
| Lucrece | 9th May 1594 | John Harrison | 1594 | John Harrison | Richard Field |
| Sonnets | 20th May 1609 | Thomas Thorpe | 1609 | John Wright | G. Eld for T. T. |

[1] *Thomas Creede.* Entred for his copie under thand of master Cawood Warden a booke intituled. *The famous victories of Henrye the Fyft conteyninge the honorable battell of Agincourt.*

[2] *Edward White.* Entred for his Copie under thandes of bothe the wardens a booke entituled *The moste famous Chronicle historye of Leire kinge of England and his Three Daughters.*

[3] *Simon Stafford.* Entred for his Copie under thandes of the Wardens A booke called ' the *Tragecall historie of kinge Leir and his Three Daughters &* ' As it was latelie Acted.

[4] *John Wright.* Entred for his Copie by assignement from Simon Stafford and by consent of Master Leake, *The Tragiall history of kinge Leire and his Three Daughters* Provided that Simon Stafford shall have the printinge of this booke.

# TABLE E

| | | | | | Transferred from Ling to Smethwick |
|---|---|---|---|---|---|
| Richard II | 1597 | Entered to Wise | 1603 | Transferred to Law | |
| Richard III | 1597 | Entered to Wise | 1603 | Transferred to Law | |
| 1 Henry IV | 1598 | Entered to Wise | 1603 | Transferred to Law | |
| 2 Henry IV | 1600 | Entered to Wise and Aspley | | | |
| Much Ado About Nothing | 1600 | Entered to Wise and Aspley | | | |
| *Merchant of Venice | 1600 | Entered to Hayes | | | |
| *Midsummer Night's Dream | 1600 | Entered to Fisher | | | |
| The Taming of a Shrew | 1594 | Entered to Shorte | 1607 | Transferred from Burby to Ling | 1607 |
| Love's Labour's Lost | No entry | | 1607 | Transferred from Burby to Ling | 1607 |
| Romeo and Juliet | No entry | | 1607 | Transferred from Burby to Ling | 1607 |
| Hamlet | 1602 | Entered to Roberts : Bad and Good Quartos printed for Ling. | | | 1607 |
| Titus Andronicus | 1594 | Entered to Danter | 1602 | Transferred from Milligton to Pavier | |
| *Contention | 1594 | Entered to Millington | 1602 | Transferred from Millington to Pavier | |
| *The True Tragedy | No entry | | 1602 | Transferred from Millington to Pavier | |
| *Henry V | [1594 | Creede entered Famous Victories] | 1600 | Creede's ' rights' set over to Pavier | |
| *Merry Wives of Windsor | 1602 | { Entered to Busby / Transferred to Johnson } | | | |
| *King Lear | 1607 | Entered to Butter and Busby | | | |
| Troilus and Cressida | 1608 | Entered to Bonian and Walley | | | |
| Othello | 1621 | Entered to Walkley | | | |

* Included in the Pavier Shakespeare (see p. 38).

# TABLE F

| | Total | Blank | Rhyme | Songs. etc. | Prose | % ot Double Endings | % of Run-on Lines | Number of Endings | |
|---|---|---|---|---|---|---|---|---|---|
| | | | | | | | | Light | Weak |
| C.E. | 1754 | 1147 | 378 | — | 229 | 17 | 13 | 0 | 0 |
| T. S. | 2553 | 1915 | 157 | 3 | 478 | 18 | 8 | 1 | 1 |
| T. G. | 2191 | 1496 | 111 | 15 | 569 | 18 | 12 | 0 | 0 |
| T. A. | 2523 | 2335 | 149 | — | 39 | 9 | 12 | 5 | 0 |
| 1 Hen. VI | 2676 | 2371 | 296 | — | 9 | 8 | 10 | 3 | 1 |
| 2 Hen. VI | 3087 | 2503 | 94 | — | 490 | 14 | 11 | 2 | 1 |
| 3 Hen. VI | 2902 | 2761 | 139 | — | 2 | 14 | 10 | 3 | 0 |
| Rich. III | 3610 | 3374 | 162 | — | 74 | 20 | 13 | 4 | 0 |
| John | 2570 | 2410 | 160 | — | — | 6 | 18 | 7 | 0 |
| Rich. II | 2755 | 2215 | 540 | — | — | 11 | 20 | 4 | 0 |
| R. J. | 2995 | 2087 | 463 | 39 | 406 | 8 | 14 | 6 | 1 |
| L. L. L. | 2518 | 582 | 1135 | 42 | 759 | 8 | 18 | 3 | 0 |
| M. N. D. | 2102 | 751 | 933 | 24 | 394 | 7 | 13 | 0 | 1 |
| M. V. | 2554 | 1883 | 130 | 10 | 531 | 18 | 22 | 6 | 1 |
| 1 Hen. IV | 2993 | 1680 | 68 | — | 1245 | 5 | 23 | 5 | 2 |
| 2 Hen. IV | 3229 | 1498 | 56 | 20 | 1655 | 16 | 21 | 1 | 0 |
| M. W. W. | 2635 | 215 | 72 | 30 | 2318 | 27 | 20 | 1 | 0 |
| Hen. V | 3213 | 1852 | 84 | 9 | 1268 | 21 | 22 | 2 | 0 |
| M. A. | 2541 | 654 | 40 | 37 | 1810 | 23 | 19 | 1 | 1 |
| A. Y. L. I. | 2611 | 926 | 150 | 98 | 1437 | 26 | 17 | 2 | 0 |
| T. N. | 2430 | 752 | 118 | 64 | 1496 | 26 | 15 | 3 | 1 |
| T. C. | 3319 | 2063 | 172 | 30 | 1054 | 24 | 27 | 6 | 0 |
| M. M. | 2666 | 1565 | 56 | 28 | 1017 | 26 | 23 | 7 | 0 |
| A. W. | 2736 | 1174 | 279 | 14 | 1269 | 29 | 28 | 11 | 2 |
| J. C. | 2453 | 2234 | 32 | — | 187 | 20 | 19 | 10 | 0 |
| Ham. | 3799 | 2511 | 146 | 77 | 1065 | 23 | 23 | 8 | 0 |
| Oth. | 3248 | 2534 | 76 | 26 | 612 | 28 | 20 | 2 | 0 |
| Lear | 3224 | 2222 | 70 | 108 | 824 | 29 | 29 | 5 | 1 |
| Timon | 2314 | 1517 | 151 | — | 646 | 25 | 33 | 16 | 5 |
| Mac. | 2086 | 1714 | 234 | — | 138 | 26 | 37 | 21 | 2 |
| A. C. | 3019 | 2711 | 32 | 6 | 270 | 27 | 43 | 71 | 28 |
| Cor. | 3305 | 2539 | 26 | — | 740 | 28 | 46 | 60 | 44 |
| Cym. | 3276 | 2597 | 90 | 126 | 463 | 31 | 46 | 78 | 52 |
| W. T. | 2960 | 2094 | 34 | 58 | 774 | 33 | 38 | 57 | 43 |
| Temp. | 2016 | 1424 | 59 | 91 | 442 | 35 | 42 | 42 | 25 |
| Hen. VIII | 2807 | 2652 | 70 | 12 | 73 | 47 | 46 | 52 | 38 |

*The figures in Cols. 1-5 are from* The Cambridge Shakespeare, 1891 ; *the percentages in Cols. 6-7 are from König ; and the numbers in Cols. 8-9 from Ingram, N.S.S. Trans.* (1874).

# INDEX

# INDEX

236